QUEER GAME STUDIES

Queer

Game

BONNIE RUBERG AND ADRIENNE SHAW, Editors

Studies

University of Minnesota Press
Minneapolis
London

Chapter 6, "Playing Outside," by Leigh Alexander, originally appeared in *The New Inquiry,* http://thenewinquiry.com/, June 17, 2013; reproduced by permission from *The New Inquiry.* Chapter 18, "The Nightmare Is Over," by Katherine Cross, originally appeared as "The Nightmare Is Over: They're Not Coming for Your Games," at http://www.polygon.com/, July 29, 2014; reproduced by permission from Polygon.com and Vox Media Inc.

Published by the University of Minnesota Press
111 Third Avenue South, Suite 290
Minneapolis, MN 55401-2520
http://www.upress.umn.edu

Printed in the United States of America on acid-free paper

The University of Minnesota is an equal-opportunity educator and employer.

23 22 21 20 19 18 17   10 9 8 7 6 5 4 3 2 1

Library of Congress Cataloging-in-Publication Data
Names: Ruberg, Bonnie, editor. | Shaw, Adrienne, editor.
Title: Queer game studies / [edited by] Bonnie Ruberg and Adrienne Shaw.
Description: Minneapolis : University of Minnesota Press, [2017] | Includes bibliographical references and index.
Identifiers: LCCN 2016036903 (print) | ISBN 978-1-5179-0036-6 (hc) | ISBN 978-1-5179-0037-3 (pb)
Subjects: LCSH: Video games—Social aspects. | Electronic games—Social aspects. | Games—Social aspects. | Gender identity. | Gays. | Queer theory.
Classification: LCC GV1469.17.S63 Q44 2017 (print) | DDC 794.8—dc23
LC record available at https://lccn.loc.gov/2016036903

Contents

Introduction
Imagining Queer Game Studies

ADRIENNE SHAW AND BONNIE RUBERG

After decades spent relegated to the margins, sexuality and gender are finally taking their place as key subjects in the study of video games. In recent years, a veritable wave of queer games and queer game scholarship has crashed on the North American games scene. Collaborations between game studies and queer studies, as well as between queer game makers and queer game scholars, are creating myriad new opportunities for exploring difference in games and exploring games as different. Leading the charge at this moment of shift, queerness has emerged as a focal point in the push to diversify both games culture and games critique. Providing a valuable framework for interrogating the very systems that structure the medium, queer thinking has the potential to simultaneously destabilize and reimagine video games themselves. In this way, exploring queerness in games means much more than studying LGBTQ content, players, or game creators. Rather, drawing from queer theory and the perspectives of queer subjects, the authors of the essays in this volume turn to queerness to challenge a variety of dichotomies that have long structured how scholars and designers alike understand games (e.g., narratology/

ludology, production/reception, control/agency, success/failure). They see queerness as an ethos that pushes us, as Naomi Clark writes in the pages that follow, to locate "unspoken norms by which a field of activity or knowledge is operating" and to find "points of rupture that destabilize those assumptions, opening up those fields to a wider and potentially more liberatory set of possibilities."[1] Drawing on the insights of queer theorists from Judith Butler to José Esteban Muñoz, queer game studies is about imagining game studies otherwise, by studying games queerly in addition to studying queer game subjects.

By destabilizing assumptions, queerness offers a new way of seeing video games, a way that operates via the paradigm we are naming "queer game studies." Through queerness this paradigm lays claim to video games of all kinds. It refigures games as systems of pleasure, power, and possibility, excavating the queer potential that can be found in all games. Moreover, as a paradigm, queer game studies stands as a call to action, an argument for the scholarly, creative, and political value of queerness as a strategy for disrupting dominant assumptions about how video games should be studied, critiqued, made, and played. As demonstrated in this volume, we can use it to consider the way queer failure, queer growth, and queer bodies are implicated in game structures; rather than understanding games as rule-based structures (ludology) or just in terms of representation (narratology), we can view games as spaces where we play within and against rules and explore representation beyond explicitly named queer content. Queer game studies opens up possibilities for queer game play that is not about finding the "real" meaning of a game text, but playing between the lines with queer reading tactics. It considers gaming counterpublics as a space for reimagining whom games are for and who is for games. Indie queer designers, utilizing nontraditional game-making tools like Twine, are pushing against the boundaries of what counts as a game and outside of concerns over commercial success. Games in all of their manifestations are a powerful place to imagine a queer utopia, not by simply imagining a better world but by giving players/makers/scholars the tools for enacting new and better worlds. Queerness, as its heart, can be defined as the desire to live life otherwise, by questioning and living outside of normative boundaries.

The present volume is inspired by the recent surge in feminist and queer game studies scholarship, as well as the numerous appeals from journalists, bloggers, designers, and player constituencies for an expanded engagement with the politics of subjectivity and embodiment in video games. On one front, a significant number of popular, academic, and industry writers have addressed the importance of LGBTQ representation in games, gaming audiences, and the games industry.[2] Driven by popular attention to what has been called a "queer games scene," the successful organization of queer gamer events like GaymerX, academic conferences like the Queerness and Games Conference (QGCon), talks by queer game makers and scholars at the Game Developers Conference (GDC), documentaries like *Gaming in Color,* and new games journalism that looks at games beyond mainstream gaming audiences, the mainstream game industry has demonstrated an unprecedented awareness of issues concerning LGBTQ players. In many cases, this attention to increased LGBTQ inclusivity reflects capitalistic concerns; while LGBTQ players have in fact been playing video games for as long as games have existed, many game companies now see them as a "new" untapped market. Simultaneously, sparked in part by the online harassment of LGBTQ game critics and makers (which we will discuss in more depth below), a number of online LGBTQ gamer communities have also begun pushing back against the marginalization they have experienced in the games industry and game fandom. Tanya DePass's #INeedDiverseGames, for instance, an organization and online community committed to addressing the under- and misrepresentation of marginalized groups in games, stands as just one example of how players from diverse backgrounds are coming together to demand long-overdue changes in the production and culture of video games.

Queer theorists—drawing from long-standing critiques of popular culture, art, communities, and capitalism—have also started turning their attention to games. In part this stems from a turn toward the digital in humanities scholarship broadly defined. As the digital humanities have gained prominence, and as queer theorists like Jack Halberstam have pushed for queer studies to increase its engagement with popular digital media forms, queer and feminist scholars from fields like media studies and literary studies have demonstrated an increasing interest in the influential role of video games in the contemporary cultural landscape. Designers, too, are driving the push to change the way queerness is understood in relation to games. Compelling work from queer game makers like Mattie Brice and Anna Anthropy has received national attention. This work models the power of video games to address queer identity at both personal and societal levels. These creative voices are shifting the discourse around games in crucial, though sometimes contentious, ways.

This is the diverse range of work that we bring together here under the banner of "queer game studies." Like queerness, queer game studies is difficult to define; this difficulty is itself highly productive for questioning the limitations of dominant conceptual frameworks. Existing academic categories prove insufficient for capturing queer game studies' uniquely hybrid emphasis on both the content of games and how games are analyzed. Queer game studies is neither sufficiently rigid nor ensconced in the academy enough to be called a discipline. At the same time, it represents more than a mere subdomain of game studies or queer studies. To call queer game studies a subdomain would imply that this work exists as an offshoot of either queer studies or game studies—whereas, in truth, it stands at the intersection of the two. The terms "field" and "area of study" are likewise misfit as descriptors of queer game studies, since they signify an engagement with a specific topic. By contrast, queer game studies refers not so much to the specific topic of queerness in games as to the application of a set of critical tools derived from queer theory and queer thinking. Far from a subfield, then, queer game studies is best understood as a paradigm. The politics of queer game studies are the politics of the paradigm shift. This tool set provides a methodological framework for disrupting the logics that underlie much existing game scholarship—including the impulse to define video games themselves. This framework uncovers the related lines of inquiry that underlie both queerness and games: how power structures shape agency, how lived experiences challenge structure, and how systems afford for opportunities of resistance. Game scholars and makers have wrestled over questions of diversity in games for decades. At times, it appears that both sides have come to an impasse: though it is obvious that video games need to be more inclusive in their representation, the pressures of industry and the reactionary response of gamer communities make game developers reluctant to enact significant change. Queer game studies stages an intervention at both a conceptual and a practical level. The frameworks of queer theory offer lenses through which to reclaim the medium, giving voices to the experiences of queer player subjects and bringing to light the fact that games are queer (or at least queerable) at their core.[3] Such frameworks have the potential to show those who make games that queerness represents far more than a niche issue or an untapped demographic.

In the spirit of queer theory, the goal of this volume is not to dictate what counts as queer game studies. Such work is rich, varied, and nascent; the full array of insights that will emerge from the intersection of queerness and video games has yet to be seen. Instead, we have deliberately chosen to represent a diverse array of perspectives and approaches to queerness in games. This volume's chapters range from the scholarly to the personal. They are written by academics, journalists, game makers, educators, organizers, and activists. By forming the volume in this way, we demonstrate the complexity of the dialogues that have emerged among these stakeholders. We also strive to welcome readers from many fields and backgrounds. Some of these pieces speak to theory, some to design, and others to the invaluable first-person experiences of carving out queer spaces inside heteronormative, mainstream gaming culture. Unlike much of the writing about LGBTQ issues and video games that has come before, many of these pieces are driven by a desire to explore queerness beyond representation. Through the paradigm of queer game studies, these authors locate queerness not only in queer characters or queer romance, but also in queer modes of play, design, research, and community building. It is our hope that this collection will lay the groundwork for future intersectional and interdisciplinary dialogues about queer games—and that this, in turn, will help make game cultures more felicitous spaces for all players. Together, the essays included here invite us to continue broadening conversations around gender, sexuality, and games. They inspire us to see video games as spaces of queer possibility.

Historicizing Queer Game Studies

By mapping the paradigm of queer game studies, and indeed by arguing for the importance of queer game studies itself, this volume calls in part for a break with existing trends in LGBTQ game scholarship. The key distinction we are making here is between scholarship that takes as its primary focus LGBTQ topics—from LGBTQ players or designers to games with LGBTQ representation—and work that seeks to understand video games through the conceptual frameworks of queerness. As a brief review of existing LGBTQ game scholarship demonstrates, a sizeable amount of research has been conducted on LGBTQ subjects in games. Although this work is immensely valuable in its own right, we believe that the time has come to push further, to embrace queerness as an approach that opens new possibilities in all games and challenges the very foundations of game studies.

Like most game studies scholarship, LGBTQ game studies can be grouped into three main areas: community/cultural research, textual analysis, and design studies. To date, the bulk of this research has focused on fan cultures and online gaming. Given that online game play has dominated much game studies work, it is not surprising that studies of queerness and games have emphasized virtual worlds.[4] Some scholars have looked at how players navigate homophobia in gaming spaces.[5] Others use online forums to understand how players react to queer game content.[6] Shaw has researched online gay gamer communities' reactions to homophobia and LGBTQ representation in games, which she talks more about in her chapter in this volume.[7] The second major area of LGBTQ games research focuses on LGBTQ characters and same-sex relationships in games. An early example of this is Mia Consalvo's work on *The Sims*' queer relationship options.[8] As several essays in this volume point out, however, same-sex relationships are indicative of homosexuality, and sometimes provide the possibility of bisexuality, but are not inherent examples of queerness. Until recently, scholarship on queer game content was sparse and focused on only a handful of games, mostly of the massively multiplayer online game (MMOG) variety.[9] Even Brenda Braithwaite's canonical *Sex in Video Games* makes only passing references to gay sex (though this is probably due to a lack of examples to study).[10] Given how long queerness has been a part of games, the pool of existing research has been small. Unlike the essays in this volume, much of the existing literature is focused on LGBTQ content rather than queerness as a mode of critique.

By contrast, much of the work that constitutes queer game studies locates queerness in games beyond representation.[11] Ruberg, for example, has addressed queer failure as a game play mode and elsewhere reframes play experiences that reject "fun" as queer worldmaking opportunities.[12] Many of the works in this volume (such as those by Jack Halberstam, Amanda Phillips, and Jordan Youngblood) are similarly interested in locating queerness in games that do not, at first glance, appear to include explicitly LGBTQ content. Other essays included here move beyond representation by interpreting the medium of video games through queer theory; the contributions by Kathryn Bond Stockton, Derek Burrill, and Christopher Goetz all fall into this category. Still others pieces, like those by game designers Colleen Macklin and Naomi Clark, explore the ways that queerness can inform game mechanics. The essays in this volume suggest the myriad ways that queer game studies reconfigures the relationships between queerness and video games. Building on this work, we hope this volume can push game scholars and designers to think in new ways about queerness and games, queerness in games, and queer approaches to games themselves.

In addition to suggesting new ways forward for queer game studies, many of this volume's essays draw from, challenge, and/or re-invigorate long-standing debates about what games are and how we should understand them. This interest in definitions and redefinitions is unsurprising; most introductory games books start with a discussion of what makes games unique as media objects.[13] Defining games is, for example, the core issue behind the so-called ludology and narratology debate that began in the early 2000s. Ian Bogost reviews this debate via different interpretations of the game *Tetris* in his book *Unit Operations*.[14] Janet Murray, he relates, argues that you can read a "story" in *Tetris*: specifically, an allegory of contemporary American life.[15] Murray's interpretation is then dismissed by Markku Eskelinen, who emphasizes the participation properties made available in the game as a rule-based object.[16] For his part,

Bogost concludes that "in both interpretations, something is lacking."[17] Instead, Bogost argues for assessing games through their "procedural rhetoric," a method he develops further in *Persuasive Games*.[18] Though the ludology and narratology debate continues today, it has become a bit of an anathema in certain circles.[19] Some scholars have suggested alternative approaches to game analysis that account for both ludic and narrative properties.[20] T. L. Taylor, for example, argues for considering the assemblage of factors that come together to create games:

> Games, and their play, are constituted by the interrelations between (to name just a few) technological systems and software (including the imagined player embedded in them), the material world (including our bodies at the keyboard), the online space of the game (if any), game genre, and its histories, the social worlds that infuse the game and situate us outside of it, the emergent practices of communities, our interior lives, personal histories, and aesthetic experience, institutional structures that shape the game and our activity as players, legal structures, and indeed the broader culture around us with its conceptual frames and tropes.[21]

Like Taylor, many of this volume's authors unpack games' richness and complexity. These contributors examine assemblages and intersections. They are inspired by the contradictory and multivalent ethos of queerness, as well as queer studies' focus on vectors of power and resistance, to analyze games themselves as systems, both ludic and social. Rather than restricting themselves to the study of a game's narrative or even rules, they seek out the queer implications of its hardware, of its code, of the individual experiences of nonnormative subjects as they play. The scholarship in this volume approaches the topic of queerness and games from so many varied perspectives because sexuality, gender, and identity in games by nature defy definition. Desire and selfhood in games can never be fully explained, contained, or constrained by a standardized set of ontological limitations.

The Queerness in Queer Game Studies

Of course, we are not the first to bring together queer theory and games. Queer theory has influenced many feminist game scholars before us, even those who do not directly address queer subjects. Jennifer Jenson and Suzanne de Castell, for example, use queer theory to analyze gender construction in games.[22] Laine Nooney uses queer theory to analyze gender and video game history.[23] T. L. Taylor and Helen Kennedy cite queer theorists in their research on game cultures and texts.[24] When we say "queer game studies" we are looking to work that does not simply cite queer theory, but that uses queerness as a method or paradigm to dramatically rethink game scholarship. We have to be aware, moreover, of the fact that some readers might only think of queer theory in relation to literary studies. Certainly, in academia, queer theory emerged from literary studies with the work of scholars like Eve Sedgwick and Judith Butler.[25] However, in the intervening decades, queerness has been adopted as a lens by a wide array of disciplines. Foundational figures like Alexander Doty and Richard Dyer put queer studies into dialogue with film.[26] Larry Gross, Lisa Henderson, and Katherine Sender are among the key figures in queer communication and media studies.[27] We might equally point toward the work of queer ethnographers like Mary L. Gray and David Valentine, queer critical theorists like Gayle Salamon, Sara Ahmed, and Lisa Duggan, queer legal scholars like Dean Spade, and queer historians like Susan Stryker.[28] Queer studies' rich multiplicity offers multiple methods for scholars, designers, and players to study games. To reach its fullest and richest potential, queer game studies must build not only on queer literary studies, but also on queer film studies, media studies, sociology, anthropology, political science, and all of the interdisciplines. It must emerge as an area of research that does not limit itself to the status of a subdiscipline of either queer or game studies, but provides space for seeing how these existing fields of research intersect.

At the same time that it blazes trails for new lines of inquiry, queer game studies needs to recognize its potential blind spots and the directions in which it must continue to evolve. Queer studies' focus on sexuality, particularly notable in early queer theory, has at times obscured the importance of race, gender, and class. In response, queer of color scholars—including Juana María Rodríguez, Mel Chen, Chandan Reddy, and Jasbir Puar—have dismantled the limited version of queer theory, queer politics, and queer activism dominant during the 1990s.[29] More recently, scholars examining asexuality through queer theory have constructively challenged the centrality of sex itself in sexuality studies.[30] Disability and socioeconomics are similarly pressing areas of inquiry, previously overlooked by dominant trends in queer theory, with which queer studies scholars are now finally engaging. Queer game studies must work to keep this intersectional thinking at its heart. We look forward to future work in this area that increasingly and even more explicitly puts issues of queerness and games into dialogue with these fundamentally interrelated concerns of access, visibility, subjecthood, agency, and voice. In a pamphlet titled "Queers Read This," published anonymously by Queers and handed out at the 1990 New York Pride parade, the authors wrote, "Being queer . . . means everyday fighting oppression; homophobia, racism, misogyny, the bigotry of religious hypocrites and our own self-hatred."[31] Similarly, Michael Warner argues in 1993's *Fear of a Queer Planet* that the goal of queer theory and queer activism is not simply acknowledgment of LGBTQ lives, but dismantling systems of oppression and normalization.[32] A queer game studies paradigm must inevitably be tied to this type of activist project: not just expanding representations of gender and sexuality in games, but in refusing the normalizing tendencies of game studies projects that seek only to build taxonomies of players, create narrow definitions of games and play, and reduce importance of a medium to commercial success. It is only by using the queer methods of embracing difference and resisting reductive categorization that games as an industry, culture, and realm of meaning making can be made to be more open.

We are standing now at a critical and exciting moment in video game history. At the same time, the concept of "now" is slippery. "Now" implies immediacy, a connection to the present. Yet the traditional academic publishing process moves slowly, and work such as this runs the risk of feeling dated by the time it reaches the public. Many of these essays were written in 2013, though we solicited some later works to address events like the #GamerGate. As we finalize this book, we find that the ground beneath our feet is still shifting. Queer game studies and the network of those invested in exploring queerness in games is ever broadening. That so many collaborators came together to realize this project demonstrates just how vibrant, present, and "now" the combination of queerness and games has felt to us all. But how can we reconcile this "now" with that "now," let alone all the future "nows" in relation to which this book will be someday read?

Perhaps "now" is something of a misnomer. Maybe we would do better to imagine this collection as a snapshot. Instead of an anthology that offers the definitive word on queer game studies—for now and for the future—we view this book as capturing a transitional historical moment. Much like David Eng, Jack Halberstam, and José Muñoz do in their "What's Queer about Queer Studies Now?" introduction to their special *Social Text* double issue, we see this volume as mapping the most urgent political concerns of queer game studies.[33] Like the 2006 inaugural issue of the journal *Games and Culture,* in which scholars were asked to address a similar question ("Why game studies now?"), these essays point to where this field might go.[34] They are as much about a future as they are a "now."

Along with many others, we felt that 2013 represented a turning point for rethinking what it meant to do queer work in video games. Two community-oriented, diversity-focused conferences began in 2013: Different Games (April) and QGCon (October). At these events, queer analyses of games took center stage. Meanwhile, at the 2013 Game Developers Conference (GDC), a group of designers organized #LostLevels, "a radically-casual 'unconference' about games and play" that aimed "to be hyper-inclusive."[35] And in August 2013, GaymerX, an LGBTQ gaming fan convention, was first held, attracting 2,300 attendees.[36] All of these gatherings have since happened annually. Steadily increasing attendance demonstrates that conversations around queerness and games are growing. In the same period, popular coverage of queer game content, players, and design also increased dramatically. Much of this coverage focused on mainstream games' inclusion of non-heterosexual relationships and characters, or on queer gamer communities. Additionally, media outlets have highlighted independent queer game designers who are pushing the boundaries of game design and questioning AAA game-industry norms.[37] Anna Anthropy's *Rise of the Videogame Zinesters* is perhaps the most widely known and earliest attempt to chronicle how free game design tools and new game distribution hubs have allowed a wider array of people to make and share games.[38] Building on this work, we hope this volume can push game scholars and designers to think in critical new ways about queerness and games, queerness in games, and queer approaches to games themselves. By spring 2014, Nintendo, the most mainstream of mainstream gaming companies, came under fire for not including same-sex relationships in their game *Tomodachi Life*.[39] If that is not a sign that the times are changing, what is? Many pressing conversations that intersect with queer game studies, such as those around representations of race and disability in games, have yet to gain the visibility currently driving the queer games discourse. We see queer game studies as a vanguard: the nowness of queer thinking in video games paves the way for the emergence of a diversity of approaches to understanding video games that stand just on the horizon: a range of lenses informed by the concerns of social justice and founded on experiences of difference.

Unfortunately, the last few years have also been notable for their challenges. By August 2014, many designers and writers invested in socially conscious gaming faced new levels of rage and vitriol. Attacked by those who rallied under the #GamerGate banner, the so-called social justice warriors who had been imagining more inclusive futures for games found themselves the targets of harassment. It is impossible to summarize #GamerGate, as it is a phenomenon that has cut across online platforms and types of fandom; it remains diverse in both its stakeholders and targets. In the simplest of terms, #GamerGate began as a Twitter hashtag that brought together various actors who felt attacked by calls to make games more inclusive (the very same calls we are foregrounding here). Some made the argument that "outsiders" were trying to change established games culture. Others insisted that games were already sufficiently inclusive, and that critics who said otherwise were unfairly mischaracterizing the objects of their fandom. Katherine Cross's essay in this volume unpacks this line of thinking in relation to Susan Faludi's metaphor of the "terror dream." After years of feeling like games were under attack from reactionary social commentators and politicians, a subset of mainstream gamers came to see game criticism as censorship—or, worse, an attempt to "take away" video games themselves. Once more, however, queer theory proves itself a valuable tool in reframing the terms of this debate. It encourages us to push past the simplistic dichotomies between the "enemies" and "defenders" of the medium reflected in the rhetoric of #GamerGate. Video games are contradictory: spaces of freedom and possibility, they are simultaneously normative and oppressive. Adrienne Shaw's essay in this volume speaks to this multiplicity concerning community formation. On the one hand, games have indeed offered a refuge for players who have experienced ostracization in other areas of their lives. Yet this refuge is itself defined by norms that limit who is granted the privilege of accessing this space. Games are both a subculture and an increasingly omnipresent feature of the mass media mainstream. Those who rail against critiques of games often insist that games should be understood as fantasies—just "for fun"—and therefore impervious to scrutiny. To the contrary, as queer studies knows well, fantasy is always already political. As for claims that critique equates to censorship, queerness reveals this presumption to be erroneous. Given a lengthy history of oppression from legal, medical, and other social apparatuses, queerness eschews dogmatic assumptions about what "good" representation is. It rejects the idea that certain subjects, stories, and desires should not be seen.

As a result of #GamerGate, several designers and journalists dedicated to addressing the importance of gender, sexuality, and difference in video games have stopped working in the field—including some authors originally included in this volume.[40] Others experiencing harassment continue to work in games but have become wary of engaging in Twitter conversations, sharing personal information, and speaking at public events. Of course, #GamerGate did not invent harassment; it has a long history in games culture.[41] As editors, though, we now find ourselves balancing this project's optimism with an awareness of its stakes. Summing up both the difficulties and the potential of this moment in her introduction to a series of queer games special issues of the journal *First Person Scholar,* Ruberg wrote, "As GamerGate has made clear, speaking up for diversity in this hostile environment takes real courage. Now more than ever, it is crucial that we create safe spaces for discussing sexuality, gender, race, and difference in videogames."[42] This is the "now" that is defining the paradigm shift of queer game studies, but our vision for queer game studies remains hopeful.

In the words of José Muñoz, "Queerness is primarily about futurity and hope."[43] For him, queerness has unique world-making potential precisely because expressions of queerness are so often impeded: "From shared critical dissatisfaction we arrive at collective potentiality."[44] Given the relative absence of queer thinking in existing game scholarship, and the current culture of online harassment against those who speak up for diversity in games, we believe it is fair to say that the authors whose work contributes to the paradigm of queer game studies are dissatisfied with where things stand. Together, the writing we have collected here demonstrates how the "collective potentiality" of that dissatisfaction can re-create game studies. These pieces make manifest the drive to mobilize in response to our dissatisfaction with the state of games, game communities, and the games industry. At the same time, in the spirit of Muñoz's queer utopia, these pieces also look ahead to possibilities for futurity and hope. What unites the works we have included here—indeed, what unites queer game studies and what queer game studies more than any other conceptual framework stands poised to offer video game criticism more broadly—is a commitment to seeing differently, to finding the marginalized in between the lines, and to unlocking the nonnormative potential that has been waiting in video games all along.

Structure of the Book

In the last few years, it has become increasingly clear that while parallel conversations are happening in game design, game criticism, and game studies, there is frequently insufficient overlap between these conversations. As much as possible, we have structured this volume to promote dialogues across perspectives, forms, and histories. Presented side by side, these authors model discussions between game design, journalism, and scholarship. What they have in common is their passion for new ways of imagining nonnormative gender and sexuality in ludic spaces. Each of the sections outlined below addresses one key area in queer game studies.

Defining Queerness in Games

We open with four pieces that explore definitions of queerness in games. First, in "What *Is* Queerness in Games, Anyway?" Naomi Clark maps key themes in recent discussions of LGBTQ issues and video games. Pushing back against the popular drive to make games "useful," Clark asks us to consider what we lose when don't allow games to remain deviant, offensive, and queer. In "Queergaming," Edmond Chang argues for understanding queerness as a counter-hegemonic play style. As a rallying cry, queergaming demands that game makers and players resist oppressive norms by embracing queerness that goes beyond surface-level representations of identity. Inspired by Michel Foucault and Judith Butler, Derek Burrill's "Queer Theory, the Body, and Video Games" argues for the importance of embodiment in game studies. Queer game studies, says Burrill, stands at the perfect intersection of theoretical traditions to bring the body to the fore. Finally, in "Queering Games History: Complexities, Chaos, and Community," Zoya Street questions what it means to write a history of queer gaming experiences. Street points us toward a mode of history making that allows queer players to tell their own stories, and acknowledges the impossibility of rendering gaming's complex systems into simple interpretations.

Queering Game Play and Design

Many of today's games are still governed by normative assumptions, but games as a medium can create counter-normative, emancipatory experiences. In this section, authors explore how we might actively queer play and game design. In "*Ending the Cycle*: Developing a Board Game to Engage People in Social Justice Issues," Peter Wonica presents a postmortem of his game *Ending the Cycle,* which began as a series of collaborative workshops. By iterating on an initial prototype, workshop participants learned about the systems of oppression that queer women face when they attempt to exit abusive relationships.

Queer gaming can be an educational tool, but it can also be a call to action. "Playing Outside" is Leigh Alexander's passionate polemic about diversifying games. By welcoming a wider range of game makers and players to the medium, says Alexander, games can move beyond fun and address difficult social issues. Hanna Brady's "Building a Queer Mythology" explores what games can learn from science fiction and fantasy. To bring queerness to games, Brady urges us to turn to fantasy and its worlds of possibility. "For Play? Literary Ludics and Sexual Politics" by Aubrey Gabel encourages us to think about "play" in discussions of queer games, and connects gaming to a literary tradition of playful language from Rabelais to Oulipo. Mattie Brice's "Play and Be Real about It: What Games Could Learn from Kink" argues that, much as kink allows partners to play with complicated personal and cultural histories, game design should create a space for engaging with the real world, not just stepping away from it. Finally, in "Queering the Snapshot: Ambient Mobile Play," Larissa Hjorth and Kim d'Amazing explore the relationship between mobile phone practices, performativity, and alternative concepts of play. Drawing on interviews with queer-identified phone users, Hjorth and d'Amazing unpack social media photo sharing as a mode of performing selfhood, affect, and sexuality. They link these practices to ambient mobile play, which transcends traditional game space boundaries and makes camera phone usage (and the selfie's bodily presence) a diffuse and ongoing game.

Reading Games Queerly

Moving from design and play audiences, in this section we consider how game texts themselves might be analyzed queerly. First, Robert Yang's "On 'FeministWhorePurna' and the Ludo-material Politics of Gendered Damage Power-ups in Open-World RPG Video Games" delves into the controversy over a misogynistically labeled power-up in Deep Silver's game *Dead Island*. Rather than see it as an obscure joke, Yang argues that the game's inclusion of "FeministWhorePurna" reflects widespread problems of sexism and accountability in the games industry. In "Welcome to *My* Fantasy Zone: *Bayonetta* and Queer Femme Disturbance," Amanda Phillips uses film studies to consider the queerness of Bayonetta, the titular character from the

2009 Platinum Games title whose design is often condemned as hyper-sexualized and fetishistic. Using Micha Cárdenas's concept of "femme disturbance," Phillips recasts Bayonetta as a queer force of disruption who manipulates the gaze, taunts players with castration, and is driven by controller techniques that recall female masturbation. Next, Todd Harper asks whether we, as players, can bring queerness to games by approaching them through alternate perspectives. This is the experiment he undertakes in "Role-Play as Queer Lens: How 'ClosetShep' Changed My Vision of *Mass Effect*." Only in the third game of the *Mass Effect* trilogy did developer BioWare offer male–male romance options for its protagonist, Commander Shepard. To make sense of this shift, Harper sets out to replay the series while imagining Shepard as a closeted gay man throughout the first two games. In "Queer(ing) Gaming Technologies: Thinking on Constructions of Normativity Inscribed in Digital Gaming Hardware," Gregory Bagnall turns to the material technologies of games. The controller-design standards for console gaming, argues Bagnall, reflect heteronormative thinking. Moving forward, Bagnall calls for a queering of gaming hardware that models itself on fluidity and possibility rather than hetero-masculinity. The section concludes with merritt kopas's "On *Gone Home*," a deeply personal response to what kopas describes as "a game about girls in love." Connecting her play-through of *Gone Home* with her own childhood, kopas describes her encounter with the game as an opportunity to live out a queer youth she missed and for which she still mourns.

Queer Failure in Games

Failure has been of interest to both queer studies and game studies in recent years. In this penultimate section, we turn to the obstacles faced by queer players, designers, and scholars, as well as the generative possibilities of queer failure. Reflecting on #GamerGate and the need for safe queer gaming spaces, Adrienne Shaw's "The Trouble with Communities" encourages readers to think about community as a series of multiple and overlapping subcommunities rather than a monolith of sameness. Far from collapsing differences, says Shaw, community provides an opportunity for "finding camaraderie despite difference." Next, Gabriela T. Richard addresses the difficulty of navigating who belongs in safe spaces. In her piece, "'Play Like a Girl': Gender Expression, Sexual Identity, and Complex Expectations in a Female-Oriented Gaming Community," Richard reflects on the policing of gender and sexuality in the (initially) all-female PMS clan and its associated all-male clan, H2O. In "The Nightmare Is Over," Katherine Cross compares reactionary gamers' outrage to what Susan Faludi has called the "terror dream." Gamers who grew up in the 1980s and '90s have lived through the trauma of social stigmatization, says Cross. Today, when faced with critiques of toxicity within games, these fans relive their trauma and lash out because they fear that video games will be taken away from them. Considering the ability of queerness to reimagine failure, Jack Halberstam's "Queer Gaming: Gaming, Hacking, and Going Turbo" builds on his previous work on animation in order to think about game play through the concept of the glitch. For Halberstam, the glitch usefully disrupts dominant value systems, an approach that he applies to three games: *Monument Valley, Thomas Was Alone,* and *Braid.* At the 2013 QGCon, Halberstam and Jesper Juul were invited to discuss the striking similarities between their recent books, *The Queer Art of Failure* (Halberstam) and *The Art of Failure* (Juul). The lively dialogue that ensued is transcribed here as "The Arts of Failure." Drawing connections between queer failure and failure in games, Halberstam and Juul discuss losing and loss as opportunities for nonnormative pleasure, cultural reflection, experimental design, and resistance through play. Jordan Youngblood concludes this section with his own analysis inspired by Juul's and Halberstam's books, which he uses to perform a close reading of failure in the *Metal Gear Solid* series. His article, "'I Wouldn't Even Know the Real Me Myself': Queering Failure in *Metal Gear Solid 2*," reframes the Raiden character as an analogue for the player, one whose experience and selfhood are defined through failure. In contrast to the hyper-masculinity of Solid Snake, the standard protagonist of the series, Raiden fails at masculinity, at his straight relationship, and even at being "real."

Queer Futures for Games

We end this collection on an optimistic note. What is possible when, against the odds, queer game communities come together? This section opens with a piece by queer theorist Kathryn Bond Stockton, today's leading thinker on the relationship between growth and queer theory. Part critique and part performance, "If Queer Children Were a Video Game" reads gaming through "lateral growth." The gamer who refuses to "grow up"; the child with such technological proficiency he seems to have grown up too fast; the childish, candy pleasure of addictive mobile games: these are the set pieces in Stockton's trip through the queerness of games and childhood. Building on Stockton's work, Christopher Goetz's "Queer Growth in Video Games" addresses a tension between two threads in current debates around queer games and growth. On the one hand, says Goetz, proponents of diversity in games want the medium to outgrow its juvenile content and immature gamer culture. On the other hand, queer game scholars celebrate gaming's invitation to revel in childish pleasures and anti-reproductive "sideways growth." Goetz himself suggests that the game's terrain is the queer sideways fantasies of childhood. In "Finding the Queerness in Games," Colleen Macklin instructs us to look for queerness in the fabric of games themselves. Referencing Muñoz, she describes games as queer utopias where players can explore "other ways of being in the world and ultimately new worlds." In "Organizing New Approaches to Games," Bonnie Ruberg interviews Chelsea Howe, Toni Rocca, and Sarah Schoemann about the unique difficulties and rewards of organizing diversity-focused video game events. Speaking about QGCon, GaymerX, and Different Games, respectively, Howe, Rocca, and Schoemann share insights to help future activists and organizers bring together the queer games community. Finally, the collection closes with Ruberg's "Forty-Eight-Hour Utopia: On Hope and the Future of Queerness in Games." Reflecting on her experience co-organizing QGCon, she asks, What is the value of creating a welcoming but temporary space for diversity in games? Change comes slowly, Ruberg admits, but that change begins with moments of excitement and hope. Imagining a different future for queerness and games means opening ourselves to joy and community, however briefly.

Conclusion

Queer game studies has emerged now precisely because now is when queer game studies is needed the most. We need queer game studies now because there has never been a more energizing, inspiring time to look for the queerness in games. Queer game makers are receiving international recognition. Thousands of queer players are coming to conventions. As diversity-focused game conferences continue to grow and scholarly interest in queer theory and game studies spreads, this new area of interdisciplinary work will surely take its place as an important new paradigm that speaks to both games scholarship and queer scholarship. Queer studies, game studies, and even queer content in games all have long histories. Here and now, those histories intersect—but the results of that intersection are still in flux. Today, we have the opportunity to open up a multitude of avenues for new inquiry. These authors all speak to this moment of convergence. Whether implicitly or explicitly, they each offer answers to this volume's key questions: Why queer game studies now? What is queer about video games? What is queer about queer game studies?

This is an exciting time, but also a turbulent and upsetting one. It is crucial that we address the current toxic games environment and condemn the ways that feminist and queer game makers, players, critics, and scholars have been attacked. Yet we also need to make room for hope, for optimism, and for the future. We must provide a sober assessment of the past and current climate, but we must also value the important work that our contributors are already doing to make the games industry and game culture better. This is not the first time that queer communities have faced backlash at moments of progress. When we are being made to feel like our voices should be silenced, we need a chance to be heard. Queer game studies offers such a chance. It points directly to the ways that systems of power produce opportunities for oppression but also resistance.

The editors would like to thank Danielle Kasprzak and the rest of the University of Minnesota Press staff for making this book a reality. Thanks as well to the two reviewers who offered valuable insight into how best to frame and shape this collection. We are grateful to our colleagues Ben Aslinger, Mattie Brice, Christopher Goetz, Chelsea Howe, and Staci Tucker, who each played a role in shaping this volume. Thanks also to Nicholas Taylor for copyediting, and to Cathy Hannabach for writing the index. And, last but not least, we are grateful to all of our contributors, who stuck through the long publishing process so that we could share their wonderful writing with the world. We are honored to feature their work here and we look forward to the new scholarship, thinking, and design it will inspire.

Notes

1. This volume, chapter 1.

2. Lesbian, gay, bisexual, transgender, and queer. Other authors in this volume use LGBT, where queerness is not central to the analysis, or LGBTQI to be inclusive of people who are intersex. Different acronyms are used in different communities for a variety of reasons. We have chosen to allow authors to use the acronym that best fits what they are talking about and where they are coming from, rather than standardize the acronym used.

3. An example of scholarship that engages in this sort of thinking is Shira Chess's "The Queer Case of Video Games: Orgasms, Heteronormativity, and Video Game Narrative," *Critical Studies in Media Communication* 33, no. 1 (2016): 84–94.

4. Jonathan Cabiria, "Virtual World and Real World Permeability: Transference of Positive Benefits for Marginalized Gay and Lesbian Populations," *Journal for Virtual Worlds Research* 1, no. 1 (2008): 1–12; Alexis Pulos, "Confronting Heteronormativity in Online Games: A Critical Discourse Analysis of LGBTQ Sexuality in *World of Warcraft*," *Games and Culture* 8, no. 2 (2013): 77–97; Jenny Sundén, "Desires at Play: On Closeness and Epistemological Uncertainty," *Games and Culture* 7, no. 2 (2012): 164–84; Jenny Sundén and Malin Sveningsson, *Gender and Sexuality in Online Game Cultures: Passionate Play* (London: Routledge, 2012); Christian Schmieder, "World of Maskcraft vs. World of Queercraft? Communication, Sex, and Gender in the Online Role-Playing Game *World of Warcraft*," *Journal of Gaming and Virtual Worlds* 1, no. 1 (2009): 5–21; Nathan James A. Thompson, "Queer/ing Game Space: Sexual Play in *World of Warcraft*," *Media Fields Journal* 8 (2014): http:// mediafieldsjournal.squarespace.com/queering-game-space/.

5. Jonathan Alexander, "A Real Effect on Gameplay: Computer Gaming, Sexuality, and Literacy," in *Gaming Lives in the Twenty-First Century*, ed. Gail E. Hawisher, Cynthia L. Selfe, and James Paul Gee (New York: Palgrave Macmillan, 2007), 167–202; James B. Kelley, "Gay Naming in Online Gaming," *Names* 60, no. 4 (2012): 193–200.

6. Megan Condis, "No Homosexuals in *Star Wars*? BioWare, 'Gamer'

Identity, and the Politics of Privilege in a Convergence Culture," *Convergence* 21, no. 2 (2014): 198–212; James Kelley, "'Hot Avatars' in 'Gay Gear': The Virtual Male Body as Site of Conflicting Desires in *Age of Conan: Hyborian Adventures*," in *Conan Meets the Academy: Multidisciplinary Essays on the Enduring Barbarian*, ed. Jonas Prida (Jefferson, N.C.: McFarland, 2013), 144–73.

7. This volume, chapter 16; see also Adrienne Shaw, "Talking to Gaymers: Questioning Identity, Community, and Media Representation," *Westminster Papers in Culture and Communication* 9, no. 1 (2012): 67–89.

8. Mia Consalvo, "Hot Dates and Fairy-Tale Romances: Studying Sexuality in Video Games," in *The Video Game Theory Reader*, ed. Mark J. P. Wolf and Bernard Perron (New York: Routledge, 2003), 171–94.

9. Robert Alan Brookey and Kristopher L. Cannon, "Sex Lives in Second Life," *Critical Studies in Media Communication* 26, no. 2 (2009): 145–64; Arne Schröder, "'We Don't Want It Changed, Do We?' Gender and Sexuality in Role Playing Games," *Eludamos* 2, no. 2 (2008): 241–56; Stephen Greer, "Playing Queer: Affordances for Sexuality in *Fable* and *Dragon Age*," *Journal of Gaming and Virtual Worlds* 5, no. 1 (2013): 3–21; Linzi Juliano, "Digital," review of *A Love Story*; *Bully*; *Grand Theft Auto IV*; *Portal*; and *Dys4ia*, *Theatre Journal* 64, no. 4 (2012): 595–98.

10. Brenda Brathwaite, *Sex in Video Games* (Newton Center, Mass.: Charles River Media, 2007).

11. Jordan Youngblood, "'C'mon! Make Me a Man!' *Persona 4*, Digital Bodies, and Queer Potentiality," *Ada* 2 (2013): http://adanewmedia.org/2013/06/issue2-youngblood/; Kazumi Hasegawa, "Falling in Love with History: Japanese Girls' *Otome* Sexuality and Queering Historical Imagination," in *Playing with the Past: Digital Games and the Simulation of History*, ed. Matthew W. Kapell and Andrew B. R. Elliott (New York: Bloomsbury, 2013), 135–49.

12. Bonnie Ruberg, "Playing to Lose: The Queer Art of Failing at Video Games," in *Identity Matters: Race, Gender, and Sexuality in Video Game Studies*, ed. TreaAndrea Russworm and Jennifer Malkowski (Bloomington: Indiana University Press, in press); Bonnie Ruberg, "No Fun: The Queer Potential of Video Games That Annoy, Anger, Disappoint, and Hurt," *QED: A Journal of Queer Worldmaking* 2 (in press).

13. Torill Mortensen, *Perceiving Play: The Art and Study of Computer Games* (New York: Peter Lang, 2009); Garry Crawford, *Video Gamers* (London: Routledge, 2012); Geoff King and Tanya Krzywinska, *Tomb Raiders and Space Invaders: Videogame Forms and Contexts* (London: I. B. Tauris, 2006);

Katie Salen and Eric Zimmerman, *Rules of Play: Game Design Fundamentals* (Cambridge, Mass.: MIT Press, 2004).

14. Ian Bogost, *Unit Operations: An Approach to Videogame Criticism* (Cambridge, Mass.: MIT Press, 2008).

15. Janet H. Murray, *Hamlet on the Holodeck: The Future of Narrative in Cyberspace* (Cambridge, Mass.: MIT Press, 1997).

16. Markku Eskelinen, "The Gaming Situation," *Game Studies* 1, no. 1 (2001): http://www.gamestudies.org/0101/eskelinen/.

17. Bogost, *Unit Operations*, 100.

18. Ian Bogost, *Persuasive Games: The Expressive Power of Videogames* (Cambridge, Mass.: MIT Press, 2010).

19. Janet Murray, "The Last Word on Ludology vs. Narratology in Game Studies," address delivered at the Digital Games Researcher Association Annual Conference, Vancouver, B.C., 2005, http://inventingthemedium.com /2013/06/28/the-last-word-on-ludology-v-narratology-2005/; Jesper Juul, "The Magic Circle and the Puzzle Piece," in *Conference Proceedings of the Philosophy of Computer Games, 2008,* ed. Stephan Günzel, Michael Liebe, and Dieter Mersch (Potsdam, B.D.R.: Potsdam University Press, 2008), 56–67; Mia Consalvo, "There Is No Magic Circle," *Games and Culture* 4, no. 4 (2009): 408–17; Thomas M. Malaby, "Beyond Play: A New Approach to Games," *Games and Culture* 2, no. 2 (2007): 95–113; Eric Zimmerman, "Jerked around by the Magic Circle: Clearing the Air Ten Years Later," *Gamasutra,* February 7, 2012, http://www.gamasutra.com/view/feature/135063/jerked _around_by_the_magic_circle_.php.

20. Frans Mäyrä, *Introduction to Game Studies: Games in Culture* (Los Angeles: SAGE, 2008); Mia Consalvo and Nathan Dutton, "Game Analysis: Developing a Methodological Toolkit for the Qualitative Study of Games," *Game Studies* 6, no. 1 (2006): http://gamestudies.org/0601/articles/consalvo _dutton.

21. T. L. Taylor, "The Assemblage of Play," *Games and Culture* 4, no. 4 (2009): 332.

22. Jennifer Jenson and Suzanne de Castell, "Theorizing Gender and Digital Gameplay: Oversights, Accidents, and Surprises," *Eludamos* 2, no. 1 (2008): 15–25.

23. Laine Nooney, "A Pedestal, a Table, a Love Letter: Archaeologies of Gender in Videogame History," *Game Studies* 13, no. 2 (2013): http://gamestudies .org/1302/articles/nooney.

24. T. L. Taylor, *Play between Worlds: Exploring Online Game Culture* (Cambridge, Mass.: MIT Press, 2006); Helen W. Kennedy, "Lara Croft: Feminist

Icon or Cyberbimbo? On the Limits of Textual Analysis," *Game Studies* 2, no. 2 (2002): http://www.gamestudies.org/0202/kennedy/.

25. Eve Kosofsky Sedgwick, *Tendencies* (Durham, N.C.: Duke University Press, 1993); Judith Butler, *Bodies That Matter: On the Discursive Limits of "Sex"* (New York: Routledge, 1993).

26. Alexander Doty, *Making Things Perfectly Queer: Interpreting Mass Culture* (Minneapolis: University of Minnesota Press, 1993); Richard Dyer, *The Culture of Queers* (New York: Routledge, 2011).

27. Larry Gross, *Up from Invisibility: Lesbians, Gay Men, and the Media in America* (New York: Colombia University Press, 2002); Lisa Henderson, *Love and Money: Queers, Class, and Cultural Production* (New York: New York University Press, 2013); Katherine Sender, *Business, Not Politics: The Making of the Gay Market* (New York: New York University Press, 2005).

28. Mary L. Gray, *Out in the Country: Youth, Media, and Queer Visibility in Rural America* (New York: New York University Press, 2009); David Valentine, *Imagining Transgender: An Ethnography of a Category* (Durham, N.C.: Duke University Press, 2007); Gayle Salamon, "Justification and Queer Method, or Leaving Philosophy," *Hypatia* 24, no. 1 (2009): 229–30; Sara Ahmed, *Queer Phenomenology: Orientations, Objects, Others* (Durham, N.C.: Duke University Press, 2006); Lisa Duggan, *The Twilight of Equality: Neoliberalism, Cultural Politics, and the Attack on Democracy* (Boston: Beacon Press, 2003); Dean Spade, *Normal Life: Administrative Violence, Critical Trans Politics, and the Limits of the Law* (Brooklyn: South End Press, 2011); Susan Stryker, *Transgender History* (Berkeley, Calif.: Seal Press, 2008).

29. Juana María Rodríguez, *Queer Latinidad: Identity Practices and Discursive Spaces* (New York: New York University Press, 2003); Mel Y. Chen, *Animacies: Biopolitics, Racial Mattering, and Queer Affect* (Durham, N.C.: Duke University Press, 2012); Chandan Reddy, *Freedom with Violence: Race, Sexuality, and the U.S. State* (Durham, N.C.: Duke University Press, 2011); Jasbir K. Puar, *Terrorist Assemblages: Homonationalism in Queer Times* (Durham, N.C.: Duke University Press, 2007).

30. Karli June Cerankowski and Megan Milks, "New Orientations: Asexuality and Its Implications for Theory and Practice," *Feminist Studies* 36, no. 3 (2010): 650–64; Karli June Cerankowski and Megan Milks, *Asexualities: Feminist and Queer Perspectives* (New York: Routledge, 2014).

31. "Queers Read This," *Anonymous Queers*, June 1990, http://www.qrd.org/qrd/misc/text/queers.read.this.

32. Michael Warner, "Introduction," in *Fear of a Queer Planet: Queer Politics and Social Theory*, ed. Michael Warner (Minneapolis: University of Minnesota Press, 1993), xxvi.

33. David L. Eng with Judith Halberstam and José Esteban Muñoz, "What's Queer about Queer Studies Now?" *Social Text* 23, nos. 3–4 (2005): 1–18.

34. *Games and Culture* 1, no. 1 (2006): 1–122.

35. "Lost Levels," nd, http://lostlevels.net/2013/.

36. Katie Williams, "GaymerX Will No Longer Hold Annual LGBT Conference," *IGN*, April 16, 2014, http://www.ign.com/articles/2014/04/16/gaymerx-will-no-longer-hold-annual-lgbt-conference.

37. Brendan Keogh, "Just Making Things and Being Alive about It: The Queer Games Scene," *Polygon*, May 24, 2013, http://www.polygon.com/features/2013/5/24/4341042/the-queer-games-scene; Alison Harvey, "Twine's Revolution: Democratization, Depoliticization, and the Queering of Game Design," *GAME: The Italian Journal of Game Studies* 3 (2014): 95–107.

38. Anna Anthropy, *Rise of the Videogame Zinesters: How Freaks, Normals, Amateurs, Artists, Dreamers, Drop-Outs, Queers, Housewives, and People Like You Are Taking Back an Art Form* (New York: Seven Stories Press, 2012).

39. Gabriel Arana, "Nintendo's Anti-gay Cop-Out: Why Its Demented Same-Sex Ban Is No Game," *Salon,* May 8, 2014, http://www.salon.com/2014/05/08/nintendos_anti_gay_cop_out_why_its_demented_same_sex_ban_is_no_game/.

40. We honor their decision, but boy, did you miss out on reading their excellent work!

41. Shira Chess and Adrienne Shaw, "A Conspiracy of Fishes, or, How We Learned to Stop Worrying about #GamerGate and Embrace Hegemonic Masculinity," *Journal of Broadcasting and Electronic Media* 59, no. 1 (2015): 208–20.

42. Bonnie Ruberg, "Introduction: Videogames, Queerness, and Beyond," *First Person Scholar,* February 18, 2015, http://www.firstpersonscholar.com/videogames-queerness-beyond/.

43. José Esteban Muñoz, *Cruising Utopia: The Then and There of Queer Futurity* (New York: New York University Press, 2009), 11.

44. Ibid., 189.

Part I   DEFINING QUEERNESS IN GAMES

Chapter **1**

What *Is* Queerness in Games, Anyway?

NAOMI CLARK

What lies at the intersection of queerness and games, and what has the bursting, proliferating dialogue centered around? Thankfully and unsurprisingly, we can find a multiplicity of answers to this question, but two large and slightly divergent currents stand out. One focuses on diversifying the content of games and representation of marginalized identities in the industry, while the other begins to investigate how to queer the structure of games.

"Queerness in games" has appeared in the media and public discourse mostly as a question of representation and inclusion: Who has been making most of our games, as opposed to who *could* be making them? What kind of people and experiences appear in the fictional universes that games can summon into existence, and whose life experiences are brought to bear on the stories told by or emerging from games? The status quo, to nobody's surprise, is that games have seldom been made by or for queers, or even with queers in mind; they're mostly created by young and middle-aged white and Asian men, to be sold to a similar if slightly younger and slightly browner audience of consumers. Just as in analogous battles in other forms of culture

and areas of public discourse, the struggle for inclusion and representation of queers has joined calls for more (and less stereotyped)
representation of women and people of color.

At a 2014 Game Developers Conference panel titled "How to Subversively Queer Your Work," game scholar Todd Harper provided
one summation of inclusivity's value proposition for the wider game
industry. With greater diversity of stories, characters, and voices,
Harper said, comes increased scope for the empathic possibilities of
games: "Empathy is the ability to see what matters to other people.
It's the ability to see what matters to someone who isn't you. Empathy is a muscle, and like any muscle you have to flex and use it
over and over until it becomes strong." Harper also suggested that
flipping the identity characteristics of protagonists in games could
broaden existing game narratives: a "bald, white, cismale space marine" could become "a half-shaved head, purple-haired, trans-woman
Latina space marine."[1]

In contrast to the focus on representation in game content, other
queer game creators have taken up the question of what happens
when we question norms and conventions about how games, or specific game genres, are expected to function. Avery McDaldno and
Joli St. Patrick gave a workshop at the 2013 Queerness and Games
Conference that explored a dozen potential techniques for independent non-digital role-playing and story games; among other things,
McDaldno and St. Patrick dismantled the notion, established since
the 1970s and influential on countless video games, that a character
in a role-playing game is controlled by and represents a single human
player.[2] In a workshop given at New York University's Game Center,
merritt kopas elaborated on McDaldno and St. Patrick's techniques
and urged participants to deconstruct existing game genres to find
the fundamental assumptions driving patterns of play, then queer
the genres by twisting, flipping, or undermining those conventions.[3]
These tactics bear more in common with the approaches of queer
theory to history, economic analyses, even information science—
locating unspoken norms by which a field of human activity or
knowledge is operating, and finding points of rupture that destabilize those assumptions, opening up those fields to a wider and potentially more liberatory set of possibilities.

Outside the culture of games, in spaces concerned with LGBTQ activism and political organizing, the queer politic is often understood to be at odds with more dominant "gay rights" rhetoric. The latter is characterized as a drive toward acceptance into existing institutions such as legally recognized marriage or military service. Anti-assimilationist queer activists, exemplified by documents such as the Against Equality online archive, instead choose to advocate from the marginalized position of queerness to ask bigger questions about who's excluded from or harmed by these institutions, and how existing structures are invisibly designed to support the status quo, the smooth operation of capitalism, the yoking of human beings into "productive members of society," and so forth.[4] It's tempting to try to look at calls for representation and inclusion in big-budget games as being akin to the assimilationist rhetoric, but there are several nuances to consider.

Game writer Samantha Allen, another panelist from "How to Subversively Queer Your Game," has described the move to push for a greater number of LGBT-inclusive games as "a lifeline to lost gamers," among them "young, closeted queer people" who may not yet be aware of more experimental, lesser-known games done by queer creators outside the big-budget studio model.[5] Her point that "we have to employ a plurality of tactics to bring down the monolith" can apply just as readily to the process of creating independent games as to advocating for the kinds of games that get made. Unlike political organizing and fund-raising, where attention and money are divided between causes that benefit people with differing relationships to established institutions, a creative process can encompass both approaches.

In 2012, during a discussion about Anna Anthropy's *Rise of the Videogame Zinesters,*[6] a senior colleague asked me what kind of benefits I thought a more diverse pool of creators, including queer creators like myself or Anthropy, had for games. My response was that creators with marginalized experiences and subaltern viewpoints have a different capacity to make new kinds of games that we hadn't even seen yet. This answer was based largely on my experiences with two of Anthropy's own games. *Mighty Jill Off* (2008) matches a narrative theme expressing the dynamics of a queer BDSM relationship with game play that forces the player to submit to a cruel and repetitive task. What I found remarkable about *Mighty Jill Off* was not simply that game play and narrative content aligned to represent submission and dominance, but that the mode of interaction and goals also highlighted a related and broadly applicable way of seeing games, with the designer as the domme providing tasks, seemingly arbitrary outside of the system of play, that the player must willingly submit to in the pursuit of pleasure. Game designers[7] and philosophers[8] writing about games have echoed this understanding of games for years, but *Mighty Jill Off* was the first time I had seen the theme bound to overt narrative content—a possibility only realizable by the expression of queer lives in games.

Anthropy's *dys4ia* (2012) goes further in the direction of queering established notions of games, to the point where game designers like Raph Koster opined that "a lot of *dys4ia* could have been built in PowerPoint and isn't a game."[9] Koster later retracted this take, which was rooted in the convention that games must have choices that let a player alter the state of the system. *dys4ia,* however, does something more subtle with its interactive aesthetics: it's presented as an autobiographical story, but one in which situations from life are represented by systems that the player must understand in order to navigate, rather than solely by words or images as in other forms of autobiography. *dys4ia* manages to destabilize one of the rarely questioned tenets of what a game *must have* to be considered a game, while also blazing new territory into overt autobiography. These two explorations are linked; unlike earlier pseudo-autobiographical games dealing in impressionistic representation of and musings on the creator's life, such as Jason Rohrer's *Passage* (2007) or Rod Humble's *The Marriage* (2007), *dys4ia* recounts actual past events from the creator's life. If Anthropy had followed the conventional rubric of games and allowed player actions to determine the course of the game, the autobiographical fidelity of *dys4ia* would have become mutable and subject to player whim.

Anthropy is far from the only queer game creator whose works combine representation of queer lives. *Realistic Kissing Simulator* (2014) by Jimmy Andrew and Loren Schmidt, uses two largely degendered heads to represent players, eluding the recently fashionable choice of "gay relationship or straight relationship" that has become a feature of games in franchises like *Dragon Age*. The game simultaneously does away with conventional notions of designer-ordained goals, mimetic realism (despite its title), and the automatic assumption of consent at the beginning of play, leaving players to figure out how and why to collaborate and encounter each other via a system of elongated, floppy tongues. Mattie Brice's EAT (2013) is a system of rules meant to be applied to the player's everyday life in order to approximate the challenges of her own existence as a black trans woman, student, and writer; the system is daunting enough that it's unclear whether anyone has ever been determined and brave enough to play it. The games of Christine Love often adopt the form of an East Asian–style visual novel or dating sim, but supplement purely romantic or sexual content with explorations of changing notions of privacy and multivalent reactions of women to repressive patriarchal society; most of the player's actions in *Analogue: A Hate Story* (2012), prior to a moment of judgment, involve reviewing an epistolary account of the past. Love's games also frequently involve "impossible" challenges that may appear to be goals for gamers, but elude the player without cheating or hacking the game.

merritt kopas's *Lim* (2012) has frequently been cited as an example of a queer game due to the way it systemically represents the experience of attempting to "pass" as one gender or another but ultimately failing and being subjected to harassment. (It's worth noting that via abstraction, *Lim* contains the potential to be played as a metaphor for multiple kinds of passing, such as passing as multiple racial identities.) Beyond the act of representation, another, less-cited aspect of *Lim* deeply queers the experience: the collision of objects in the system, representing harassment of a non-passing protagonist, sometimes grows so violent that the protagonist is pushed through the walls constraining the space of play and into an empty, lonely space beyond. kopas has refused to clarify whether this effect was part of her intention as the creator, or a glitch that arose from the code of the game—an unintentional "flaw" that happens to harmonize with the rest of the game to create a possibility of utter refusal emerging from trauma and movement beyond the confines of a harsh system. By keeping this possibility ambiguous, kopas leaves open the possibility that this is a discovery of players, not a top-down artifact of authorial intent.

Studies of game design have long succumbed to a kind of dualism, a bifurcation of the game experience into two supposedly separate aspects that are often portrayed as being in tension. The narrative content of a game, sometimes called the dramatic elements,[10] includes characters, plot, fictional world, spoken dialogue, and so forth, while the systemic structure of a game, also known as the formal elements,[11] consists of things like the rules, pieces, interactions and choices available to the player, underlying algorithms or mathematical models of economies or physics, and so forth. Theoretical arguments between "narratologists," supposedly advocating the importance of dramatic elements, and their opponents, the "ludologists," date back to 1997; the formal elements have long been held up as the *unique provenance* of games, that which distinguishes them from other forms of culture (many of which, of course, involve narrative content but not playable systems).[12] The two sides of formal/narrative dualism are often described as being in an irreducible tension that designers must do their best to manage or mask, lest "ludonarrative dissonance" color the player's experience.[13]

Vocal critics, many of them consumer fans, have attacked many of the games described above—as well as other games with queer themes, such as the Fullbright Company's *Gone Home* (2013)—on the basis that they're "not real games" or "just very simple games." This understanding is based entirely on the formal elements of the game, as was Koster's initial critique. Reducing a game to its formal elements, whatever the rationale (e.g., "It's the aspect that only games can do") seems akin to insisting that invertebrates, as a class, must primarily be understood by examining and evaluating their internal bone structure. Giving primacy to the skeleton of a game, this approach flays off the skin and flesh, the distinguishing characteristics of experience that are the first encountered by a player, to prioritize the skeletal system that more expert forensic analysts (most of them game designers or theorists) can take apart to gain a supposedly truer understanding of the game.

When fleshed of content and linkage to the context of lived experience, the systems of many queer games may appear to such a "forensic examination" to be identical to older interactive forms. Traditionalists describe *dys4ia* as akin to a PowerPoint presentation, or games made with Twine are equivalent to *Choose Your Own Adventure* game books. It's only when looked at in context, clothed in flesh, that this illusion of retrogression vanishes and we can see that new relationships between different aspects of games can arise from queer modes of creation—which, it should be added, are nearly always operating outside of a profitable market context or financial support from publishers.

Ironically, it's the refusal to obey orthodox conventions about games, and a willingness to embrace bare systems, that makes it easier for queer games to achieve striking new forms of interplay and consonance between the experiences and aspects of queer existence they represent and the structures of interaction that players encounter. The relationship between experience and systemic representation in the games by queer creators mentioned above is often crisply straightforward—sometimes simply revolving around what's placed on or removed from the canvas of possibility. These simple approaches manage to sidestep the complex, yet supposedly inevitable and frustrating, clash between "ludo" and "narrative." Queer game creators have already imagined queer modes of game play in which ludonarrative dissonance, at least, is not a vivid concern.

Although we may wish to question the taken-for-granted dualism of narrative and game play and we can dismiss the false either/or binary of "push for inclusion of marginalized identities in big-budget games" *or* "queer existing norms of game play to create new types of work," it's still worth asking a final question: if different approaches to queerness and games aren't necessarily in tension with each other, what *are* they in tension with?

One possible answer returns to the question of assimilation of marginalized identities rather than maintaining the possibility of an outside, questioning, and destabilizing voice. Rather than associating assimilation with the demand for greater representation in game fictions, it may be useful to consider assimilation as *the legitimization of games as a social good.*

Games, much like queers, have a long history of being maligned and regarded as frivolous, jejune, or degenerate. Sports were regarded separately for much of games' history, and many of the most widespread games played by adults were games of chance used for gambling—

associated with the lower classes, soldiers, criminals, and so forth. In the nineteenth-century United States, game creators began to try to rehabilitate the image of games when they sought to sell games to families. Some game creators replaced dice, strongly associated with gambling, with a new random-number-generating spinner (the "teetotum"); other board games, like *The Mansion of Happiness,* added content to the traditional race game genre that promoted Christian morals.[14]

Twentieth-century stereotypes about games and gamers are much more familiar to today's gamers and game developers: parents accusing *Dungeons & Dragons* players of placing suicide curses on their children, video games becoming secondary culprits in school shootings, studies of game addiction and whether games cause violence.[15] Rather than thuggish gamblers, the popular conception of gamers is now that of an overweight, unshaven, socially maladjusted, immature white man. Game academics, gamers themselves, and the game industry have continuously struggled against these perceptions by deploying counter-studies, reactionary anger of the sort that exemplified the #GamerGate movement, and public relations tactics, respectively. The game industry, in particular, has benefited from a broadening of market categories (the introduction of "casual gamer," for instance) that helps normalize the idea of games and creates the perception that most average people play games.

The most enduring perception of games, however—so fundamental to commonly held notions of games that it has structured human–game relations throughout history—is that games are "only" a leisure activity, a "pass-time" engaged in for pleasure rather than productivity, as an escape from work and possibly from mundane reality. This notion can be seen as a generative base for other stereotypes: games are frivolous, meant for children's abundant free time rather than for serious adults, save for moral degenerates who may become so enthralled by the possibility of escape from the ordinary that they become delusional, unable to distinguish fantasy from reality. This primal understanding of games is also the most recent to be the subject of an attempted rehabilitation: the Games for Change movement suggests that games can be deployed on serious subjects to convey political consciousness, while the use of games as productive components of education has most lately been practiced under nomenclature like game-based learning. Gamification, meanwhile, seeks to use games in whole or part to adjust player motivations, at their own behest or in accordance with institutional goals. These approaches have two things in common: goals involving harnessing games for more "productive" and "useful" ends than leisure, and Jane McGonigal.

McGonigal exemplifies the intersection of various productive uses for games; she advocates the potential for games to prevent PTSD in trauma victims, creates games that teach or raise consciousness about an issue, and designed a gamified system to cultivate positive motivation and psychological reinforcement toward a player's self-defined goals.[16] Her vision for games doesn't just involve rehabilitating and assimilating them into a "productive member of society," participating in established institutions from education to the nonprofit industrial complex; she orates about the potential for games to become a savior, the *most* productive aspect of society. The goals McGonigal advocates and designs for—awareness of peak oil problems, recovery from traumatic injury, motivated physical exercise, learning about public libraries, planting community gardens—are difficult to impugn. The conversion of play into a resource to be harnessed, however, is perhaps the most ambitious attempt to assimilate games into usefulness. According to McGonigal, the libidinous energy of engagement with games—the pleasure of unproductive play, the nebulous notion of "fun"—can potentially be channeled towards all sorts of productive goals. By the same token, this energy could also be harnessed for goals diametrically opposed to the positive ends that McGonigal champions.

The work of philosopher Bernard Suits forms one of the foundations of McGonigal's approach to game design, specifically the definition of games from his 1978 text, *The Grasshopper: Games, Life, and Utopia.* According to Suits, a game must involve "voluntary obstacles"—another lens on the system that a player submits to in order to play a game. McGonigal sees this aspect of games as explaining "everything that is motivating and rewarding and fun about games."[17] Her method of design involves placing voluntary obstacles—challenges that one decides to overcome—along the way to a goal that's productive or improves life in some way. Unlike McGonigal, however, Suits rejects the notion of productive goals for games. In *The Grasshopper*, the titular protagonist is a version of the same character in Aesop's fable about the ant and the grasshopper—an insect who eschews work for pleasure. Suits reimagines the grasshopper as a philosopher who seeks ultimate goods—activities that are pursued for their own ends, and for no other reason. The laboring ants, preparing for the winter, are working for a purpose, but the grasshopper seeks only happiness for its own sake, and concludes that games are the way to this utopia. In an ideal world, he reasons, we would do nothing but play.

Although Suits may not have been entirely serious in his characterization of games as the main ingredient in utopian living, the cast he gives to the inherently unproductive nature of games is striking; in light of movements to rehabilitate and instrumentalize games for productive ends, we must ask what we are losing in the rush to raise games out of the scorned red-light district of trivial, immature pleasures. Games can be legitimized by yoking them to support the institutions of education, propaganda, nonprofit organizations, and behavioral psychology—but should they be yoked? Games are even on a climb toward legitimacy as an art form, and the debate over whether games "can be art"[18] is nearly a foregone conclusion as the Museum of Modern Art adds games to its collection.[19]

Even Eric Zimmerman, who in 2013 predicted that the twenty-first century will be the "Ludic Century" where games become the preeminent creative form,[20] wrote to discourage the assimilation of games as an accepted form of art exactly a year later: "Once games are just another department in the academy, just another section in the newspaper, just another kind of festival or marketplace or catalog then they no longer have the disruptive power that makes them so special. Art is the name for establishment culture—works that have ceased to challenge and offend."[21]

Anyone who has engaged with video games in the last three decades is familiar with the primary institution that games *have* been successfully deployed in service of: the consumer marketplace. Games were once created and mutated as a form of folk creativity, distributed and taught by word of mouth; the rehabilitation of games' association with morally degenerate gambling made the family-friendly board game market possible, and the computing revolution enabled an explosion in the number of increasingly disposable product choices available for consumers. Further assimilation in the service of established institutions could herald a turn toward other productive uses for games besides profit and employment. But the queer question must remain: What will we lose in the process as we make additional bids for legitimacy?

Notes

1. Todd Harper, "How to Subversively Queer Your Work," panel discussion at Game Developers Conference, San Francisco, March 20, 2014.

2. Avery McDaldno and Joli St. Patrick, "Beyond Representation: Queer Mechanics in Tabletop Games," conference presentation, Queerness and Games Conference, Berkeley, Calif., October 27, 2013.

3. merritt kopas, "Interrupting Play: Queer Games and Futurity," workshop, New York University Game Center, Brooklyn, February 28, 2014.

4. *Against Equality,* nd, http://www.againstequality.org/.

5. Samantha Allen, "Closing the Gap between Queer and Mainstream Games," *Polygon,* April 2, 2014, http://www.polygon.com/2014/4/2/5549878 /closing-the-gap-between-queer-and-mainstream-games.

6. Anna Anthropy, *Rise of the Videogame Zinesters: How Freaks, Normals, Amateurs, Artists, Dreamers, Drop-Outs, Queers, Housewives, and People Like You Are Taking Back an Art Form* (New York: Seven Stories Press, 2012).

7. Marc LeBlanc, "Eight Kinds of Fun," *The Collected Game Design Rants of Marc "MAHK" LeBlanc,* nd, http://8kindsoffun.com/.

8. Bernard Suits, *The Grasshopper: Games, Life, and Utopia* (Calgary: Broadview Press, 2005).

9. Raph Koster, "Two Cultures and Games," *Raph's Website,* July 6, 2012, http://www.raphkoster.com/2012/07/06/two-cultures-and-games/.

10. Tracy Fullerton, *Game Design Workshop: A Playcentric Approach to Creating Innovative Games* (Boca Raton, Fla.: CRC Press, 2008), 33–43.

11. Ibid., 26–33.

12. For narratology, see Janet Murray, *Hamlet on the Holodeck* (Cambridge, Mass.: MIT Press, 1998). For ludology, see Espen J. Aarseth, *Cybertext: Perspectives on Ergodic Literature* (Baltimore: Johns Hopkins University Press, 1997).

13. Clint Hocking, "Ludonarrative Dissonance in *BioShock*," *Click Nothing*, October 7, 2007, http://clicknothing.typepad.com/click_nothing/2007/10/ludonarrative-d.html.

14. Julia Keren-Detar, "Discovering Grim History through Games: Tales Told by Early American Board Games," address delivered at IndieCade East, Museum of the Moving Image, Astoria, N.Y., February 14, 2014.

15. For more on legal efforts of concerned parents against *Dungeons & Dragons*, see David Waldron, "Role-Playing Games and the Christian Right: Community Formation in Response to a Moral Panic," *Journal of Religion and Popular Culture* 9, no. 1 (2005): http://www.utpjournals.press/doi/abs/10.3138/jrpc.9.1.003.

16. Jane McGonigal, *SuperBetter: A Revolutionary Approach to Getting Stronger, Happier, Braver, and More Resilient* (New York: Penguin, 2015).

17. Jane McGonigal, *Reality Is Broken* (New York: Penguin, 2011), 19–20.

18. For a prominent example of public debate on this topic, see Roger Ebert, "Games vs. Art: Ebert vs. Barker," *Chicago Sun-Times*, July 21, 2007.

19. Olivia Solon, "MoMA to Exhibit Videogames, from *Pong* to *Minecraft*," *Wired*, November 29, 2012, http://www.wired.com/2012/11/moma-videogames/.

20. Eric Zimmerman, "Manifesto for the Ludic Century," September 9, 2013, http://ericzimmerman.com/files/texts/Manifesto_for_a_Ludic_Century.pdf.

21. Eric Zimmerman, "Games, Stay Away from Art. Please," *Polygon*, September 10, 2014, http://www.polygon.com/2014/9/10/6101639/games-art.

Chapter **2**

Queergaming

EDMOND Y. CHANG

Queergaming is a provocation, a call to games, a horizon of possibilities. Queergaming is a refusal of the idea that digital games and gaming communities are the sole provenance of adolescent, straight, white, cisgender, masculine, able, male, and "hardcore" bodies and desires and the articulation of and investment in alternative modes of play and ways of being. Queergaming is a challenge to this stereotypical, status quo intersection of game players, developers, cultures, and technologies, what I have elsewhere called the "technonormative matrix,"[1] the digitized, gamified version of Judith Butler's heteronormative matrix, "the matrix of power and discursive relations that effectively produce and regulate the intelligibility of [sex, gender, or sexuality] for us."[2] Ultimately, queergaming is heterogeneity of play, imagining different, even radical game narratives, interfaces, avatars, mechanics, soundscapes, programming, platforms, playerships, and communities. It is gaming's changing present and necessary future.

Queergaming, a term I am coining as a response to the normativities of games, asks the following question: How might we think about ways to play games and make games that recognize and work around the limitations and flexibilities of digital computers, player expectations, and the "playing it straight" cultures at large? As I have argued elsewhere, "given the binary nature of digital computers—from platform to programming—the difficulty of queering games remains a challenge. After all, what is a game but a matrix of code, power relations, and constraints? . . . In other words, games always constrain players via normative narratives and mechanics."[3] How then might games embrace and enhance queer transformations, happy accidents, glitches, and switches that allow for non-technonormative practices, opportunities, and endgames? In other words, how might we think about what Alexander Galloway calls *countergaming* or "redefining play itself and thereby realizing [gaming's] true potential as a political and cultural avant-garde"?[4] Drawing on Peter Wollen's definitions of the countercinema of the 1960s, Alexander Galloway in *Gaming: Essays on Algorithmic Culture* argues for countergaming, which "exists in opposition to and outside the gaming mainstream" and which models not only what avant-garde gaming should look like but what it should play like, juxtaposing and experimenting with form, genre, function, and experience.[5] Wollen articulated seven values of "old" cinema versus avant-garde cinema (holding Jean-Luc Godard up as an exemplar) including narrative transitivity (continuity, logical progression) versus narrative intransitivity (interrupted continuity, episodic, digression), transparency (naturalizing and disappearing the technology of film) versus foregrounding (making the mechanics of film apparent), and closure (a self-contained, bounded, resolved whole) versus aperture (open-endedness, excess, intertextuality). Galloway adapts Wollen's seven values to the medium of digital games that not only identify "alternate formal strategies but the active employment and gleeful exploration of those strategies."[6] Galloway's *six* values of countergaming include:

1. *Transparency versus foregrounding.* (Removing the apparatus from the image versus pure interplay of graphics apparatus or code displayed without representational imagery.)
2. *Game play versus aestheticism.* (Narrative game play based on a coherent rule set versus modernist formal experiments.)

3. *Representational modeling versus visual artifacts.* (Mimetic modeling of objects versus glitches and other unexpected products of the graphics engine.)
4. *Natural physics versus invented physics.* (Newtonian laws of motion, ray tracing, collisions, et cetera, versus incoherent physical laws and relationships.)
5. *Interactivity versus non-correspondence.* (Instant, predictable linkage between controller input and game play versus barriers between controller input and game play.)
6. *Gamic action versus radical action.* (Conventional gaming poetics versus alternative modes of game play.)[7]

Though Galloway's list foregrounds primarily the manipulation and experimentation of the look and feel of games, he recognizes, "We need an avant-garde of video gaming not just in visual form but also in actional form. We need radical gameplay, not just radical graphics."[8] In other words, the challenge of new, different, alternative, even radical games requires a thoughtful reconfiguring and reimagining of more than just screen, pixel, interface, content, and controller. Queergaming dances with the possibilities of noncompetitive, nonproductive, nonjudgmental play, as well as the uncertainty and inefficiency of glitches, exploits, and other goofiness and the desire for queer worlds as opportunities for exploration, for different rules and goals, and even for the radical potential of failure.

To date, most "queer" games focus on superficial content, on same-sex *sex,* and queer marriage or couple plots. From BioWare's *Mass Effect* and *Dragon Age* series to the *Sims* franchise by Electronic Arts to Lionhead's *Fable* series to casual games like Digicub's *Mini Gay Boyfriend,* queerness in games is still largely window dressing, menu-driven identities (to quote Lisa Nakamura), a yes-or-no, date-him-or-her, have-sex-with-man-or-woman choice, which replicates the rather limited binary of hetero or homo, gay or straight, and even more insidiously the conservative belief that sexuality is a simple choice.[9] For example, in *Mass Effect 3,* playing as the male main character, Shepard, the player can choose to romance Kaidan, a non-player character controlled by the game. To woo and win Kaidan as a lover, the player must discover, maintain, and satisfy a series of in-game "choices" and requirements that unlock the availability and feasibility of the subplot. From the start of play, the path through the game's decision trees have already been plotted, predestined, and taking a wrong turn, making an incorrect response, means the queer match is lost. Given this inflexibility, in a sense, queer-friendly games and game design seem still mired in the limited and unproductive binary of narratology versus ludology, story versus playability. In these mainstream games, the solution to difference and diversity in games is token inclusion or flattened representation, and what it means to be inclusive is still narrow, often stereotyping, and problematic.

Queergaming *queers* countergaming, inflecting and infecting it with what Eve Kosofsky Sedgwick calls the "open mesh of possibilities," a challenge to normative structures, narratives, and technologies—a wholly different kind of adventure.[10] Or as Anna Anthropy, an independent, openly transgender game maker, argues, "In this world, 'gay' is a checkbox on a character sheet, a boolean, a binary bit, not an experience that greatly changes one's life, identity, and struggle."[11] Anthropy, best known for games like *dys4ia*, enunciates the need for alternative formal, ludic, narrative, and player strategies that collapse and complicate the terms and tensions that frame queer(ish) games: content versus experience, Boolean checkboxes versus the multiplicity of identities and embodiments, and the inescapable binary structure of digital computers. To that end, I propose an adaptation and repurposing of Galloway's countergaming values organized around intersections rather than binary oppositions. These queergaming values are outlined below.

Queer(er) design. From the platform up and from the player experience down, queergaming demands more than window dressing, more than binary choices, and more than the politics of representation. Building in a queer character or allowing for a queer plotline is not enough. Rather, a queerer game design takes up Anthropy's challenge when she argues, "Token characters are not the product of queer experiences. Actual queer experiences offer perspectives on identity, on struggle, and on romance that could be entirely different."[12] Representation must inform mechanics, and mechanics must deepen and thicken representation. For instance, BioWare's newest title in the *Dragon Age* series, *Dragon Age: Inquisition* (which debuted in late 2014), includes a "fully gay" non-player character, Dorian. Too-obvious Oscar Wilde reference aside, what does it mean for a character to be "fully" gay? Ostensibly, the answer is that Dorian will only be romance-able by a player character of the same gender, unlike earlier *Dragon Age* titles where characters were ostensibly "fully" bisexual, coded with hetero- and homosexual romance plots. Dorian's homosexuality is fixed, flattened into witty repartee and flamboyant stereotype. Unfortunately, as with other mainstream games, inclusion is defined as simply adding another checkbox, another token, another plotline. Granted, the fact that such a character is visible and playable is a step in the right direction, but how might games and game design enact queerness that is "procedurally relevant," more fully purposeful and "integrated with the narrative *and* ludic dimensions of the game"?[13] How does being "fully gay" affect not only narrative but also game play, mechanics, consequences, and possibilities? How does being gay differ or more importantly matter not just in terms of the plot or game world but also in terms of platform, programming, and player? Finally, how might we imagine and interact with a queer character and queer experience not organized solely around sex and romance?

Queer(er) play. Extending Galloway's hope for new "grammars of action" or "radical action" in games, which resist conventional gaming aesthetics, goals, and poetics, queergaming engages different grammars of play, radical play, not grounded in normative ideologies like competition, exploitation, colonization, speed, violence, rugged individualism, leveling up, and win states. Games should be about much more than bigger guns, grislier gore, and "pwning" (owning, topping, defeating, humiliating) other players. How might we develop game play and end states that invite exploration, cooperation, complexity, meditation, ambivalence, alternative spaces, even failure? What would it mean to play against the intent of the game's design, to repurpose or resist the rules, to play as a collective? For example, in the massively multiplayer online role-playing game *World of Warcraft*, a player character named Everbloom of the Feathermoon server maxed out their character (at the time, level 85) without killing a single in-game creature.[14] Going against the easy and obvious route, the player instead relied on wandering the game world and developing character skills in healing, herbalism, and mining. In fact, as Jenova Chen, designer of alternative games like *Flower* and *Journey*, says, "To me the measure of a human's greatness is the value they can contribute to society. The game industry doesn't need another shooter; it needs something to inspire them . . . If the entire game industry is focusing on excitement and adrenaline rushes . . . well, then I will look at peace, or love. That way we can expand the perception of what games can be and can accomplish."[15]

Queer remediation. Beyond queering the ways we design games and the ways we play games, queergaming describes the ways games and players respond to, reflect on, and remediate themselves and one another. J. David Bolter and Richard A. Grusin define remediation, in part, as the borrowing, appropriating, repurposing, and transforming of one medium by another. For example, video games often rely on the accepted and familiar logics of film like point of view or cut scenes. Bolter and Grusin say, "We call the representation of one medium in another 'remediation,' and we will argue that remediation is a defining characteristic of the new digital media. . . . The electronic medium is not set in opposition to painting, photography, or printing; instead, the computer is offered as a new means of gaining access to materials from these older media, as if the content of the older media can simply be poured into the new one."[16]

Queergaming takes up this idea of borrowing, appropriating, and repurposing to describe the strategies in which games and players take existing game titles, characters, stories, and worlds and queer them, remediate them to refashion and reimagine not only content and play but their very own relationship to ostensibly non-queer games and communities. Queergaming then is a response to the lack of queer representation, narratives, game play, game worlds, and gaming communities. Queergaming expands what it means to create, consume, and play to include game mods (or modifications) and Easter eggs (hidden messages, jokes, and surprises), paratexts like game wikis and player-created websites, walkthroughs, and "Let's play" videos, and even fan fiction, parodies, machinima, and cosplay (costume play). Queer remediation deploys what Henry Jenkins calls "textual poaching" or "a participatory culture which transforms the experience of media consumption into the production of new texts, indeed a new culture and a new community."[17] Jenkins argues:

> Fandom's very existence represents a critique of conventional forms of consumer culture. Yet fandom also provides a space within which fans may articulate their specific concerns about sexuality, gender, racism, colonialism, militarism, and forced conformity. These themes regularly surface within fan discussions and fan artworks. Fandom contains both negative and positive forms of empowerment. Its institutions allow the expression both of what fans are struggling against and what they are struggling for; its cultural productions articulate fans' frustration with their everyday life as well as their fascination with representations that pose alternatives.[18]

In other words, players have been imagining queerness in games and in their relationship to games long before inclusion and the commodification of queerness became fashionable.

Queer futures. Queergaming is all of the above and more. These are merely possibilities, potential lines of flight and tactics of change and transformation. Queergaming is a flickering of the screen, the taking of a different path. Queergaming is utopia, what José Esteban Muñoz calls "a structuring and educated mode of desiring that allows us to see and feel beyond the quagmire of the present . . . that thing that lets us feel that this world is not enough, that indeed something is missing."[19] It is a different kind of gamification—a queergamification—that does much more than offer more menu choices and decision trees, high-definition graphics and immersive sound, points and epic loots. It is a response to the failure of games to think beyond and outside the checkboxes of so-called target demographics to see that both games and players have been and will be more than a homogenous body and normative field. Queergaming is a direct challenge to the reality that "much of the pleasure of videogames comes at the expense of women and people of color, both literally and figuratively," and at the expense of those deemed different, monstrous, even dangerous.[20] It is optimism that cannot be paid for with the hopes and dreams and blood and bones of others. Like Galloway's call for a radical countergaming, queergaming is stepping out of "the rigid conceptualization that is a straight present" into "a collective temporal distortion" into queer fun, fantasy, even ecstasy.[21] All in all, queergaming is a demand for full, dimensional, consequential, variegated, and playable queer experiences, lives, bodies, and worlds.

Notes

1. Edmond Y. Chang, "Technoqueer: Re/Con/Figuring Posthuman Narratives" (PhD diss., University of Washington, 2012), 58.

2. Judith Butler, *Bodies That Matter: On the Discursive Limits of "Sex"* (New York: Routledge, 1993), 42.

3. Edmond Y. Chang, "Love Is in the Air: Queer (Im)Possibility and Straightwashing in *FrontierVille* and *World of Warcraft*," *QED: A Journal of GLBTQ Worldmaking* 2, no. 2 (2015): 8.

4. Alexander Galloway, *Gaming: Essays on Algorithmic Culture* (Minneapolis: University of Minnesota Press, 2006), 126.

5. Ibid., 108.

6. Ibid., 111.

7. Ibid., 124–25.

8. Ibid., 125.

9. Lisa Nakamura, *Cybertypes: Race, Ethnicity, and Identity on the Internet* (New York: Routledge, 2002), 102–3.

10. Eve Kosofsky Sedgwick, *Tendencies* (Durham, N.C.: Duke University Press, 1993), 8.

11. Anna Anthropy, "Now We Have Voices: Queering Videogames," *Auntie Pixelante*, January 12, 2013, http://www.auntiepixelante.com/?p=1888.

12. Ibid.

13. Todd Harper, "Gay-for-Play: Addressing the Challenge of Relevant Gay Game Content," *Gambit*, October 2011, http://gambit.mit.edu/readme/lectures/gay-for-play-addressing-the-ch.php#004952.

14. Tom Goldman, "Peaceful *World of Warcraft* Player Hits Max Level without Kills," *The Escapist*, April 10, 2011, http://www.escapistmagazine.com/news/view/109134-Peaceful-World-of-Warcraft-Player-Hits-Max-Level-Without-Kills.

15. Simon Parkin, "Jenova Chen: Journeyman," *Eurogamer,* July 21, 2015, http://www.eurogamer.net/articles/2012-04-02-jenova-chen-journeyman.

16. J. David Bolter and Richard A. Grusin, "Remediation," *Configurations* 4, no. 3 (2006): 339.

17. Henry Jenkins, *Textual Poachers: Television Fans and Participatory Culture* (New York: Routledge, 1992), 46.

18. Ibid., 283.

19. José Esteban Muñoz, *Cruising Utopia: The Then and There of Queer Futurity* (New York: New York University Press, 2009), 1.

20. Lisa Nakamura, "'It's a Nigger in Here! Kill the Nigger!' User-Generated Media Campaigns against Racism, Sexism, and Homophobia in Digital Games," in *The International Encyclopedia of Media Studies: Media Studies Futures, Volume VI,* ed. Kelly Gates (New York: Blackwell, 2013), 9.

21. Muñoz, *Cruising Utopia,* 185.

Chapter **3**

Queer Theory, the Body, and Video Games

DEREK A. BURRILL

> *The real political task in a society such as ours is to criticize the work-*
> *ings of institutions that appear to be both neutral and independent,*
> *to criticize and attack them in such a manner that the political vio-*
> *lence that has always exercised itself obscurely through them will be*
> *unmasked, so that one can fight against them.*
> —Michel Foucault, *The Chomsky–Foucault Debate: On Human Nature*

One of the defining characteristics of queer theory is its commitment to difference as pragmatics. It has histories, theorists of specific
gravity, and schools of thought, but avoids essentialist and binaristic
modes of being and representation, favoring hybridity, elision, and
discursivity. Since Teresa de Lauretis's use of the term "queer theory"
at a conference in 1990 (and in text in 1991) and through the work of
Eve Kosofsky Sedgwick and Judith Butler, concepts such as "heteronormativity" (the notion of the male/female heterosexual binary as
stable, and therefore, "natural") and "performativity" (gender, and
indeed identity, as constructed through a series of iterative performances) have helped to distinguish queer theory as a central (if not

the central) critical methodology in the understanding of identity, culture, and the body.[1] Much of this theory stems from the groundbreaking work of French poststructuralist Michel Foucault, particularly his concept of the discursive body. In his work, the body is a socially and historically constructed site of contention, inscribed, counter-inscribed, and erased by power and systems of domination and control.[2] Hence, queer theory and theories of the body are derived from common ground and concepts—difference, subjectivity, discourse, and power.

I find it to be no accident that games studies has undergone its own genesis over the same twenty-five or so years, as video games (as a product of the development of digital technologies, as well as global markets of visual and interactive pleasure) function as the media and art form ne plus ultra of the poststructuralist, decentered, and hybridized subject (including the attendant digital imaginary where the subject is objectified and subjectified simultaneously). So, it has always seemed to me that queer theory and games studies are fellow travelers that share a mutually imbricated approach. However, games studies, for the first decade of its rapid expansion toward maturity (the 2000s), failed, for the most part, to take advantage of this potential collaboration, even in terms of gender and sexuality studies in the more expansive sense.[3] This historical misstep is similar to the absence of identity and representational politics in film and TV studies for much of its prehistory (which, of course, has a great deal to do with historical realities: the slow dissemination and acceptance of critical theory and cultural studies, skepticism toward the postmodern, poststructuralist project, the changing nature of the media apparatus, etc.). So, it seems that queer games theory may be ripe for a "Mulvey moment."[4] However, in the case of games studies, so much of the fabric of queer theory, and identity politics and representational discourse in general, has already been carefully and collaboratively woven. Thus, queer games studies, in itself, might function collaboratively and with a discursive elasticity to which previous media theorists did not have ready access.

This is not to say that queer games studies (and queer game development/production) should simply co-opt the terms and dialogues from other queer/media theories and shellac them onto the study of interactive media. But, perhaps, notions such as narratology and ludology can be put to task in similar ways that other heteronormative and hegemonic theories have in the past. Often, narrative in games is assumed to be constructed from discrete units both modal and thematic, with tacit acknowledgment of player and designer exegesis. A queer understanding of narratology would necessarily focus on difference as a functional epistemology and praxis, moving beyond the binaries of plot/story, or *histoire/discours*. Jesper Juul's *Half-Real* similarly understands ludology as a methodology that postulates discourse-as-imagination, signaling a queer-inflected emphasis on the player's agency in, and resistance to, the unpacking of rules and systems of control.[5] In this sense, queer games studies would privilege neither narratology nor ludology as schema, but would perhaps instead configure a meta-hybrid approach that actively deconstructs the methodologies themselves. As the Letterist and Situationist Internationals employed *détournement* for the unmaking and reconfiguring of art and theory, queer games could employ an embodied, intermediated *détournement* as a productive strategy and tactic.

Video games sit at the center of a media matrix that paradoxically energizes the populace while it functionally satiates them, so that choice and desire become the same, where the couch in front of the screen functions as a stand-in for the supporting framework of hegemonic consumption. And, historically, queer theory, like games studies, has undergone several major shifts, has experienced troughs, peaks, and tremors, set amid a swirling backdrop of deeply embedded and ideologically momentous global traumas that themselves play out like a series of levels in a massively multiplayer online game. The game then distends to the level of the network, across the net, through the labyrinths of capital, crossing geographic boundaries and borders so that the game is at once local and global, bound and unfettered, enclosed and amorphous. The machines themselves— consoles, PCs, handhelds, server farms—are nodes in the network, buzzing feedback loops enmeshing the player in the dance of desire. Desiring machines. Machines of desire. Overlooked, ignored, and erased are the queer subjects, practices, and spaces that defy the machines of capital and commodification, and disrupt and refute the phallogocentrism and hegemony of heteronormativity. By focusing on the body—and by this I mean the body as a biological entity, a discursive force, and a culturally constructed apparatus—within digital space as well as in what someone like Sandy Stone likes to call "meatspace,"[6] queerness can enunciate itself through a vessel that serves, contains, and represents its particular notion of radical, embodied difference.

Bodies

As I suggested above, one theoretical deployment that should be central to queer games studies is body studies. Body studies, as an academic and theoretical approach, although living in and through many disciplines for decades, has only fairly recently identified itself as an approach in itself.[7] In the sense that the body is a central area of concern for queer theory, a focus on the body can also serve to enable queer theoretical approaches to games in order to break from past biases toward visuality, textuality, and formal structure. More specifically, I want to make a case for a focus on the body within queer games studies for several reasons:

(1) The body has traditionally been left out of games studies—regardless of whether it is always "present" during play—and has been effectively ignored in relation to the virtual self as focus of analysis.

(2) The body is central to queer theory, particularly bodies of difference, extension, and transition.

(3) The body is the site of digital and real labor and is largely responsible for the creation, development, manufacture, distribution, consumption, and dissemination of material games and products.

(4) Bodies are responsible, often in sweatshops and gold farms, for the production of virtual commodities and products marked for consumption in first world countries.

(5) Digital technologies are increasingly being inscribed on and within the body (Google Glass, wearable technology, ingestible micro-cameras, etc.), while digital games gradually pursue an erasure of the tactile and screened interface (Oculus

Rift, for example), in favor of an immersive and haptic non-interface, so that the body itself operates as interface.

Now, while this may seem like a transcendent boon to futurists and singularity-minded techno-shamans, there are risks here, particularly for queer gamers and their bodies. Fundamentally, the risk is the potential erasure or disembodiment of the real body and its signifying and representative power in virtual space; hence, bodies of difference face deletion, while a corporatist, homogenous, objectified, and universal body that fits all systems (regardless of how many "choices" of avatar the user is afforded) continues its steady ascendance.

Let us take our cues from Adrienne Shaw's groundbreaking work on LGBT representation in games and its attendant erasure/reprisals in industry product, Alexis Pulos's trenchant analysis of embedded heteronormativity in *World of Warcraft,* and Jenny Sundén's ethnographic erotics and emphasis on the affective turn in her evocative essay, "Desires at Play: On Closeness and Epistemological Certainty."[8] Each of these works illustrates a queering of games studies, one that critiques the excesses of oleaginous Big Gaming and the inchoate nature of embodied media criticism itself, while illustrating a progressive maneuverability around and through heteronormative and habitual modes of analysis.

Key Concepts

Key theorists for the queer games theory project are Judith Butler, Donna Haraway, and Sara Ahmed. In compelling complexity, Butler finds that gender (and therefore gendered bodies) is an enactment, a performance of iterative acts that fabricate the illusion of stable gender categories. Butler writes that "the tacit agreement to perform, produce, and sustain discrete and polar genders as cultural fictions is obscured by the credibility of those productions—and the punishments that attend not agreeing to believe in them."[9] Additionally, Butler emphasizes that the most seemingly essential parts of the body—organs, genes, hormones—are already discursively situated, to the extent that the parts of the body are always already inscribed with preexisting sexual, gender, and racial baggage, both material and conceptual. For queer games theory, Butler's work is crucial in that it reminds us to constantly question reductive thinking and systems of essentialized normativity, particularly in relation to the playful performativity of so much of queer games, gaming, and gamers.

Since writing "A Cyborg Manifesto: Science, Technology, and Socialist–Feminism in the Late Twentieth Century," feminist biologist and science historian Donna Haraway has doggedly argued for nonessentialized hybridity in the form of the cyborg, a post-human being that is machine and organism, male and female, self and other.[10] Her work on and advocacy for species companions is prescient. It invites us to reconsider the organic in our daily, technologized lives, assuredly drawing our attention to the ubiquitous destruction of the natural world wrought by patriarchal technoscience at all levels. Haraway's work is key for queer games theory; the cyborg is, if anything, queer, and reminds us that we all are hybridized by culture, identity politics, and technologies. Some embrace this as a strategy, some as a means of expression, some as a mode of survival (in and out of game space). Finally, her work reminds us that the object and apparatus of study—digital tech and the body—comprise energy and material, both of which are unevenly developed and distributed.

Finally, in *Queer Phenomenology*, Sara Ahmed reorients the language of queer theory, using a phenomenological understanding of the word "orientation," navigating Butler's bodies that matter and Haraway's cyborgs into the realm of space and habitation.[11] In her schema, bodies in motion materialize space, so that orientation becomes a spatialized, advancing series of movements (and moments), where one's disorientation, through proximity, distance, alignment and flux, offers revolutionary potential. Her "lines of thought" have clear affinities with the way we talk about digital bodies and space-as-movement in virtual worlds, but with a strong emphasis on instability and elision as signifiers and modes of divergence.

Queer Bodies, Queer Games

In the first issue of *Games and Culture: A Journal of Interactive Media*, media and cultural theorist/sociologist Toby Miller advocates for a variegated methodological approach as a means of analyzing games:

I think we need a combination of political economy, textual analysis and ethnography if we are to make gaming studies into a major player in the public sphere of popular criticism, state and private policy creation, social movement critique, and labor organization. That will allow us to consider who makes the games, who profits from them, how they target audiences, what the games look like, what they are like to play, and how they fit in with social life . . . Follow the money. Follow the labor.[12]

Included in this mixed approach, indeed central to it, must be queer theory and queer bodies. Queer theory—and queerness itself—through its inherent variance and fluidity, serves as a model for the productive and radical possibilities of virtual worlds that resist formations of control, predictability, and homogeneity. Let's not confuse neoliberalism with progress, competition as edict (even though so many games are competitions), and individuality-at-all-costs as an unassailable logic.

Queerness is difference, but difference as *détournement,* an assemblage of multiplicities. The great lie of the market is that (the vast majority of) game development companies have given us games for everyone. Why then is difference not equally represented in all the "choices," particularly considering the vast array of concoctions digital code engenders? Let's not accept blind capitalist individualized meritocracy as the only game in town, with its attendant shaming of divergence and difference. This entitled myopia has the added benefit of ignoring microchip sweatshops, hit-point farming misery, and the ecological catastrophe that is e-waste (focusing on bodies in the queer games movement means that we also foreground the environment, digital, and real as something to be nurtured, not controlled). To boot, #GamerGate has shown us all that the malignancy of entrenched power metastasizes virulently and that the "gamer" identity is itself a fiction; these should (and will) be replaced by discursive modes of address and reception engendered by radical potential and independent production.[13] Queer games should be collective, shared, productive, and liberating, a means of celebrating difference without sacrificing fun. And queer games theory should be prepared to not only analyze and critique games and gaming, but to lead in the fabrication and development of concepts, games, and worlds suited for queer bodies, the queer community, and beyond.

Ending with (and reiterating) Judith Butler, particularly her three-part identity-formation schematic, I want to emphasize what comes after identification ("I am this") and repudiation ("I am not this"): disidentification ("I used to be this, but now *I no longer believe in it*"). Our bodies are prime sites of disidentification; they are objects, subjects, and spaces where we can break up our binary patterns, chart our points of disidentification—the things with which we no longer identify, the things in which we no longer believe. In doing this, all of our psychological, cultural, and physical differences can become queer, strategic empathies in preparation for the Great Game of our own making.

Notes

1. Teresa de Lauretis, *Sexual Difference: A Theory of Social–Symbolic Practice* (Bloomington: University of Indiana Press, 1990) and *Alice Doesn't: Feminism, Semiotics, Cinema* (Bloomington: University of Indiana Press, 1984); Eve Kosofsky Sedgwick, *Tendencies* (Durham: Duke University Press, 1993), *Epistemology of the Closet* (Berkeley: University of California Press, 1990), and *Between Men: English Literature and Male Homosocial Desire* (New York: Columbia University Press, 1985); Judith Butler, *Gender Trouble: Feminism and the Subversion of Identity* (New York: Routledge, 1990), *Undoing Gender* (New York: Routledge, 2004), and *Bodies That Matter: On the Discursive Limits of "Sex"* (New York: Routledge, 1993).

2. Foucault, *The History of Sexuality, Vol. 1: An Introduction*, trans. Robert Hurley (New York: Vintage, 1990), *The History of Sexuality, Vol. 2: The Use of Pleasure*, trans Robert Hurley (New York: Vintage, 1990), and *Discipline and Punish: The Birth of the Prison*, trans. Alan Sheridan (New York: Vintage, 1995).

3. For an excellent discussion of this period see Henry Jenkins and Justine Cassell, "From *Quake Grrls* to *Desperate Housewives*: A Decade of Gender and Computer Games," in *Beyond Barbie and Mortal Kombat: New Perspectives on Gender and Computer Games*, ed. Yasmin B. Kafai, Carrie Heeter, Jill Denner, and Jennifer Y. Sun (Cambridge, Mass.: MIT Press, 2008), 4–19; as well as Jennifer Jenson and Suzanne de Castell, "Gender, Simulation,

and Gaming: Research Review and Redirections," *Simulation and Gaming* 41, no. 1 (2010): 51–71; and McKenzie Wark, *Gamer Theory* (Cambridge, Mass.: Harvard University Press, 2007).

4. This is in reference to Laura Mulvey's seminal feminist film theory essay, "Visual Pleasure and Narrative Cinema," *Screen* 16, no. 3 (1975): 6–18, an essay that concretized notions such as the gaze, voyeurism, and scopophilia, all concerns central to queer studies, games studies, and the body.

5. Jesper Juul, *Half-Real: Video Games between Real Rules and Fictional Worlds* (Cambridge, Mass.: MIT Press, 2006).

6. Allucquère Rosanne Stone, *The War of Desire and Technology at the Close of the Mechanical Age* (Cambridge, Mass.: MIT Press, 1995).

7. Routledge, for instance, published *Body Studies: An Introduction* in 2014, a sure sign of the codification of a discipline's approaches and vocabularies. See Margo DeMello, ed., *Body Studies: An Introduction* (New York: Routledge, 2014).

8. Adrienne Shaw "Putting the Gay in Games: Cultural Production and GLBT Content in Video Games," *Games and Culture* 4, no. 3 (2009): 228–53; Alexis Poulos, "Confronting Heteronormativity in Online Games: A Critical Discourse Analysis of LGBTQ Sexuality in World of Warcraft," *Games and Culture* 8, no. 2 (2013): 77–97; Jenny Sundén, "Desires at Play: On Closeness and Epistemological Uncertainty," *Games and Culture* 7, no. 2 (2012): 164–84.

9. Butler, *Gender Trouble,* 179. See also *Undoing Gender* and *Bodies That Matter.*

10. See Donna Haraway, *The Haraway Reader* (New York: Routledge, 2003) and "A Cyborg Manifesto: Science, Technology, and Socialist–Feminism in the Late Twentieth Century," in *Simians, Cyborgs, and Women: The Reinvention of Nature* (New York: Routledge, 1991), 149–81.

11. Sara Ahmed, *Queer Phenomenology: Orientations, Objects, Others* (Durham, N.C.: Duke University Press, 2006), 10.

12. Toby Miller, "Gaming for Beginners," *Games and Culture: A Journal Interactive Media* 1, no. 1 (2006): 8–9.

13. Anastasia Salter and Bridget Blodgett, "Hypermasculinity and Dickwolves: The Contentious Role of Women in the New Gaming Public," *Journal of Broadcasting and Electronic Media* 56, no. 3 (2012): 401–16.

Chapter **4**

Queering Games History
Complexities, Chaos, and Community

ZOYA STREET

Over the past couple of years, through conducting oral histories and publishing open calls for essays, I have come across at least a dozen different accounts of gender play in people's personal histories of gaming. I've never directly asked anybody about game avatars or gender, but it has been a topic that people raised again and again, suggesting that to people—straight, queer, trans, and cis alike—cross-gender digital play is often a significant experience in their gaming lives. It is not some mundane non-event that researchers ascribe meaning to, but something that people found remarkable when thinking about their own histories. Often, this is because someone else found out that they were playing across gender lines, and suddenly they felt pressed to explain their behavior to someone who found it unusual.

Contemporary, mainstream, commercial games culture is often strictly gender normative, but it seems that our private histories of game play often involve countercultural deviations. As a historian, it's tempting to try to answer the question: Have videogames given us permission to be more queer?

I've often wondered whether I should try to gather more accounts about this, to try to make sense of how games history has affected the social history of gender. However, I worry that the historical methodologies I'm comfortable working with would not do justice to the material. If I am not mindful, then my attempt to incorporate marginalized experiences into my histories will only colonialize them.

Esther MacCallum-Stewart's oral histories are a testament to the complexity of cross-gender play as one example of an experience that queers games history.[1] In these histories, the normativity of framing gender in a ludic context starts to emerge: women's bodies are instrumentalized and placed under a gaze that challenges arguments about personal identification. For MacCallum-Stewart, the history of female characters in games has resulted in a naturalization of cross-gender play into something safe and normative that needn't interrupt one's cis-heteronormative performance. Analyses like these are important, not least because they challenge the exotifying gaze that frames a choice to perform femininity as deviant and exciting.

I don't have any clear answers yet, but I wanted to share some reflections on how and why we might aspire to the approach I would call "no history without queer history," and no method without queer methods.

The college where I did my undergraduate degree had two libraries. One was the regular library with ugly metal shelves and paperback books with poorly designed covers from academic publishers. This was the library you would actually use for studying anything from the past three hundred years. The other was an ornamental library. Tourists were charged a fee to come and visit it. It had extremely old, beautiful books and these marble busts of the college's esteemed alumni, all of them great white men. They were made extra white by the marble.

When I began studying there, one of the matriculation rituals involved going up to this library on your own and walking down this long corridor to sign your name in a big book that contained the names of more great men. This ritual was part of the seduction that convinces students to buy into their newly acquired privilege. These were incredible people who knew so much and changed the world, and by signing my name in that book I was supposed to feel like I was destined to be one of them.

But the more I studied, the more I felt that I was not one of them. The world outside that library was not mine to know. I'm not one of those great men who knew lots of things. I don't have that right.

I was at that college studying something that seemed to those around me to be of little value: Japanese studies. This included Japanese language, history, ethnography, and politics. You can't directly apply Japanese studies to anything productive. You can't go out and make a Japan.

I used to justify my degree to people by saying that history and culture can uncover things about how we live and work now, and how things might change in the future. It was a natural explanation to turn to when surrounded by physicists.

The problem is that descriptive theories about history easily become prescriptive. Just because people's lives have gone a certain way in the past, it does not logically follow that our own lives will operate in a similar way. Yes, I could use those testimonies about gamers' experiences of gender play to change our theories about history to account for queer experiences, but queerness is fundamentally about that pushback against prescriptive assumptions. History is not like physics, and I cannot sensibly treat my sources like test subjects. History cannot be known that way.

The way I was taught to do history was, broadly, that you find source material, find some relevant secondary sources that will include other histories that have been written about that subject and some relevant theories, and then compare the primary sources to those secondary sources. The hinterland of historical knowledge will be rendered afresh, and human thought will be enriched.

This is what I thought I might do with all those accounts of gender play in personal histories. But the more I thought about the content of those sources, the more suspicious I felt about the endeavor.

To try to assuage this concern about pushing theories onto other people's lives, when writing up the interviews for *Dreamcast Worlds* I sometimes sent drafts to the subjects themselves, so that I wouldn't publish something with which they weren't comfortable.[2] This taught me a lot. People don't necessarily read their past the same way that you do. I might think that someone who is transgender now was therefore transgender as a child, though maybe nobody knew it at the time, but they might not feel the same way. Likewise, each new account turned my assumptions and models upside down.

Queerness might be described as a resistance against that coercive attempt to claim knowledge of other people's experiences.

The fact that I even assumed I was in any position to interpret those stories is in retrospect quite troubling. It doesn't seem terribly different to the Great British Tradition of plundering other countries for artifacts so that Great British Men can study them back home. Often it feels like the purpose of study is to become one of those men, to get the authority to make knowledge about other people's lives.

I remember my heart swelling as I read in my prospectus (a guide that U.K. universities produce to advertise themselves to potential students) that studying at that university would make me an "expert in the field." Yay! After a lifetime of being nothing more than a child, I get to be an expert in something! Of course, here I am on the other side of that degree course and another on top of that and I'm still not an expert in anything, let alone Japan. Japan isn't mine, so how can I live off my knowledge of it? Likewise, studying queer histories of gaming would not make me an expert in how people queerly game.

Knowledge is about ways of seeing. I do nobody any favors by trying to teach them how to see their own past.

So now I'm trying to work out what the alternatives are to the historical methodology in which I've been trained. Since it was oral history that upturned my view of history as practice in the first place, I first looked to other areas where oral history is prominently used. I like the idea of community histories, because it re-centers authorship in the community itself, and this has been particularly well done in parts of the world where history is fragile, poignant, falling outside of the interests of the people who keep records.

My hometown is one of those places: a huge part of the language and culture I grew up with was created by the mining industry, which is now almost entirely gone. The Kiveton Park and Wales History Society collects photographs and oral histories from the community to record the experiences that created that culture. It is history by the community, for the community, and about the community, and it replaces that assumption that someone is coming in and gaining knowledge to become an expert with a sense of responsibility to let people tell their own stories. In some ways I see my independent e-zine *Memory Insufficient* as a similar project to this.[3]

In my search for other community history projects I came across the public history project that has been taking place at the Chicago Historical Society since the mid-twentieth century. Public history is not quite the same as community history, since its primary goal is presenting history to the public, but the CHS is one example of a public history institution that began bringing the public back into the process of creating historical knowledge; objects were collected from the community, and exhibitions such as "We the People" tried to disrupt established ideas about American life, to account for the lived experience of Chicago's diverse population.[4]

While other forces, such as the rise of an academic class of museum directors, still pull the public history projects into an authoritarian direction at times, that push to write history with the public and not for the public is needed if we're going to queer histories of gaming. As the historian, I'd rather not know anything because I think that better work is done upturning knowledge than setting it right.

I interned in a somewhat similar institution a few years ago in Japan. It was a public institution, in that it was owned and run by the city government, and its main remit was to archive items donated by the local community and to support historical education. It was located in an earthquake-proof concrete reproduction of a castle, based on guesses about what the original might have looked like.

The English name for this institution was Chiba City Folk Museum, but the Japanese name of "kyoudo hakubutsukan" is really all about local-ness rather than folk-ness. The museum displays lovely things like swords and samurai armor and religious statues, and the guidance materials tell the story of how the Chiba clan took over the area, how people came to worship gods in the stars, and, in a small display in the basement, how Chiba was destroyed through firebombing in World War II.

Hidden in the archives are amazing things that will likely never be shown to the public for political reasons, such as a huge collection of World War II propaganda music records. History museums are a great place to witness how knowledge exists in service to our deep-seated fears.

This inclination to domesticate history at the same time as we popularize it was criticized by heritage studies academic David Lowenthal in *The Heritage Crusade and the Spoils of History.*[5] A parallel could be drawn with the "naturalization" in MacCallum-Stewart's oral histories of cross-gender play. At the heart of this work is something messy, personal, perhaps a little painful, but it gets rationalized into something safe that doesn't challenge the status quo.

When we collect these objects from the community, only to hide them from view, heritage serves the same authority that traditional history would. Likewise, collecting personal accounts of queer histories of games only to then have them mediated by the priorities of the historian, or of whatever theories happen to be in vogue in the dominant class of thinkers at the time, does not necessarily serve the marginalized stories that I'm trying to re-center. Or at least, it re-centers them only in a narrow way.

A community history that includes queerness and other marginalized experiences has to give up on expert authority and reimagine new metaphors for the historian's goal. Maybe knowledge isn't the right metaphor for what community histories try to achieve.

This search for a way of queering histories—writing them without being the knowledgeable authority on other people's lives—has brought me into contact with the work of sociologists such as John Law, who are interested in foregrounding the complexity of the world rather than trying to distill it into a digestible narrative. Work like Law's can bring historical research into contact with an interesting set of metaphors that allow us to rethink the methodologies we might apply to a complex world.[6]

Games are complex things. They are not stable objects but processes that come to life as network effects, and queerness further complicates games by challenging how we imagine the actors in that network. How can we even hope to tell a history that is true to this level of complexity? I've worked with actor-network theory in the past, and even that seemed too tidy as a metaphor: what we call a network is really just a huge, chaotic mess.

John Law says that events "necessarily exceed our capacity to know them."[7] Queer histories of gaming have taught me that, in reality, histories of games cannot really be known.

Instead of attempting to organize every media experience into tidy categories of "normative" or "subversive," a queer history needs to highlight the constant work that games culture puts into producing normativity despite the strange, private experiences people have when testing the boundaries of a liminal space. MacCallum-Stewart's work highlights how games culture has managed to contain gender fluidity, for example through ludic systems that make sexualized female bodies such as Chun Li's synonymous with skilled mastery—but she also quotes players interested in femininity as a form of hidden knowledge. All gender play can't be taken at face value as clearly queer, but neither can its rationalizations be understood as perfectly tidy.

Knowledge is constantly being constructed, and the action of history contributes to the production and performance of knowledge. Essay writing is a ritualistic craft activity. Part of what is required when writing histories of gaming that don't erase things like queerness is to become interested in knowledge as a thing being crafted in the moment, from the point of view of the interviewee as well as the historian, the game designer, the PR executive, and so forth.

Historical knowledge has its own performativity, and maybe it's possible to play with that creatively, to embrace the fluidity of our role in its constant social construction.

Queering history does not just mean including queer experiences in accounts of gaming histories. It also means challenging the normative structures of history as practice, making it more open and flexible and less authoritarian. It means finding ways to embody the role of the historian in an authentic way, rather than posturing in a way that privileges some voices over others. It means abandoning knowledge. It means not knowing anything.

Notes

1. Esther MacCallum-Stewart, "Real Boys Carry Girly Epics: Normalising Gender Bending in Online Games," *Eludamos: Journal for Computer Game Culture* 2, no. 1 (2008): 27–40.

2. Zoya Street, *Dreamcast Worlds* (Rotherham, U.K.: Rupazero, 2013).

3. Zoya Street, ed., *Memory Insufficient* (Silverstring Media, 2013–16), http://meminsf.silverstringmedia.com.

4. Catherine Lewis, *The Changing Face of Public History: The Chicago Historical Society and the Transformation of an American Museum* (DeKalb: Northern Illinois University Press, 2005).

5. David Lowenthal, *The Heritage Crusade and the Spoils of History* (Cambridge, U.K.: Cambridge University Press, 1998).

6. John Law, *After Method: Mess in Social Science Research* (Oxford, U.K.: Psychology Press, 2004).

7. Ibid., 6.

Part II   QUEERING GAME PLAY AND DESIGN

Chapter **5**

Ending the Cycle
Developing a Board Game to Engage People
in Social Justice Issues

PETER WONICA

Project History and Ideology

Held as a workshop during the Fall 2013 semester at the University
of Texas at Dallas, "Putting the Pieces Together" used a board game
to communicate the challenges faced by queer women leaving abusive relationships. While the workshop provided a unique view on
the complex systems that keep queer women from leaving abuse, the
most effective educational experience was the community-driven
development experience. For the event, I was commissioned to create a game by the Carolyn Lipshy Galerstein Women's Center, which
organizes LGBT programming on campus. Instead of personally developing the project, I enlisted the help of the campus community to
design a board game that serves as an abstracted model of relationship abuse. Using the concept of play as an entry point into social
justice discussion, a group of participants expanded their knowledge
and ability to enact positive changes in real-life systems.

While the process did produce an educational board game that
was featured in the Fall 2013 workshop, the greater emphasis was
on the collective design process. The project provided participants a

safe space to discuss sensitive issues and explore possible solutions. The intensity of our discussion around these complex systems often made participants tense and uncomfortable. Following these discussions, participants were in need of catharsis. This provided them with the motivation to enact change in real-life environments. The production of the board game thus sparked greater motivation to take action around issues of abuse and empowered people through game design.

The design of this workshop was heavily influenced by the work of scholars and video game critics studying the topic of critical play, such as Mary Flanagan and Gonzalo Frasca. Critical play, according to Mary Flanagan, "means to create or occupy play environments and activities that represent aspects of human life."[1] Play becomes a social environment in which people explore sensitive and serious topics in an engaging, safe way. Frasca's writing connects video games to the work of Augusto Boal, a Chilean dramatist who created the "Theatre of the Oppressed." This participatory form of theater turned audience members into improvisational actors who addressed and explored different perspectives in politically charged events. Writing about Boal's work, Frasca notes that "instead of being 'inside the skin' of the character, [Boal] wanted [the audience] to be at a critical distance that would let them understand their role."[2] For this experiment in game-based education, instead of learning through singular situations, players were encouraged to consider the cultural rules that perpetuate systemic discrimination. The perspective of a game designer establishes a critical relationship to the material. Instead of being immersed within a system, as in traditional role-play, designers act as detached critics working to understand the complexities of a system. This mode of critical play creates new opportunities for the creation of learning environments capable of intimately addressing complex social issues.

Workshop Cycle

At the University of Texas at Dallas, the Women's Center provides funding and support for large on-campus events focused on LGBT issues. One consistent feature of their programming is a series of events called the Advanced Safe Zone Dialogues, a collection of lectures, discussions, and workshops. As part of this event series, the goal of the workshop was to educate college students and staff about the unique challenges faced by queer women in escaping abusive relationships, such as access to resources, legal problems, and connection to family and friends.[3] While previous programs in the series focused on lectures, this workshop used play to start a conversation about abuse and systemic discrimination.

Over the course of a month, a group of interested participants and I met to discuss the creation of a model that teaches abusive relationships in a board game. The initial intention was to develop a board game communally, yet that idea was simplified in order to make the experience accessible to people of all gaming literacies and backgrounds. To this end, I constructed a simple prototype to serve as a starting point for continued development. Rather than starting from scratch, participants used the prototype to discuss the validity and realism of an abstracted model of abuse. Through play, they began to discuss their personal experiences in a collective attempt not only to improve their own knowledge, but also to start addressing discrimination.

The following steps represent a brief description of the workshop process.

Play-Testing and Observation

At the start of each session, participants played through the current version of the game. For the first session, the game was a prototype developed to spark discussion and critique. In following sessions, I used a prototype that had been altered by the previous participants. The group included both new and returning individuals. New participants often contributed novel perspectives and research to the discussion.

Reflection and Critique

After playing the game, all the participants had an opportunity to share their reactions. By deconstructing the systems of the game, participants were able to evaluate the best way to create a model of unhealthy relationships while still producing a playable work.

Examples of questions raised by play-testing included: What defines the end of an abusive relationship? What constitutes safety for somebody who has escaped? What is the likelihood that a queer person will face discrimination from those who are supposed to help, such as lawyers, cops, or even women's shelters? What patterns of behavior do abusers use to keep women in these relationships?

Many of these questions emerged during game play as we realized our need to better understand issues related to abuse. Participants brought different perspectives and opinions, and some shared their own experiences of abuse. All of this information, which was expressed through the game-design process, helped contribute to answering questions and sparking further investigation into the issues.

Re-creation

In this phase, game rules were added or modified to develop a more accurate simulation of relationship abuse. In discussing the rules of the board game, our conversations addressed the rules of real-life systems. Eventually, conversations often shifted to how people could create more equitable and fair rules in real life. From these discussions emerged a newfound desire and ability to enact real-life change, a crucial outcome of this project. For example, individuals explored the resources available to queer women escaping from abusive partners. In creating game rules for women's shelters, they gained a greater understanding of the flaws of the shelter system, especially within their local city. With an understanding of these gaps in support, there came an understanding of ways to improve domestic violence shelters.

Each session followed these steps. I posed different questions for each phase and let conversation evolve naturally as participants explored these issues. Over the course of a month, the seed of a prototype grew into a full game that was playable at our final workshop event.

The Process in Action

The original iterations of the board game were often the most problematic, and early participants worked hard to find an appropriate way to create an educational experience about abuse. As an example of the early problems of the project, the first prototype was nick-named "Oppression Olympics: The Board Game" because of how it emulated the traditional Privilege Walk exercise.[4] A sketch of the prototype, seen below, shows that players have a movement track for different gender/sexual identities. Game-play mechanics consisted of playing cards that moved characters forward or backward. The desire to escape became a race, in which the queer characters would be severely handicapped in relation to those who are heterosexual or cisgender. However, this was deemed a flawed model because it gave the player limited opportunities for action and inaccurately depicted issues of abuse. This prototype put undue focus on transgender (an idea originally designed to reflect the sheer level of discrimination such individuals face in real life), diminishing the experiences of other characters.

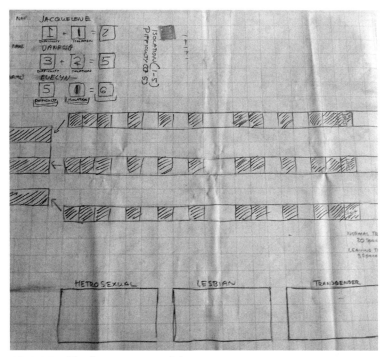

FIGURE 5.1. The first prototype of the game.

This was a learning opportunity. Participants took turns discussing their thoughts on the prototype, contributing knowledge, personal experiences, and reactions to the way the information was presented. Following the initial observation phase, participants deconstructed the ideas behind the prototype with the following questions: Why is this a poor way to present abusive relationships? Does this model of oppression lend itself to overemphasis on quantification? Is this an offensive depiction of systemic oppression?

During the deconstruction phase, participants considered these questions and discussed systems of abuse and privilege. Through their discussions, they uncovered parallels to comparative models of privilege often found in similar workshops. Working from experience and knowledge, participants then discussed rule additions or modifications that would help the game more accurately model abusive relationships. Through this process, many people developed a better understanding of how information, while depicted in a well-intentioned way, can have negative consequences and underplay the complexity of an issue. Once the session was over, a new version of the game was created, which in turn was modified by future participants.

The final version of the game focused on providing people with routes to escape abusive relationships. Three players each assume the role of a character who must face their own set of challenges. Participants play cards that allow them to create a "Life Path," a representation of the actions taken by their character. Card effects were hidden until played, simulating an unstable and tense atmosphere. Each player had different family, social, and financial scores that affected their ability to take action. Difficulty checks also affected players' ability to utilize their resources. A player's difficulty was increased through stress and discrimination. Difficulty was decreased through positive events and self-care. The players would then roll to determine if they accomplished a desired action. With every action taken they added onto their character's Threat Dial, a simulation of the abuse cycle. When they hit a certain point on their Threat Dial, they would draw an Abuse Card, which would negatively affect the character's ability to continue playing. Overall, the game was a simple but relatively accurate model that helped people understand some of the experiences these women faced. The post-play session of the final game encouraged critical discussion about the rules that perpetuate oppression that go beyond individual characters and situations.

During the debriefing, every mechanic provided a new opportunity for a critical discussion. For example, the end condition of the game was left purposely vague to foster discussion about when an abusive situation truly ends. What does it mean to escape an abusive relationship? What happens if you return to the relationship, and what would cause this? These questions helped participants explore the topic of abuse and share their own knowledge and personal experiences. By presenting the material in the form of a game, the conversations became more accessible and engaged a wider array of participants.

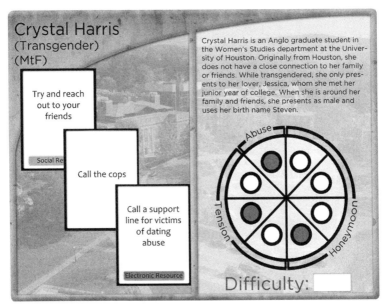

FIGURE 5.2. The character sheet and cards are on the left. The "Life Path" is on the right.

Conclusions

After a year and a half, the project has grown further to become *Ending the Cycle,* a commercially available game. Developed as my Masters of Fine Arts thesis, the project took the basic premise of the workshop and improved the accuracy of the simulation and accessibility of the game play. The new iteration became more inclusive and included a variety of gender expressions and sexual identities, not simply queer women. Yet, the project still incorporates community-driven experience by allowing players to modify the rules of the system to better explore their understanding and expectations of real-life situations. The current version of the game includes different tools to modify and even add new components, continuing the pattern of participatory design from which this project grew.

For me, the focus on participatory design has likely been the most empowering and educational aspect of this project. Demonstrating that game design can be easily accessible serves to demystify the field and make complex systems more approachable. Designing can simply be the act of having a conversation about societal issues and thinking critically about ways to address them. In taking this approach, one of my goals was to help players conceptualize the oppressive context in which abusive relationships exist as a system. By learning that systems can be analyzed and discussed in this way, players developed a greater understanding of the world and the rules that govern oppression and discrimination. My hope is that the training they received in modifying the rules of game systems might empower them to modify the rules of real-life systems.

Notes

1. Mary Flanagan, *Critical Play: Radical Game Design* (Cambridge, Mass.: MIT Press, 2009), 6.

2. Gonzalo Frasca, "Rethinking Agency and Immersion: Video Games as a Means of Consciousness-Raising," *Digital Creativity* 12, no. 3 (2001): 170.

3. Naomi Freedner, Lorraine H. Freed, Y. Wendy Yang, and S. Bryn Austin, "Dating Violence among Gay, Lesbian, and Bisexual Adolescents:

Results from a Community Survey," *Journal of Adolescent Health* 31, no. 6 (2002): 469–74.

4. T. J. Young, "The Privilege Walk Workshop: Learning More about Privilege in Today's Society," *College Success 1: College, Career, and Lifelong Success,* March 11, 2006, http://www.collegesuccess1.com/.

Chapter **6**

Playing Outside

LEIGH ALEXANDER

If video games want cultural legitimacy, designers will have to concede that it's not all about fun.

Video games are bone weary with growing pains, though the signs are that the medium has arrived: The multibillion-dollar game industry draws curious investors and heavy hitters. Franchises like *Call of Duty* and *World of Warcraft* have become cultural institutions and tradable names, and on the back of his success the CEO of leading game publisher Activision in 2013 received an 800 percent pay raise, to nearly $65 million.

Interactive entertainment hasn't just been succeeding financially; it has begun attracting a new cultural legitimacy as well. The soundtrack to *Journey,* one of 2012's most celebrated games, earned a Grammy nomination, and the game itself crushed the annual awards cycle, an impressive feat for an indie game based on Joseph Campbell's monomyth and the sentimental concept of unvoiced collaboration with strangers. The Tribeca Film Festival hosted a panel on *Beyond: Two Souls,* a game heavy with the vaunted promise of mature storytelling—and featuring the voice and facial-mapped performance of Oscar-nominated actress Ellen Page.

These are the kind of radar blips that attract attention from the "proper" art and technology world, those who might have previously consigned gaming to the realm of the incomprehensible plaything, mere power fantasy for males of a certain age. Gamification is mostly marketing-friendly snake oil as far as anyone who actually makes real games is concerned, but the idea that game-design concepts can affect and influence productivity and social change has turned a lot of heads.

There's a growing vibe in the games industry that while the wider world still might not "get" video games, they might be willing to entertain a reevaluation of their prejudices. This is, after all, the era of the smartphone, and games are the most popular category on Apple's App Store, even eclipsing books.

The growing outsider interest in the medium is partially a result of patient insistence on visibility by charismatic innovators like Will Wright (of *Sims* fame) and game critics and journalists, and partially the result of the games industry's dogged pursuit of legitimacy.

Outcasts and weirdos in the late 1970s and early 1980s founded what would become gaming culture. Rogue programmers and witty, countercultural Steve Jobs–types built awkward, secretive text adventures and later led the early rush to colonize the Internet with ways for people to role-play and explore fantasy realms together. The modern games industry we see today—the one made to answer for mass shootings and to serve in-jokes to the TV programs *Family Guy* and *South Park*—emerged more slowly, the result of a certain lack of self-esteem that maybe isn't surprising for a medium born of nerds.

The industry of the 1990s viewed itself as an earnest second cousin to film and generally consented to help hardware makers mobilize their young male audience with promises of immersive interactivity and "in your face" special effects. Since *Doom* and *Counter-Strike* began colonizing student computer labs all across the nation, the muscle-bound first-person shooter has been the dominant paradigm, though far from the sole one.

Japanese role-playing games, comedy-sketch adventure stories, and sprawling, stat-heavy fantasy campaigns became safe zones for the uncool. You could be a social outcast or a geek, but as long as your parents could afford a PC or a Nintendo 64, you could have access to a world where every variable, every event could be controlled, where every conflict had a predictable win condition, if only you were skillful enough.

The downside of developing a lexicon that only you and your friends value and understand is that it's by definition inscrutable to everyone else. Advertisements for hyperrealistic war landscapes and parades of unrealistic, objectified female bodies intimidate or alienate most people. And all gamers have some story of the time they tried to show a non-gamer friend some rich, transporting universe with which they'd fallen in love, and despite bravely hefting a controller—these days they include twin sticks, a directional pad, four buttons, and four rear triggers—the friend struggled to make the character stop walking determinedly into a wall.

But passionate game fans willfully ignore the communication gap between the games industry and everyone else. "Are games art?" is a question raised so often in social media–enabled gaming fandom that it's almost a joke. When the late, great film critic Roger Ebert declared years ago that video games "can never be art," he must have had no idea of the nerd war he was about to launch. He eventually recanted that position in 2010—not because some revolutionary work of interactive entertainment had changed his mind, one imagines, but because he'd simply become exhausted by Internet trolls and declared a truce.

Gamers are a force to be reckoned with online, uniting with absurd fervor to defend their medium. They see the mainstream world's dubiousness about the value of their safe space as a further rejection, more teasing from the jocks. Some are so attached to those old high school dynamics that they have a hard time seeing that interactive entertainment, as the product of digital artists and experienced designers, has a real shot at broader recognition.

Sexism is such a hot topic in the games industry these days because new voices are virtually banging down the industry's doors to be recognized, included, and heard. The geek tree house is terrified at the idea of change. The obsessively earnest Internet comments and tweets about how games absolutely are an expressive art form that deserves as much respect as anything else are paired with claims about how feminism and "censorship" are going to ruin everything for them, naturally.

In most ways, gaming culture is much like any other insular, ideologically driven group faced with the fact that their little world needs to start meaning more things to more people. One finds the same political problems among passionate leftists—white men who feel especially sorry for themselves in ways that countermand their expressed desire for respect and change.

But these attitudes may no longer be financially viable. The main arm of the commercial games space—colloquially called AAA because of their $100 million budgets, hundreds-strong studio teams, and obsession with the ideal of visceral realism—is contracting despite the increases in executive pay. A significant portion of gaming's founding fan base has quietly turned into grown-ups and parents, more hesitant than they might have once been to put war simulations and high-resolution breast physics in front of their colleagues and kids. As game play shifts more toward participatory online multiplayer, muddling in the trenches with a lot of slur-slinging, phobic Internet trolls is an ever less attractive proposition.

With decreasing time budgets, shorter—and less expensive— art-house games and smartphone-market "distractionware" become a more appealing proposition. Much of gaming's historical audience would rather integrate gaming into their adult lives than cling to a militantly geeky platform.

But the game industry, laboring under a dated marketing vision that still dreams of the seventeen- to twenty-five-year-old gadget geek with the bottomless wallet, hasn't grown up at the same rate. Risk taking and creative innovation are receding amid a destructive feedback loop in which appealing to a niche audience becomes increasingly critical the more that audience's contribution to the bottom line shrinks. As a result, the games currently lining store shelves are increasingly impossible to distinguish from one another. Game companies bet on becoming the single most attractive option in the same homogenous field rather than branching out to create something new and risking expensive failure.

When games writer Jason Schreier wrote a *Kotaku* post expressing annoyance and fatigue with yet another set of unrealistic anime breasts in the fantasy-action game *Dragon's Crown,* he drew a wave of ire—and even a homophobic gibe from the game's Japanese artist. Shouldn't an artist be allowed to *express himself*? myopic fans demanded to know in regard to a top-heavy cartoon sorceress. And aren't games just for fun, anyway?

The idea that, at the end of the day, games are obligated to serve the purpose of "fun" above all others has been the main wrench in the works of the gaming industry's machinations for legitimacy. Why should games be mature, cope with social issues, reflect society, or demonstrate the genuine artistic vision of a grown-up creator? Ultimately, they're just for *fun,* say gamers when they've run out of defenses against the mainstream industry's embarrassing, stagnant homogeneity.

Alarmingly, professional game creators often contribute to that echo chamber, too. Traditional game production is a ruthless wringer of a career, demanding eighty-hour weeks and making widows of wives (creators are still predominantly male and heterosexual). A developer who has led a product that's managed to achieve commercial success is virtually canonized for his sacrifice. Veteran game developers are masters of creating "fun," and understandably they lead the charge against the idea that games can or should be anything else. But if genuine legitimacy for games lies in the idea that they can be a form of creative expression and tools for global communication and teaching—that's the evolutionary purpose of play, after all—fun decreases in relevance. Culture-changing entertainment is rarely described as "fun."

Games' twenty-first-century culture war could be consigned to end in attrition. The form has become an economic heavy hitter, colonizing every modern technology platform and spawning a fervent and accessible independent games scene that's as relevant to the medium as festival flicks are to cinema. But, now that all the opportunities are finally at hand, will the industry's slavish commitment to economics, best practices, and the grail of "fun" keep wider legitimacy at arm's length?

The future doesn't need to repeat itself. A tiny but reverberating kernel of game makers, tired of waiting to be embraced by veteran developers busy planning how to make an even more realistic assault weapon, have embraced new technology that allows them to create independently.

Development tools used to represent a significant barrier to entry. To make a game once involved a highly specialized skill set, access to programming or digital art and design education, and high-end technology for both practice and creation. But game tools have been quietly skewing closer to Web development tools, becoming easier to use. Tools with pricey licenses are getting dislodged by tools with lower barriers to entry, like Unity, GameMaker, RPG Maker, the visual novel generator Ren'Py, and a flexible, free interactive text tool called Twine.

This mass democracy of tools has meant that women, gender-queers, minorities, outsider artists, and a broad, brand-new wave of individual creators who haven't necessarily grown up on the insular vocabulary of "video gaming" have been drawn to experimenting with games, digital play, and interactive entertainment. The popular wisdom in game design has long been to lavish on players the idea that they are the ultimate storytellers and that the job of the game designer is simply to provide a framework for the players to create their own experiences. That approach is not inherently invalid, but it just feels huge that after decades of rationalizing and defending nerd fantasies as high art, personal expression and authorship now have the opportunity to become a major trend in games.

One nominee in the Excellence in Narrative category of the 2013 Independent Games Festival (the industry's Sundance, in a sense) was *dys4ia,* a game by Oakland-based designer and author Anna Anthropy, about the intimate struggle she endured undergoing hormone therapy for gender transition. Anthropy has long been one of indie games' most beloved and contentious Angry Young Women, developing indie games that deal with themes of identity, kink, relationships, and personal storytelling. Her manifesto, *Rise of the Videogame Zinesters,* urged aspiring artists of all kinds of get their hands on the broadening menu of accessible game-creation tools and be heard in interactive entertainment.

dys4ia didn't win at the IGF, which traditionally celebrates young white guys experimenting with the language of design through well-liked but increasingly familiar twee, retro aesthetics. (Disclosure: this festival is run by the same organization that owns one of my longtime employers, the industry news and features site Gamasutra.) But this year, the festival's grand prizewinner was another harbinger of a new, deeper way of viewing what game experiences can mean. Richard Hofmeier, another independent game designer, made *Cart Life,* a grueling simulation of the daily life of someone relying on a sidewalk cart's income to survive. Its bleak grayscale art and the ruthlessness of even its smallest rituals, like showering, buying food, and remembering to pick your child up from school, represented a shift in the "life sim" genre, highlighting the humble heroism in simply facing the world every day without privilege rather than the power fantasies with which games are usually associated.

Hofmeier took a further step once he received the award. He turned over his booth on the well-trafficked expo floor to his friend, critic, writer, and text-game creator Porpentine so she could showcase her game *Howling Dogs,* a fascinating, brilliant text experience in confinement, depression, and escapism.

Since then, the individual games movement has exploded, attracting curious creators and new experimenters in droves. It's also attracted its share of detractors, veteran game designers who look at the narrative-driven, personal-storytelling games as "cool, but 'not games.'" They may see a betrayal of their sanctified best practices of systems design, player agency, and reaction driven by conditions. Their resistance has begun to seem as political as it is professional, a desire to close a door to underrepresented voices just as those individuals have begun to step through it.

It's within this growing personal games movement that we can see the genuine potential of games as art and communication. The geek community has been validated for long enough by economic growth and a product industry that panders to them even at their own expense. Let them have that niche if they're so desperate to choke it into irrelevance.

Cart Life, Howling Dogs, dys4ia, and their contemporaries are touching and occasionally brutal, antithetical to games' holy doctrine of fun. But they are important. The high-end AAA gaming business will hopefully start to learn from the brave experiments of indie artists with everything to say and nothing to lose, folding some of the movement's most resonant lessons into its experience design. That's the road to a healthy culture and a genuinely mature, artistically legitimate games industry. But for now, individual outsider games are gently bringing game creation back to its spiritual origin—this time, in ways that could include everyone.

That non-gaming friend who views even the most innovative among console games as a foreign language can pick up *dys4ia, Howling Dogs,* or any of their contemporaries and understand their purposes, receive their intended messages, and be touched by empathy. They can be changed—maybe enlightened about a lived experience that isn't necessarily their own. They won't just be walking into walls.

Chapter **7**

Building a Queer Mythology

HANNA BRADY

The rules of a story or game are not what's in the story or game.

The rules are the recipe, the structure, not the ingredients.

Rules about ingredients aren't the rules of storytelling and they aren't the rules of any genre. Throw them boisterously out of the window.

The Un-universal

Once upon a time a hero is born and when he is grown (or nearly so) he goes on a quest. He looks like, speaks like, loves like the dominant demographic of whatever ancient or contemporary is telling us the story. He crosses a few thresholds and finds a magic solution and saves the day for the ordinary world and the magical one, all at once. He gets the girl. He goes home and lives happily ever after.

VerySimilitude

A game functions based on certain rules—lines of code or where and when you pass the ball. SFF (science fiction and fantasy and speculative fiction) needs coherence; it needs to feel like it works. It needs the lie to have some truth. It needs conviction.

Both need someone to act like they believe it.

A game needs the agreement that these are the rules we are playing by—a goal has to go here and the cracks in the sidewalks are lava—and SFF needs that agreement in order for dragons and garudas and spaceships to fly.

One of the rules could easily be that everyone in our SFF (or) game is transgendered. Or gay or asexual.

SFF starts with zero rules about what the story needs to be.

We're made of stories: real ones and true ones and made-up ones. The more different stories that make us up, the more broad our experience, the more capacity we have for compassion.

Tell a Story

Once upon a time, a great hero went on a quest to rescue a princess. He traveled far, fought monsters, defied fate, and when he'd finally climbed the tower and defeated the villainous knight guarding her door he found that she'd escaped with the maid, and they were already living happily ever after.

The Magic Is in the Telling

Stories don't exist by themselves.

They need a voice or a director. A hundred computer graphics artists or a pen and paper. They need to be told visually, orally, or physically, or all of the above. They need someone to tell them.

And they need an audience.

They need someone to ask, "Then what happens?" with the press of a button or the turn of a page or with wide-eyed attention. That's how a storyteller knows a story is working.

A story that gets that question, a story that tugs the audience along in the tide, is more than the building blocks, be they pixels or bits of ink. Such stories have what the poet Coleridge called "a semblance of truth sufficient to procure for these shadows of imagination that willing suspension of disbelief which constitutes poetic faith."[1] A story needs to be true, especially when none of it is real.

Tell It Different

Once upon a time, there was a boy who stayed home. He loved his home. He would never have thought of leaving, except that one day another boy came through the door. This second boy said, "You are my elixir. You are what I need to save the world."

Story Relics

Stories used to be essentially mutable. They were passed from voice to voice, impermanent. Now so many are fixed and static and vastly distributed. There are so few versions of Cinderella, so few stories about what poverty is like or what makes a hero.

No. That isn't true. There are millions of remembered and evolving Cinderellas, and the story of poverty is different for every person living or remembering or imagining it, and there exist a multitude of heroes—but one variant controls the signal, one story is dominant and told so frequently that it drowns out the others and becomes perceived as the authentic surrounded by variants.

The dominant and common variants aren't bad stories, but their overwhelming signal strength homogenizes our frame for the world and lies to us by saying there is a right story instead of infinite stories.

And since we are stories . . .

Beginnings in the Middle

Once upon a time, a great queen was about to have her firstborn. The seers prophesized that the child would be a boy, a great man who would save the world. And when the child was born, it was a girl. The seers were shocked and flabbergasted.

Her mother laughed.

"What better son could I ask for?" asked the queen.

Stardust and Stories

We're made of the same stuff. We are made of stories.

Humans tell stories to define ourselves to ourselves and to others, to explain our culture and family, to make people laugh and like us. To give our families something to remember. Stories are the fabric of our history and our ghosts. Sometimes they reflect what is real and sometimes they do not. But they create what is true. A story can as easily erase history and hide ghosts.

And since we are stories . . .

Tell It Again

Once upon a time, a hero was on a quest.

On the way he met a woman, a sorceress of great strength who offered to help him on his journey. They agreed to travel together. On the second morning of their fellowship, the hero awoke to discover that the sorceress was a sorcerer.

Astounded, the hero inquired whether the transformation occurred every night. The sorcerer replied that it did. The hero offered to seek out a cure for this affliction. The sorcerer replied that it was no affliction, but simply the way he was and that any cure would strip him of his magic.

The hero apologized and the two continued together for a long time and through many adventures.

Suspension of Disbelief

Because our worlds are constructed from stories, we don't like them to be variable. It's uncomfortable and unstable. It's easier to keep track of things if we know that what this news channel says is true or that your aunt is a liar and that this story is fiction because it has dragons.

However, fiction and nonfiction aren't mutually exclusive. They live on a spectrum. Meaning and communication are more complicated than simple black and white. It's more like sea and sky. But whereas humans are more uncomfortable with variants, with plurality and with ideas that contradict our world and self, stories are closer to the fiction end of the spectrum.

We encounter stories of monsters and cry for imagined beasts and beauties. If we can find empathy for such constructions, surely we can find empathy for a more nuanced perspective on gender and orientation.

The combination of accepting the improbable or impossible for the sake of story and of accepting that we are story-stuff ourselves is a powerful tool for creating empathy. The more improbable or impossible, the wider our minds and imaginations cast and the more room there is to tell and to understand a different story.

That's what makes SFF so important and so powerful a place for creative social change.

Again!

Once upon a time there was a girl who was trapped inside the body of a boy. She met a boy trapped inside the body of a girl. They set out together to find a witch to help them.

Modern Mythology

Some of the fantastic, some SFF, is straight-up mythology—modernized, twisted, bastardized, or restored. Old gods become superheroes. Sleeping beneath the heroes, and beneath the myths, curled tight under these popular interpretations, are dead religions. At the heart of every religion is a collection of stories.

Heir to these stories, to their vocabulary and symbols and places in the human heart, is SFF in all forms. The fantastic, building on the mythic, is at its best and worst able to harness the power of religious narrative.

This new mythology, this religion of pop culture, needs queerness and the full spectrum of the human experience.

Once More

I stepped up to the gates of obsidian and ruby, carrying a sword that wasn't a sword and a chalice that wasn't a chalice. I called out my challenge and the gates answered me back:

"What are you, to stand on the threshold and challenge me? Are you a man or are you a woman?"

"I am me," I said, "I am both," and the gates swung wide.

Step into My Shoes

Empathy and compassion are rooted in creativity. The games of pretend we play as children so often start with, "Today I am something I am not." It's the same as the most basic empathy exercise: "How would I feel if I were you?"

We start our lives with the inclination to ask.

A player steps into a fantasy knowing that the suspension of disbelief is going to be more necessary. It props open our imaginations and our empathy. The very childishness sometimes criticized in SFF can allow access to that primal part of our personhood, which can be hard to reach through the "real world."

Once Below a Time . . .

A child was living happily ever after, but it didn't feel right. The child thought that maybe the story that zhe walked through was not the one zhe needed. The child picked up one foot and set it back behind zher, testing with zher toes to see if maybe there was a different path to take.

The Point

Let the stories of our cultural mythology reflect the full rainbow of queer. Our art tells the story of what we are, and SFF encourages us to dream of what we might be.

SFF can be a dark and miserable reflection of the human spirit, and there is a place for that. There is a place for the traditional space operas and dragon-filled fantasies with pointy-eared heroes. But there is a hunger for more. For a way forward or sidewise that is neither so bleak nor so bleached.

So make fantastic queer games. Make queer fantastical games. Make something. Tell a story.

Note

1. Samuel Taylor Coleridge, "Biographia Literaria," in *The Norton Anthology of English Literature,* 8th ed., vol. 2, ed. Stephen Greenblatt (New York: Norton, 2006), 478.

Chapter **8**

For Play?
Literary Ludics and Sexual Politics

AUBREY GABEL

Often when we discuss "queer games," the word we are debating the most is "queer." What does it mean to be "queer" and to whom? How broadly should the term be used and what policing of its use (if any) should happen? What are the practices and stakes of queering? In the games context, these concerns are often reformulated in terms of the making and playing of predominately twenty- and twenty-first-century video, board, and role-playing games. How does a "queer" game alter player behavior and game mechanics? What kinds of queer identities are expressed in certain games and not others, and which are enabled by playing a game "incorrectly," or "failing" (to borrow Jack Halberstam's term) at gendered practices implicit in the game's structure?[1] Without downplaying the importance of such questions, which are as political as they are pragmatic, I want to point out that, when we debate these specific terms, we take others for granted. The discussion of "queer games" could benefit equally from an analysis of the term "game," as it does from debates surrounding the term "queer."

At first, it may seem obvious what does or does not constitute a game, especially as a material object. However, historically, the category of "games" has included many forms that have not yet entered discussions about queerness or games. These games have ranged from lighthearted parlor wordplay and conversational banter to metaphysical debates about the production of creative thought. We might also expand the definition of "game" to include that of "play": bringing to mind not only the structured behavior and seriousness of games like chess, but also the unstructured, creative freedom of "play" and its assumed lack of seriousness, bordering on frivolity.[2] No doubt we could also debate contiguous or derivative terms, and the way in which they internalize or reject abstract binaries like play/game or seriousness/frivolity. Are such binaries always mutually exclusive? "Foreplay," for example, connotes a kind of joyous, erotic antics. It is a pleasure-seeking sex act conceived in opposition to historically loaded terms like "procreation," which normativize sex by assuming it is inherently purposeful, penetrative, and pleasureless. But just because "foreplay" is posited against the grain of such terms, is it any less serious? Can't "foreplay" also be played according to rules (as in "role-playing")? And does an unserious tone always betray a lack of seriousness? In this essay, I hope to enrich discussions of queerness and games by giving a brief overview of the concept of literary ludics, or what I am calling "for play": it is an interrogation of what it means to "play" and "game" in the literary field, and of what forms "play" and "game" take in literature. While queer game scholars are no strangers to literary analysis, juxtaposing ideas about "play" and "game" from the fields of literature and new media studies will expand our perspective to include other practices and historical contexts.

One simple way of approaching literary ludics is through philosopher Jacques Henriot's notion of "le jeu" (or "play/game"), which is simultaneously an act, an attitude, and a set of rules.[3] Let me begin with a short excerpt from *Gargantua*. Written by the sixteenth-century French author François Rabelais (given here in Donald Frame's translation), this poem illustrates how "le jeu" can function as a mode of poetics at work in literature: "Shithard / Squirthard / Farthard / Turd spray / Your bum / Has flung / Some dung / Our way. May you burn in Saint Anton's fire! / Unless / You dress / Your mess, / And wipe it clean ere you retire!"[4] Believe it or not that was a poem. There is a rhyme and a certain thematic trend. This is a poem about shit. Rabelais's *Gargantua* is a grotesque epic, a parody of the epic form that seeks to offend its audience as much as possible. At this moment in the text, the epic's antihero, Gargantua, is making the serendipitous discovery of the *torche-cul,* or the ass wipe, along his journey to manhood. This seemingly unpoetic (and rigorously unheroic?) discovery is not without poetic interest for Rabelais, however. He craftily challenges the very concept of poetry not only by constructing such a well-wrought facetious poem (with its rhyme of the pejorative suffix "-ard"), but also by touching on quintessentially unserious—and even grotesque—subject matter: the lesser feats of the embodied self, with all of its dirty details. And he wasn't alone: after all, hadn't his contemporary, Clément Marot, written poems about rhyming, imploring creditors, and even saggy teats?[5] And hadn't his successor, Joachim du Bellay, even written epitaphs for cats and dogs and a poem mocking a fellow poet's experience of going deaf?[6]

Literary ludics, like those on display in Rabelais's poem, are at once formal and thematic. In this way, they can be understood as an investment in play, or in experimenting with poetic, novelistic, and other literary forms, but also in *foreplay,* which draws thematically on the gritty embodiment and bawdy humor of the grotesque tradition. On the one hand, play/game can refer to an act of literary formalism. It rewrites established rules of poetry making, by rethinking canonical literary forms (like the rondeau we see here). But play/game can also describe a particular attitude toward that act: a sense of humor with respect to textual production, which purposefully exploits taboo subjects like sex and shit. In this respect, Rabelais's play with form works on several levels. He is not merely playing with rules of the poetic code, but with the expected subjects available to literary production. Why does one write a poem about shit if not to challenge expectations for what does and does not qualify as poetry? Certainly this was true in the sixteenth century. Even today, does it not ruffle our feathers a bit to read a poem about ass wiping?[7]

Moving forward in time to the twentieth century, we find more widely known examples of literary games by the French surrealists, who experimented with playful or rule-oriented means of producing texts, from fill-in-the-blank questionnaires to collectively written poems (known as *cadavres exquis*) to automatic writing. However, I would like to examine the somewhat lesser-known example of a 1960s literary group called Oulipo, or the Ouvroir de littérature potentielle (Workshop of Potential Literature). When Oulipo began in 1960, the idea was simple: to survey and actively use literary forms that had existed and could potentially exist. The play that Oulipians engaged in was often rule-oriented and their creations were often rather simple, such as a new poetic rule or a new novelistic form. Sometimes this meant trying out a riff on existing forms, like the "counter-rhyme," in which rhyming words come at the beginning instead of the end of the line. In other cases, this meant developing fairly radical ideas with respect to form by offering up either a procedural constraint, one that affects the act of writing (often limiting its time and place), or formal constraints, one that centers on the language of the text itself. Often these ludic projects were multi-layered, including several constraints or rules.[8]

While Oulipo was never overtly "queer" in its agenda (its early existence even preceded the term), the group did often investigate taboo subjects and sexual identities.[9] One important example of this interest in literary ludics and sexuality can be found in George Pererc's *Les Revenentes* (1972). The title of this novel is notoriously difficult to translate because it is a neologism. *The Returned Ones* would be the most literal, but English lacks a means of gendering "one" as feminine.[10] This novel is a wacky, "sex-crazed" text about the exploits of jewel "thievettes" who steal from a wealthy young woman, Bérengère de Bremen-Brévent (i.e., "B de BB," "The Qeen," or "The Legs"), enlisting (and having their way with) her posse of gay priests. Formally, the novel is a monovocalism, or a text written with only one vowel, the letter "e," and as such, writing it required a series of "cheats," or an alternative phonetics and orthography of the French language, which Perec based in both French and English. Perec—ever the master of "for play"—explicitly bends the rules, allowing himself the use of the letter "q" to stand in for a hard "cu" pronounced \ky\. He also writes the sound \i\, generally produced in standard French orthography with the sign "i," with the letters "ee," as in English. In order to work around the constraint, Perec also gives himself some latitude in his vocabulary, using antiquated terms like "descendre" ("to fell") rather than more standard words written with "e" like "to kill" ("tuer").

Perec, not unlike Rabelais, is playing with sex and shit. He is drawing on a tradition of ludic language ("for play") and grotesque imagery ("foreplay"), which has its roots in works like Sade's *Justine* and Georges Bataille's "Story of the Eye." Yet, Perec's novel also reads like a parody of 1970s sexploitation films, a quasi-feminist riff on an erotically charged, high-action film.[11] But Perec relies on a radically different kind of language, as the speech of one member of the Bremen-Brévent's posse, Ernest, demonstrates, here in Ian Monk's translation: "Yer henchemen 'n' the wenches even-stevens the deeds'll be the seyme, the deyngers the seyme, the effets the seyme. We fleece Bérengère's gems 'n' her necklesses, then we'll be serene."[12] Once the reader is able to parse Perec's dense language, it becomes clear that while the narrative is filtered through the vision of a heterosexual voyeur, this is not a classic heterosexual fantasy. Perec evades some readerly expectations by including male and female homoerotic acts, multiple-partner sex, and sex between partners with significant age gaps (not to mention sex between priests). Indeed, part of the inventiveness of Perec's language lies in its ability to represent a multiplicity of sex acts and gender identities, all while respecting the monovocalism by having them "begger," "bed," or "screw." In fact, Perec jams in so many sex scenes that the heist narrative almost disappears, as if the writing of sex were itself a secondary constraint.

Perec's wordplay resonates with the grotesque eroticism of foreplay in more ways than one. The indulgent form of the text, with its exclusive use of the vowel "e," symbolically replicates a kind of sexual excess. The novel's monovocalism also lends itself to a number of not so subtle in-jokes, a kind of code deployed by the author to humorously allude to the sex act at hand. For instance, the text repeatedly uses the term "enQlé," a difficultly translated term that has historically been an insult and a term for someone who is being penetrated anally—the "bottom" in colloquial terms. By avoiding the use of the letter "u" found in the standard spelling of the word "enculé," Perec asks the reader to linger over the pronunciation of the letter

"Q," which in French is homophonous with "cul," or "ass." Thus, in order to make sense of the text's strange orthography, those readers who do not get the pun right away become the butt of the joke: they have to say the word "ass" out loud.[13] In this way, readers are almost obliged to take part in the game of Perec's literary ludics, which are at their most playful—and most scandalous—when they are "for play" and "foreplay."

For some, the formal elements of Perec's text made his representations of sexuality and sexual violence less visible but not less explicit. The novel's playful language allowed it to pass under the radar of censors. There is an important lesson here. Literary ludics are not only a radically new way of thinking of game/play, but historically, as a marginal literary practice, they have also offered a safe space for the interrogation of sexuality. Might similarly playful approaches to formalism, humor, and coded speech offer today's video games the opportunity to explore sexuality safe from scrutiny? Ludic attitudes and self-imposed rules are already key to game design. This implies, in ways that modern video game scholarship has not yet considered, that modern games may be drawing on literary traditions that precede them. As my analysis of literary ludics in both Rabelais and Perec suggests, situating play/game as a historicized mode of writing or thinking could be a helpful way of further investigating terms like "queer" or "game." Literary ludics might in themselves enable game developers to imagine game mechanics as a type of formalism, with its own kind of "for play" and "foreplay," its own means of rewriting the rules in order to make room for queer desire.

Notes

1. See Jack (Judith) Halberstam's *The Queer Art of Failure* (Durham, N.C.: Duke University Press, 2011).

2. In the context of studies of "game," "play," or "ludics," in fields spanning from psychology to sociology to literary studies, there is often an implicit territory battle taking place, in which the serious work of "game" wins out over the frivolity of "play"; this theoretical division is used to legitimize certain practices at the expense of others. I will not be engaging in such a

territory battle here, as I believe that it is worth acknowledging that the terms "play" and "game" often go hand in hand, so much so that in many languages, like French, they are collapsed into the same word or series of words ("jouer" or "jouer un jeu"). It is this double stance, of both seriousness and a lack of seriousness, which is important in conceiving of literary ludics as a genre.

3. Jacques Henriot, *Le jeu* (Paris: Presses universitaires de France, 1969).

4. The rondeau, which was common between the thirteenth and fifteenth centuries, was generally set to music, and involved the structured repetition of a refrain. François Rabelais, *The Complete Works of François Rabelais,* trans. Donald Frame (Berkeley: University of California Press, 1991), 35.

5. See "Au roi" (also known as "Petit epistre au roi"), "A un creancier," "Du beau tetin," and "Du laid tetin" in Clément Marot, *Oeuvres complètes* (Paris: Garnier, 1920).

6. See "Epitaphe d'un chien," "Epitaphe d'un petit chien," "Epitaphe d'un chat," and "Hymne de la Surdité: À P. de Ronsard, Vand" in Joachim du Bellay, *Divers jeux rustiques* (Geneva: Droz, 1965).

7. I will just add, so you can appreciate my pun, that Gargantua will determine that the perfect ass wipe is a goose, because it is so soft and supple.

8. The earliest exemplary Oulipo piece, for example, was a collection of sonnets its cofounder Raymond Queneau was coaxing into existence just as the group began, *Cent mille millards de poèmes (One Hundred Million Poems),* published in 1960. The premise of the text is a formal constraint based in combinatory mathematics: Queneau wrote ten sonnets, each with the requisite fourteen lines; each line of the sonnet may be replaced by any of the nine other lines in the same line-position, meaning that there are 1,014 possible combinations of complete sonnets, or one hundred million possible poems.

9. While I would like to avoid unnecessary "policing" of the use of the term, my hesitation in calling this text or this group "queer" is factual and historical: this is a term that Oulipo never openly used in the early 1960s, precisely because the term did yet not exist, nor was "queerness" a theoretical interest of the group (even while Oulipians experimented with the representation of sexuality). Many Oulipians, as well as other ludic writers of the same era, might even shy away from such a term, because of its historical association (particularly in the French psyche) with another, later term, "identity politics," which was not popularized until the 1970s. This is not to say, however, that Oulipo does not have its place in a "queer" conference, because many Oulipians have dealt with sexuality or nonstandard sexuality and often use sexuality as a form of constraint. For example, one

might consider Anne Garréta's text *Sphinx* (1986), written prior to her induction into Oulipo in 2000, a romantic story written without any textual reference to the genders of the narrator and the narrator's lover; this is a linguistic and conceptual feat given the manifold grammatical markers of gender in French (including suffixes and past participles). Another text that makes sex a constraint is Harry Mathews's *Singular Pleasures* (1993), a series of sixty-one vignettes, all told in different styles, about different individuals masturbating.

10. Perec's translator, fellow Oulipian Ian Monk, opts for a title that avoids the problem, calling it *The Exeter Text: Jewels, Secrets, Sex.* See Georges Perec, *Three,* trans. Ian Monk (London: Harvill Press, 1996).

11. One can almost hear the voice-over: "This is the story of the skilled thievery of a group of sexy ladies, who have no trouble getting the jewels or getting it on."

12. Perec, *Exeter Text,* 88.

13. While making the reader say a dirty word or alluding to a dirty book may seem simplistic or silly, the text offers other in-jokes that make compelling arguments about sexuality in literature. Partway through the text, as the narrator innocently glances through the newspaper, he stumbles upon an ad for "Eden, eden, eden: September's best seller?" (Perec, *Exeter Text,* 72). This seemingly meaningless blip is in fact an allusion to a controversial text of the same name, written by Pierre Guyotat in 1971, the year prior to *Les Revenentes.* The text was not only prefaced by several of the academic elite, including Roland Barthes, Michel Leiris, and Philippe Sollers, but was banned for consumption by those under eighteen for obscenity. The allusion is surprising, suggesting that Perec is not merely being tongue-in-cheek but is, in fact, pointing to monovocalism, and literary ludics at large, as a means of evading censorship.

Chapter **9**

Play and Be Real about It
What Games Could Learn from Kink

MATTIE BRICE

On a regular basis, about once or twice a month, I get e-mails from journalists or researchers who want to talk to me about "empathy games." The scare quotes are theirs, but I'm also skeptical of the term and how/where it is deployed. Empathy games as a genre create a conversation that is construed as new and unexplored, while at the same time providing an excuse for the rest of games to not be concerned with empathy. The category itself reinforces games as something special while justifying them as mindless entertainment that profits off troubled aspects of culture.

This is one manifestation of the "dark side" of games' techno-determinism that Heather Chaplin picks up on in her addendum to Eric Zimmerman's "Ludic Manifesto."[1] The kind of games and design philosophies that are most often valued focus on allowing people to navigate through systems and solve problems for the games' own sake; there is actually little that is ludic about this sort of future—or, rather, it represents an obsession with game objects. If there is something that isn't widespread in design and practice, it's the use of play to connect with life or to self-reflect. We are often entertained by games and gain some meaning through those moments of play, and games in turn use this to propagate industry. Play that is used for the purpose of reflection and connection, however, is greatly under-valued and under-supported by the main institutions of video games.

Addressing the concerns of an unempathic future for games, Steve Wilcox wrote that play is actually an exercise in understanding con-texts, and that that act of understanding is empathy.[2] Games are currently imagined as a combination of players and systems of rules. The result of that is a sort of systems thinking: seeing cause and ef-fect, mentally bending problems as far as possible in order to see how this system works and to use it for the players' own devices. But what about people? Sure, we might be able to turn people into systems for play; you can map a genome or something. The problem—and most serious games and "serious games" can tell you this—is getting people to care about the subject on top of which a system is mapped. People play a "match-three" game about recycling because they want to play a match-three game, and the moment they don't want to play a match-three anymore, they are done with the experience. Without real context, people rarely connect or care.

This reminds me in particular of Anna Anthropy's talk at the first annual Different Games Conference, "How to Make Games about Being a Dominatrix," and her mantra, "CONTEXT IS EVERYTHING."[3] She uses similar language to describe how mainstream games are empathically challenged. They use imagery from social issues as a top layer that is dressing for gaming a system. Anna provides the comparison between *Mighty Bomb Jack* and her own *Mighty Jill Off*. She explains that, while the games are similar in their systems, the latter brings a context that allows the player to create a connection beyond the rules of the game. And this particular context is the kinky dynamic between a domme and her submissive.

Kink isn't just a topical analogy, as it is for masocore games; it's a good framework for challenging these contextless play experiences by reimagining the positions of the designer, player, and play, and what those positions mean. The comparison between kink and games design isn't that large of a leap; Anna talked about that as well at the Queerness and Games Conference a couple months after Different Games.[4] I recommend you read through the transcript from Anna's talk in full because she covers all the bases, but the short and crude version is this: dommes can stand in for the game-design role as the person who is crafting an experience for the submissive, and the submissive relinquishes control after negotiating with the domme the rules of the play session. This creates both a magic circle and a system of play. As Anna says in her talk, this sort of play is often transformative. It can be a safe place to explore not only yourself through rules and systems, but life and culture itself. In particular, I want to continue with the implications of the dominant as someone who receives submission, and the comparison of a designer being someone who receives play.

If we understand play as the exercising of empathy through engaging contexts, and kink as a type of play design that deeply confronts life contexts, then kink practices stand as a stronger model for engaging people with meaningful play than the overly instrumentalized and decontextualized approach to games propagated by contemporary game design. Instead of games as objects to manipulate, kink shows bodies and minds in codependent situational contexts based completely on the participants' relationship with real life. Play doesn't need systems or rules to exist and be meaningful; it needs honest engagement with context. Mainstream games completely dodge dealing with reality and don't allow people to actually be present. In contrast, see my games EAT and *Mission*.[5] They aren't encouraging people to figure out their juicy elegant systems or find the meaning of life. Most people look at these games, get what they're trying to say, and never want to play them. This is because we haven't gotten used to the idea of play as confronting contexts, as empathy. They are painful games to play, but that is the only way to engage with the contexts being examined there. As kink shows, there isn't pleasure without trial, without going through consensual pain.

And this is important to me: the technophilia of games is stymieing this outlook on design. The ludic century isn't one of play, but of VIDEO GAMES. Video games are preoccupied with tech progressivism and late capitalistic practices that bank on ripping out the sutures that connect reality to play. WE ARE ALWAYS PLAYING. WE ARE ALWAYS IN CONTEXTS. CONTEXT IS EVERYTHING. Game design rarely uses real-life contexts when trying to depict meaningful content.

Valued video games are not challenging the construction and deployment of social systems or enabling people to actually engage with and understand their place in these systems. Games designed for social impact aren't dropping players into safe spaces to experience the raw contexts of the subject matter they want to communicate. Video games are ruining the conversation around play through devaluing all other types of games and promoting instrumentalized methods of relation. Despite trying to take the "gender issue" seriously, which valued video games are honestly confronting players with the construction of gender and how it plays out in our society?

There is an experience arc to kinky play that I think games of all kinds could reference when rebuilding their relationships to actual life contexts. I encourage you to explore the philosophies of kink more on your own to draw parallels, because this is a very personal and intimate practice, and what I'm describing isn't necessarily a standard. Rather, it's my own observations.

Consent: What separates kinky and vanilla sex for me is the active recognition of consent. Because of how our (I'm speaking as an American) culture works, we aren't really supposed to talk about sex. Rather, we hop into a dark space with each other and keep our fingers crossed that the other person knows what they're doing. Consent is the process by which you find out exactly what your partner wants before you play and acknowledge what you definitely don't want to happen. In another context, the things you consent to could be seen as mean, out of place, or degrading, but consent is its own context, and it allows play to be both affective and expressive. Video games tend to obfuscate the effect they will have on the player because they place importance on content and entertainment value. If consumers knew everything about the game and how it works, the typical model of selling games wouldn't work, because PR couldn't hype up the product and convince you to trust that you will have a good experience. *BioShock* makes you wait for the narrative twist before you really understand what the game is even about. This does not allow for the cycle of wielding and receiving play between designer/game and player. It doesn't allow for consent. We only have instrumentalized fun in mainstream games because context is hard to sell.

Scene: Just because there is consent, that doesn't mean play is completely predictable. Rather, it means that the domme and sub have the same goals: to bring each other to the places on which they've agreed. It is in the scene that the power dynamic between them is established and contexts from real life are introduced into play. This is important because it means combining our culturally imbued traits with a certain relationship to power. A relationship between a non-cis, multiracial woman dominant and a white cis, submissive man carries powerful symbolic weight. The scene allows the players to be flooded with cultural contexts through kinky play: for instance, the use of sexual dominance and submission. In this space, people can engage with hyperbolized contexts, because that's where they often want to go. The power dynamic gets players to a place where faux egalitarianism in mainstream society cannot. They play these roles to deeply feel these contexts in their bodies, and through that, they practice empathy. Typically, valued games don't take players deep into cultural contexts like this. The magic circles they draw rarely allow for safe experimentation with real-life contexts.

Aftercare: Play on this level is psychologically trying, and a debriefing, bringing the players back into reality, is needed for complete contextualization. Players brought to intense places during play commonly need reminders afterward that they are good, loved people no matter where the scene went, within its consensual bounds. This allows both partners to see clearly the context of play juxtaposed against the context of their life. Players see themselves in the scene as a part of their whole identity, and aftercare aims to ease that transition process. It creates a moment for reflection and integration. It allows a person to complicate their views, complicate their identity. Video games don't often afford us the opportunity to debrief because they assume that stepping in and out of play is simple. Leaving is as easy as turning off the TV, because you aren't meant to feel much besides bemusement or an evening's worth of thoughts. These games don't expect you to be transformed or touched by anything other than superficial storytelling devices.

All kinds of play can take place in contexts that mean something to us. Empathy isn't just important in the domain of queer art games. To the contrary, it is endemic to play. It is the self-inflicted rupture between reality and play performed by most games that blocks mainstream discourse from actively engaging in meaningful play outside of entertainment. Designers are far too complicit in the promotion of instrumental play and its refusal to engage with the world when that world is not directly attached to the game. Technology and capitalism play too large role in how we talk and think about games and the existence of games in culture. I say we should take a step back and recognize how we are engaging in life's contexts with our own bodies and selves, how we gender, race, class, and elevate that kind of play when we look to create and critique games ourselves.

Notes

1. Heather Chaplin, "The Ludic Century: Exploring the Manifesto," *Kotaku,* September 9, 2013, http://kotaku.com/manifesto-the-21st-century-will-be-defined-by-games-1275355204.

2. Steve Wilcox, "Videogames and Empathy: Towards a Post-normative Ludic Century," *First Person Scholar,* July 30, 2014, http://www.firstpersonscholar.com/videogames-and-empathy/.

3. Anna Anthropy, "How to Make Games about Being a Dominatrix," *Auntie Pixelante,* May 7, 2013, http://auntiepixelante.com/?p=2025.

4. Anna Anthropy, "Boundaries of Play: Game Design and Kink," *Auntie Pixelante,* October 26, 2013, http://auntiepixelante.com/?p=2182.

5. Mattie Brice, EAT, August 10, 2013, http://www.mattiebrice.com/eat/; Mattie Brice, *Mission,* August 19, 2013, http://www.mattiebrice.com/mission/.

Chapter **10**

Queering the Snapshot
Ambient Mobile Play

LARISSA HJORTH AND KIM D'AMAZING

Yeah, I used to do it a lot when I first got my smartphone a few years ago, like all the time, maybe twenty photos a day. [Pictures of] every-thing. Mostly of myself, though, I was a bit narcissistic. I don't think I'm as bad now. But now I think I only take, I'd take an average of one photo a day.

—Tom, participant

I take photos if I want to show someone something, or if I want to upload to Facebook or Instagram . . . Random stuff. Like, what you're doing, if you want to, like sort of mark a lifetime event or show some-thing you're proud of, or you want to show people in general . . . I do my pets a bit. And if I dress up nice. That's probably the main two.

—Henry, participant

The above two participant quotes speak to the way in which camera phone practices are entangled within the movements of the every-day life. The first participant shows how once the new media is do-mesticated into the everyday and the "honeymoon" is over, it settles back into the background as a form of ambient play. The second participant talks about genres and content of camera phone images as part of marking occasions and about their performative role.

The mundane, intimate, ephemeral, tacit, and phatic all contribute to the inner workings of camera phone practices as a lens for cartographies of co-presence. Here we understand co-presence as much more a type of *psychological,* than *physical,* proximity. Conceptualizing camera phones through co-presence allows us to think through various movements and forms of engagement across the seams and ruptures between online and offline, here and there, presence and absence. Camera phones demonstrate that co-presence is reflected in rhythm and movements across places, spaces, and temporalities.

In this essay, we think about camera phones in terms of ambient play as part of queer performativities. In order to do so, we connect the debates of performativity from critical cartography and queer literature. Through interviews with five queer-identified participants who take us through scenarios of use and meaning in, and around, the photos they take and share, this study seeks to consider the role of camera phones as vehicles for ambient play. We define ambient play as an embedded part of media practice within the background or soundtrack of the everyday. Ambient play highlights the role of intimate banalities—that is, the way in which the mundane in the everyday is normalized, subverted, or redefined through sharing of photos. And camera phone practices demonstrate the endurance of intimate co-presence as a main motivation for the use of camera phones themselves. Here, expanding on the groundbreaking work of French sociologist Christian Licoppe and Japanese American anthropologist Mizuko Ito, we see co-presence taking various forms of embodiment and engagement.[1] Co-presence, like intimacy, needs to be understood as always mediated: if not by technology (and maps) then by language, gestures, and memories.

Co-presence is often an important part of the ambient texture of the everyday. Playing across physical and/or psychological distances that are made intimate by particular communication technologies, co-presence has become a key feature of what makes mobile media so compelling.[2] In order to understand the ambient and playful role of camera phones, we need to address how central geo-tagging (both as a default and also as something to resist) has become to mapping the everyday. For cultural geographer Chris Perkins, applications such as desktop mapping and geographical information systems have democratized the tools for cartography and in turn made mapping "no longer tied to fixed specifications."[3] This has transformed the relationship between places and maps as "performative." And yet these performative debates in cartography need to be connected to queer literature.

Rethinking the Performative in the Age of Camera Phone Apps

Camera phone practices shape, and are shaped by, different modes of conceptualizing and performing place. As such, they provide particular ways in which to understand the role of cartography and co-presence as an overlay between media, visual culture, and geography. That is, camera phones are key players in the idea of representing place (i.e., maps) as performative. The performative nature of maps within critical cartography shows that we shape maps as much as they shape us.[4] As Verhoeff notes, mobile interfaces are indicative of a shift from "representational cartography to navigation as a performative cartographic practice."[5] Critical cartography also highlights the role of power within the mapping process. Here we see an inherent connection to these definitions of the performative as deployed within queer literature. It is the pivotal role of power that informs Judith Butler's definition of performativity in *Gender Trouble,* in which she puts forth a poststructuralist approach to gender as being regulated through cultural norms rather than being innate.[6] And yet these conversations about the performative within playful mappings have yet to be connected with queer theorizations despite their overt overlaps—especially in fields like camera phone practices, which bring together cartographies, identity politics, power, and performativity.

Butler has not been the only scholar to discuss issues around performativity and identity, although she is often the most cited. Feminist Eve Kosofsky Sedgwick also probed the texture of the performative, especially in terms of queer identity.[7] As she noted, "Queer is a continuing moment, movement, motive—recurrent, eddying, *troublant* . . . . It is the open mesh of possibilities, gaps, overlaps, dissonances and resonances, lapses and excesses of meaning when the constituent elements of anyone's gender, of anyone's sexuality aren't made (or can't be made) to signify monolithically."[8] Queer is "relational." The technical, conceptual, and emotional role of mobile technologies in notions of performativity cannot be ignored. Indeed, mobile media apps, especially in terms of gamified apps, require us to revisit and redefine the nature of the performative and co-presence within everyday life.

Literature around co-presence within mobile communication fields has flourished as a productive way for rethinking traditional binaries that are no longer adequate in everyday life. Binaries such as here and there, virtual and actual, online and offline, absent and present have been challenged through mobile media practice. The rubric of co-presence provides a broader context for understanding intimacy and mediation not only as something that is a late twentieth- or twenty-first-century phenomenon but also as something that has been an integral part of being social and human. Today co-presence can be understood as what Esther Milne calls "the degree to which geographically dispersed agents experience a sense of physical and/ or psychological proximity through the use of particular communication technologies."[9]

As well as being transmitters for intimate co-presence, camera phone practices also involve ambient play. Ambience is often used to describe sound and music but has also been used in computing and science. As a noun, it specifically refers to a style of music with electronic textures and no consistent beat that is used to create a mood or feeling. More generally, though, the term describes the diffuse atmosphere of a place. The concept of ambience is frequently used in computing, especially around human–computer interaction (HCI). However, in the context of sound and visual practice, there are also more poetic and multifaceted definitions of ambience, which posit ambience as an affective texture of place. In short, ambience is about the texture of context, emotion, and affect. Ambient play is a more useful rubric for understanding mobile gaming's diverse experiences of embodiment and distraction beyond the problematic label of "casual." Ambient play is about a blending of forefront and background, interwoven into the rhythms of everyday life. Ambient and co-present play are what motivate users to take and share camera phone images as part of an experience of place.

For nearly a decade within game studies, Salen and Zimmerman's definition of play, which is heavily influenced by Huizinga, held prominence.[10] However, more recently, play has been the subject of more debate, notably through nuanced and ethnographically attuned approaches.[11] In *Play Matters,* Miguel Sicart explores a "nonformalist aesthetics of play, inspired by contemporary art theories."[12] In this vein, play is no longer conflated with game play but is imagined as a practice informed by social, cultural, political, and economic factors. Combining play with ambience affords a space for contesting normalization by allowing for nuanced readings. Ambient play contextualizes the game within broader processes of sociality and embodied media practices and is essential to the corporeality of play whereby play inside, and outside, the game space reflects broader cultural nuances and phenomena.[13]

Accounting for the ambience and co-present play of place requires us to understand the shift from first- to second-generation camera phone studies as a movement from *networked* to *emplaced visuality.* First-generation camera phone studies were characterized by networked visuality, while those focusing on second-generation camera phones—with geo-tagging added into the mix—can be defined as emplaced visuality.[14] While many studies have been conducted around first-generation camera phone practices, in which opportunities for sharing between users were delayed because they needed to transfer images to computers before uploading them to photo-sharing services like Flickr, second-generation practices are marked by the speed with which participants can take, share, and comment on camera phone images.[15] Second-generation practices are exemplified by apps like Instagram, which allow for quick sharing across multiple intimate publics, like Facebook and Twitter. These practices are also characterized by their connection to geo-tagging, which allows geography, intimacy, and information to be overlaid in new ways. It is with ambient play, intimate co-presence, and performative cartographies in mind that we will now discuss our case study of queer uses of camera phone practices and ambient play in the everyday.

Case Study: Moving Pictures

In order to gain insight into the ways that camera phone practices operate as ambient play, we interviewed five participants about their media usage and scenarios of use. During interviews, participants would scroll through their phone and discuss their practices. By no means definitive, this study is preliminary and provides a basis for future longitudinal, nuance-based research in which participants will be interviewed over the course of three years. Rather than focusing on the images taken by participants, this study seeks to explore the motivations around image taking and sharing.

Many of the existing studies into queer play with camera phone apps have centered on obvious, gamified apps like Grindr. For Kane Race, Grindr affords a type of speculative pragmatism around intimate encounters in Australia.[16] This is further explored by Licoppe, who conducted ethnographies into the ways in which Grindr constructed intimacy around notions of physical proximity.[17] In Larissa Hjorth and Kay Gu's study of Jiepang in Shanghai, user practices shaped apps as much as they shaped types of performativity. Jiepang was originally sold as China's Foursquare.[18] Soon, however, users were deploying the service as a type of camera sharing app much like Instagram. In addition, Jiepang was reappropriated by the queer community to function as a Chinese version of Grindr. Jiepang soon realized its adapted use and rebranded itself as a hybrid between Instagram and Tumblr. Rather than just focusing on a "queer" app, however, we wanted to gain a nuanced sense of how mobile media reflected broader notions of ambient play. In interviews with five self-identified queer participants in Melbourne, we explored the role of the photo not just in terms of sharing particular content but also in terms of the act of taking the photo itself, which has implications for how the photographers view themselves and how they are viewed by others. The act of photographing is as important to the identity of the photographer as the photograph is. In interviews, we asked participants to reflect on the camera phone images they shared and their scenarios of use.

Of late, camera phone practices have become of great interest in terms of the politics of "selfies": photos that camera phone users take of themselves. For some researchers, selfies are reenacting older, analog traditions around self-portraiture. For other researchers, selfies are demonstrating new forms of performativity that may seem to be about narcissism, but are in fact about misrecognition.[19] In these debates, the politics of identity have endured, especially given that selfies amplify socioeconomic, ethnic, and cultural norms. When we asked our participants about selfies and image management, they expressed an overt sense of obligation. They reported feeling compelled to constantly be online and perform a type of image management akin to what sociologist Arlie Hochschild defined as "feeling rules," part of the commodification of human feelings into emotional work. Feeling rules, like performativity, are socially shared norms that influence how we think we should feel in certain situations.[20] Gender, class, power, and age all shape feeling rules. The tension around feeling rules and the "intimate publics" of social media mean that often-tacit etiquette informs different understandings of the normal versus the fake or inauthentic. Our participants also echoed the tension between narcissism and misrecognition debates:

> Social media apps have moved us into this notion where we are faux celebrities, and that someone cares, and that we are the center of the universe. (Harold, male, twenty-nine)

> I guess when I get a photo taken I pose a lot. And someone once said, "Oh, why don't you just act normal?" Like they were really, like I was just, you know, being silly in a photo. And people got sick of it. It's got a negative response. (Rachel, female, nineteen)

Many participants felt a pressure to establish an online "identity" or a "presence" that was connected to, but still distinct from, their offline persona. Here we see how ambient play is embedded within understandings of online and offline entanglements. Like a form of ambient play, this form of identity creation uses photos, especially selfies, to invite favorable judgment from others. The number of comments or likes a photo receives equates to its success. Photos are a way of showing others on social media how happy or successful you are, especially in the context of queer identities. As some participants noted:

There's more of a sense of wanting to be an identity in the queer scene, right? We've all been told . . . the overwhelming feeling is (here's my rant) that as a queer person you're told that you're less. From the start. Regardless of whether that's explicitly told, or whether that's just the trickle-down effect from the patriarchal society. . . . You have to overcompensate. And that's why a lot of queers are creative, because you're constantly making. "Am I worthy now? Am I valid? If I make this, if I make this, am I OK?" . . . And the hungry beast thing! You'll never fulfill it. It will devour you, it will destroy you. It destroys queer, like queer men just want to be something special. And that's fine, like we all want to be, but we're being told that we're not enough so that overcompensation that will never get validated is self-destructive. (Harold, male, twenty-nine)

Selfies are unquestionably occupying the intersection of ambient play and performativity. That is, they are playful and yet entangled within the politics of the body, gaze, and normalizations. While participants enjoyed judging others for being inauthentic, they often saw their own presentations of self in visual and textual forms as just a projection of an ideal, quantified self. Here we see a tension between the feeling rules and emotional work of mobile media and the ways in which performativity is being understood by users. For one of our participants, Frank, the role of the selfie as a barometer for political performativity was also a matter of ambient play. In this sense, selfies can function as an important political weapon: a method of self-expression that defies, illuminates, and plays with ideas of the quantified queer body. In Figure 10.2, Frank has asked a stranger to photograph him at an art exhibition. He is wearing a suit, scarf, and bonnet that he has designed and sewn himself. This photo functions as a record of an event, a moment of confidence, and (given the text written on the shirt, "Fuck Tony Abbott!") a deliberately staged comment on federal politics.

As Frank's photo highlights, selfies can be powerful platforms for ambient play and performativity—evidencing political, social, and cultural norms as well as providing a space for subverting such normalizations.[21] Interview participants in the creative arts also deployed selfies as part of their iterative artistic process and as a means of creative dissemination. For Harold, camera apps are like shared online sketch journals that are entangled with his practice:

> I don't consider them art, for sure, definitely. I consider them, like how artists used to keep a sketch journal. I'm not a drawer, I don't draw, so I don't keep a visual journal to draw people on the tram, and I know people that do, I'm a photographer and I'm based in photography, so it's almost like a living, kind of shared photo journal where I get to practice things and share them. Like, I don't take it that seriously, but a lot of great stuff's come out of it so it's got value. If that makes sense. (Harold, male, twenty-nine)

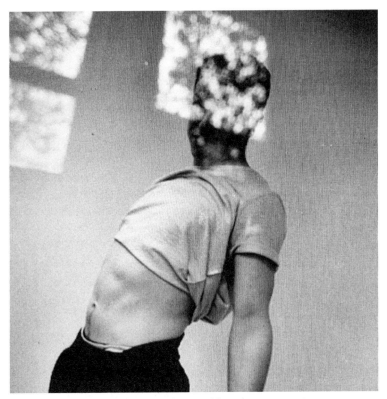

FIGURE 10.1. Social media image by Harold, male, twenty-nine.

FIGURE 10.2. Social media image by Frank, male, fifty-four.

FIGURE 10.3. Carnivalesque performativity. Image by Frank, male, fifty-four.

Conclusions: Performing the Mobile

This essay has suggested that in order to understand queer mobile media we need to put it in context: historically, emotionally, and socially. We have focused on ambient play as a way to think through the queer performativity involved in, and around, camera phone practices. Through the ambient play and co-present performativity of camera phone usage, we can begin to imagine a more complex definition of play as central to performativity in and around media. At the same time, the differing usages of performativity across media, identity, and practice need to be reconciled with performativity's feminist and political roots. Here, we have sought to bring some of the disparate debates together in order to discuss the ways in which queer identity politics is being managed through and by mobile media. Using the notion of ambient play, we have suggested that performativity, mapping, sociality, and identity are taking on new forms of engagement that shape mobile media as much as mobile media shapes its participants.

Notes

1. Christian Licoppe, "'Connected' Presence: The Emergence of a New Repertoire for Managing Social Relationships in a Changing Communication Technoscape," *Environment and Planning D: Society and Space* 22, no. 1 (2004): 135–56; Christian Licoppe, "Doing Ethnographic Studies of the Uses of Location Aware Social Networks: The Case of Grindr-Based Dating in Paris," address delivered at the Mobile Media: Making Cooperation Work Conference, Siegen, Germany, June 2014; Mizuko Ito and Daisuke Okabe, "Everyday Contexts of Camera Phone Use: Steps towards Technosocial Ethnographic Frameworks," in *Mobile Communication in Everyday Life: An Ethnographic View*, ed. Joachim R. Höflich and Maren Hartmann (Berlin: Frank & Timme, 2006), 79–102.

2. Esther Milne, *Letters, Postcards, Email: Technologies of Presence* (New York: Routledge, 2010), 165.

3. Chris Perkins, "Playing with Maps," in *Rethinking Maps*, ed. M. Dodge, R. Kitchin, and C. Perkins (Routledge: London, 2009), 168.

4. Ibid., 167–88.

5. Nanna Verhoeff, *Mobile Screens: The Visual Regime of Navigation* (Amsterdam: Amsterdam University Press, 2013), 145.

6. Judith Butler, *Gender Trouble: Feminism and the Subversion of Identity* (London: Routledge, 1990).

7. Eve Kosofsky Sedgwick, *Tendencies* (London: Routledge, 1994).

8. Ibid., 8.

9. Milne, *Letters, Postcards, Email* (New York: Routledge, 2010), 165.

10. Katie Salen and Eric Zimmerman, *Rules of Play* (Cambridge, Mass.: MIT Press, 2003).

11. T. L. Taylor, *Raising the Stakes* (Cambridge, Mass.: MIT Press, 2013).

12. Miguel Sicart, *Play Matters* (Cambridge, Mass.: MIT Press, 2014), 1.

13. Peter Bayliss, "Notes toward a Sense of Embodied Gameplay," address delivered at the DiGRA Conference, June 2007, Tokyo, http://lmc.gatech.edu/~cpearce3/DiGRA07/Proceedings/013.pdf; Paul Dourish, *Where the Action Is: The Foundations of Embodied Interaction* (Cambridge, Mass.: MIT Press, 2001).

14. Sarah Pink and Larissa Hjorth, "Emplaced Cartographies: Reconceptualising Camera Phone Practices in an Age of Locative Media," *Media International Australia* 145, no. 1 (2013): 145–56.

15. Jean Burgess, "Vernacular Creativity and New Media" (Ph.D. diss., Queensland University of Technology, 2007); Søren Mørk Petersen, "Common Banality: The Affective Character of Photo Sharing, Everyday Life and Produsage Cultures" (Ph.D. diss., IT University of Copenhagen, 2009); Ito and Okabe, "Everyday Contexts."

16. Kane Race, "Speculative Pragmatism and Intimate Arrangements: Online Hook-Up Devices in Gay Life," *Culture, Health, and Sexuality* 17, no. 4 (2014): 1–16.

17. Licoppe, "Doing Ethnographic Studies."

18. Larissa Hjorth and Kay Gu, "The Place of Emplaced Visualities: A Case Study of Smartphone Visuality and Location-Based Social Media in Shanghai, China," *Continuum: Journal of Media and Cultural Studies* 26, no. 5 (2012): 699–713.

19. Brooke Wendt, *The Allure of the Selfie: Instagram and the New Self-Portrait* (Amsterdam: Institute of Network Cultures, 2014).

20. Arlie Hochschild, "Emotion Work, Feeling Rules, and Social Structure," *American Journal of Sociology* 85, no. 3 (1979): 551–75.

21. Wendt, *Allure of the Selfie*.

Part III   READING GAMES QUEERLY

Chapter **11**

On "FeministWhorePurna" and the Ludo-material Politics of Gendered Damage Power-ups in Open-World RPG Video Games

ROBERT YANG

The video game industry often markets open-world role-playing games (RPGs) as complex simulations, but this computational fantasy rarely extends to its AI inhabitants, understood by players to be endlessly replaceable characters made of randomized traits. Such "generic identities" co-opt personal identities as formal strategic affordances for players to exploit. Deep Silver's 2011 open-world zombie game *Dead Island* offers a compelling case study, especially in light of its "FeministWhore" scandal. This incident highlights sexism in game development as a systemic bias from a technical as well as cultural perspective: a bias engineered directly in the game-play systems, user experience design, and the workflow of the game engine itself.

A History of "FeministWhorePurna"

On September 8, 2011, several consumerist game media outlets reported that a data file in the video game *Dead Island* contained the text string "FeministWhorePurna," referring to a player skill power-up for a woman named Purna that allowed her to "increase [her] damage when killing an enemy of the opposite sex."[1] In response, the developer Techland quickly released this public statement to the popular game news site *Kotaku*: "It has come to our attention that one of *Dead Island*'s leftover debug files contains a highly inappropriate internal script name of one of the character skills. . . . The line in question was something a programmer considered a private joke. The skill naturally has a completely different in-game name and the script reference was also changed. What is left is a part of an obscure debug function."[2]

According to Techland, "FeministWhorePurna" was merely an internal reference within the game engine's scripting files from an early version of the game mistakenly sold and distributed online. In all final release versions, the actual in-game text as seen by players had already been changed to "Gender Wars." To the developer's credit, the company took substantial responsibility: "This has been inexcusably overlooked and released with the game . . . This is merely an explanation but by no means an excuse. In the end that code was made a part of the product and signed with our company name. We deeply regret that fact and we apologize to all our customers or anyone who might have been offended by that inappropriate expression."[3]

Techland's public statement worked beautifully. In gamer communities and the wider public, the "controversy" seemed to run its course within the Internet news cycle, and *Dead Island* went on to sell millions of copies and grow into a lucrative media franchise with sequels and spin-off titles.[4] The story of the "Feminist Whore" was quickly relegated to trivia, a short quirky anecdote to be strategically deployed at tepid happy hours.

However, FeministWhorePurna is not just a rogue prank by a sole misogynist commercial game developer: it is a useful lens to articulate wider systemic problems of gender representation in video game culture. Specifically, there is a history of gendered combat "perks" in open-world RPG games similar to *Dead Island,* and it is very likely that many gamers would interpret the logic of FeministWhorePurna within the context of that history. What is the procedural rhetoric of gendered combat within these games, and how do these game-play systems and simulations enact a specific logic of "gender war" to be performed by players?

The Simulationist Dream of Open Worlds

To situate FeministWhorePurna within *Dead Island*, it is useful to briefly situate *Dead Island* within a larger play culture and design history of similar open-world video games.

Open-world games promise players a simulationist fantasy: instead of limiting player movement and navigation along a closed progression of set levels, these games offer an "open world" where players freely navigate a large city or small continent, complete with autonomous non-player characters (NPC) agents (wildlife, civilians, disparate factions) who interact within a supposedly vast, dynamic AI ecosystem. Marketing materials for *Grand Theft Auto V* promised "denser traffic, greater draw distances, upgraded AI, new wildlife . . . for the ultimate open world experience,"[5] while both *Elder Scrolls: Oblivion* and *Elder Scrolls: Skyrim* heavily advertised their "Radiant" AI systems. *Dead Island*'s marketing also invokes this tradition: two of six bullet points on its storefront page list "open world tropical island" and "hordes of gruesome zombies."[6] For all these games, the extent of their emergent world and agent simulation is their central selling point.

Game developers generally do not engineer, simulate, or author open worlds as continuous worlds. Instead, developers often separate the world into many regions, sectors, or lumps: smaller chunks of a larger world, which are then streamed into the game engine as the player crosses a secret boundary. When the player leaves a given neighborhood, that data is cleared from memory. As an optimization, inhabitants from past regions will often "sleep" or even vaporize entirely when the player is not present or not looking.

Most open-world engines operate as "sandboxes" that retain little or no memory of what happens within their environs. If a *Grand Theft Auto* player causes a twenty-car pileup in Downtown Los Angeles, drives away, and then returns five minutes later, there will likely be no evidence of a car accident or civilian fatalities because they were all "generic" entities, understood by players to be non-crucial actors who are infinitely replaceable by the game.

In this sense, an NPC's gender is just a random interchangeable trait like every other part of the simulation. Yellow hair here, green hair there; a man this time, a woman another time. How can such variables be made meaningful within the common game mode of player-initiated violence?

The game *Red Dead Redemption* rewards the player with an achievement trophy called "Dastardly" for placing a "hogtied" NPC woman (and only a woman) on train tracks and watching her get run over by a speeding locomotive. It specifically requires substantial complicity (you must place her there, you must watch her die) before it will reward the player with five Xbox Gamerscore points. This is probably the worst example of gendered violence as a "fun achievement" meant to provoke the player into exploring how two systems, like autonomous NPCs and an autonomous train, can collide.

Fallout 3 and its sequel, *Fallout: New Vegas,* both feature gendered damage upgrades. Acquiring the "Lady Killer" or "Black Widow" upgrades each grant +10 percent damage bonuses and "unique dialogue options" with NPCs of the "opposite" gender relative to the player avatar's gender. *Fallout: New Vegas* also has equivalent same-gender power-ups called "Confirmed Bachelor" and "Cherchez La Femme" to support gay relationships with named NPCs. For the vast majority of agents in an open-world simulation, with whom the player will never speak, these power-ups are compelling choices in the sense of their combat damage bonuses, and *Dead Island*'s "Gender Wars" is rooted in this convention.

FeministWhorePurna as Read by *Dead Island* Players

Dead Island has no developed conversation simulation like *Fallout* or other open-world RPG simulation games, so "unique dialogue options" for a gendered power-up are not relevant. Instead, the Feminist Whore or "Gender Wars" power-up for Purna players confers solely a damage bonus against hostile NPCs gendered as men. The power-up is unique to the Purna character and not available for the other female character, Xian Mei, and "misogynist" power-up equivalents do not exist for male player characters.

The ability icon for the power-up consists of a "feminist power" symbol, a Venus symbol inscribed with a clenched fist. This image implies that Gender Wars are a militant, activist, feminist vocation. This is consistent with the in-game lore for the Purna character, an autobiographical monologue (with voice-over narration) displayed prominently at the beginning of the game while the player selects a character, which casts Purna as a woman of color and an Australian ex-cop who struggles against virulent racism and sexism in her profession:

> You know how many female half-Aborigine detectives there were before me? None. You think it was easy suffering the abuse of my so-called colleagues? Half of 'em hated me because I was a

FIGURE 11.1. Character selection screen with "Purna" selected from *Dead Island* on Windows.

girl and the other half didn't like the fact that my mum was a Koori. So I came up the hard way: I busted my ass. It took me twelve years to make detective and that still wasn't enough. It's an old boys' club, you know. The whole justice system is a fucking joke. . . . No one would care because I was nothing, a nobody, an Abo bitch.

Within the context of contemporary video games about shooting things, this is an incredibly progressive portrayal of a woman of color who is angry with institutional barriers, both in her personal and professional life. However, she is still somewhat of a "straw-woman feminist" whose main character trait is that she more or less hates all white men.

Purna's "angry unreasonable black woman" attitude toward institutional sexism contrasts with the other playable woman character, Xian Mei, who is portrayed as more patient and "reasonable." She is an undercover cop from Hong Kong who resents her male bosses but remains stoic, ending her own monologue by saying "I just need the opportunity to prove myself."

However, it is questionable whether most *Dead Island* players (mostly men, one assumes) would stop to listen or read the characters' biographies, or whether most were ever exposed to these backstories, which would require them to consider playing as a female character. To the game engine, these characterizations are merely text and audio assets that could easily be rewritten and swapped out of the game without having to reprogram or redesign any game systems.

For most players, the narrative behind FeministWhorePurna and the Gender Wars power-up is secondary to its strategic value. What is the game-play logic of this power-up within the context of the simulation? How does it better afford the killing of zombies to level-up characters and become more powerful?

In *Dead Island*, players level-up their character by spending points in a skill tree. To advance further down the skill tree and access more powerful upgrades, the player must spend at least three points in a previous row above.

When considering whether to invest points into Gender Wars,

the player must also consider investing points in abilities within the same row, including Maintenance, which makes close-combat melee weapons last longer, and/or Kicks of Strength, which gives energy to the player when kicking enemies.

Given that the Purna character is presented as a "firearms expert" in the character selection screen (this is literally the first thing the player learns about her after her name; when selected, she is holding a rifle, and we learn that her "rage bonus" only applies to pistols), it is questionable whether players would choose the Maintenance or Kicks of Strength skills, which are upgrades that do not apply to gun combat.

So, Gender Wars is an obvious strategic choice for most Purna players.

Additionally, players can spend points to upgrade their upgrades. At Rank 1, Gender Wars gives a +5 percent damage increase "against opposite sex." At Rank 2, that value increases to +10 percent damage, and at Rank 3 it confers +15 percent damage. This bonus stacks with Purna's other damage upgrades. *Dead Island* players generally agree that Gender Wars is very effective; across several Internet message boards for discussing game strategy, players argue that most of the

FIGURE 11.2. Purna's "Combat" skill tree, with the Gender Wars icon highlighted at Rank 3. It is the only upgrade in that row that applies to firearms damage, her specialty.

game's monsters, especially near the end of the game, are gendered as male and thus susceptible to the damage bonus:

> It is worth it. There are no enemy female humans. Act 3-4 [of the game] has almost no female zombies and all specials are male.

> Take it. Almost every enemy is male and it gets amplified by her survival skill.

> The zombie overlords are all male.

> Its a nice damage buff versus Thugs, Rams and Butchers.[7]

> Gender Wars boosts damage against male zombies, which seem to be about half of the common zombies, and many of the tougher zombies, making Gender Wars very useful.[8]

Thus, Gender Wars is an upgrade that is central to Purna's identity as a playable character—and that identity is a woman of color who specializes in sniping men from a distance. Gender Wars' effectiveness depends on the number of generic "men" in the game, as well as generic "special" male enemies that are also freely spawned and deleted by the game engine as necessary. It turns out that the majority of hostile NPCs are male, which implies that male is the "default gender" even for seemingly androgynous or un-gendered enemies.

Technical Reading of FeministWhorePurna

Given that players would never know of Gender Wars' history unless they read the news coverage, the situation begs the following question: Why is this technical history important, and how did FeministWhorePurna function internally within the script file, within the game engine itself?

"FeministWhorePurna" was a "skill" object bound to newly created Purna-classed player characters within a text file called "default_player_setup.scr." Although this file is no longer loaded in retail versions of *Dead Island*, it seemed to control game logic and skill manifests for all four playable characters as well as default money supplies and inventories at various checkpoints within the game.

The .scr file extension likely denotes this file as a "script," a form of plain-text non-compiled code common in many game engines, that denotes game rules and initializes variables but is not part of the game engine itself. Script files are commonly the interface between the game engine (complex, low-level code that controls graphics, sound, physics, etc.) and the game code (simpler, high-level code that defines worlds, inhabitants, items, etc.). Scripting operates as a sort of bridge, a central locus of interaction between separate programming and game design departments at a large commercial game studio like Deep Silver or Techland.

The "default_player_setup.scr" excerpt in question reads as follows:

```
sub Skills_Purna ( ) {
[ . . . ]
Skill("TeamSpirit2Purna");
Skill("FeministWhorePurna");
Skill("MeleeDurabilityPurna");
[ . . . ]
}
```

Such script files are often enticing sites of intervention for game modders (end users who modify the game) to edit the text to reconfigure the game's behavior. In this case, modders edited the contents of default_player_setup.scr, and one modder described the script's functionality as "a way to alter the items you get when choosing a chapter."[9] This description sounds neither "private" nor "obscure," as described by Techland's public statement. At best, their statement is a substantial mischaracterization of this file's importance and interdependency within the game engine; editing the file would have required cooperation and cross-validation between multiple departments at Techland.

If a programmer added a new skill to the game, he or she would have to edit this script file to implement that change. If a designer wished to balance or delete any skills, he or she would have to edit this script file to implement that change. If a quality assurance tester wished to try different player equipment load-outs to test game balance, he or she would have to edit this script file to implement that change.

Multiply these cases across staff, between multiple coders, designers, or testers, and it is only reasonable to conclude that many more people than one "rogue coder" were editing this file and signing off on its contents through years of development. The credits of *Dead Island* for the Windows platform list thirty-two programmers, not including any engine or tools engineers, and zero game-design roles (which is unusual practice within the industry), but eight level designers and seven writers and thirty-four quality assurance staff. All development staff would have had to validate their changes against the rest of the file; if there was even a single errant line anywhere, it might have caused a parsing error in the game and the script file could be rendered inoperable. Testing staff might have even encountered the "Feminist Whore" text string within the game interface itself, before it was replaced for the public retail version.

So, for whatever reason, throughout *Dead Island*'s development, multiple staff members at Techland and Deep Silver likely saw the text string "FeministWhorePurna" in this highly shared, highly intersectional, commonly invoked file within the game—and this text was not changed until very late in the development process. This means that the renaming was probably a low-priority development task, postponed until more of the game was built, or until more urgent, "game-breaking" bugs were fixed.

Conclusion

This analysis insists on referring to the original 2011 incident as "FeministWhorePurna" instead of "Feminist Whore," as it was known in news media. Using "Feminist Whore" instead of "FeministWhorePurna" erases both the racial politics—only the dark-skinned "man-hating" character Purna is a "feminist whore," not the Xian Mei character—as well as the technical politics—this was a mechanic embedded at a central juncture in the game logic, which requires wide-ranging complicity across broad levels of the development team.

While much of this analysis is educated conjecture, it is still conjecture. Due to the hyperbolic levels of secrecy maintained by the triple-A game industry, it is exceptionally unlikely that the public will ever know the specific details and processes that led to FeministWhorePurna, and games media journalism regularly assumes that such details are trade secrets that cannot be discussed—and so no one ever asks. Techland's public statement relied on this expectation to characterize FeministWhorePurna as the work of a rogue misogynist working alone, rather than a symptom of institutional misogyny that allowed such behavior to go unchecked until right before the game's release. Such assumptions are dangerous because they encourage development communities to clean up and hide evidence of toxic behavior, rather than address root causes and the reality of a hostile work environment.

But even in its sanitized version, *Dead Island*'s in-game portrayal of Purna is still deeply racist and sexist, implying that "gender wars" are performed only by angry women of color, and never perpetuated by stoic, patient, lighter-skinned women (Xian Mei) or men (Sam B and Logan). Only Purna has access to this ability, and her play style leads most players to invest in it. This game-play logic eerily mimes Techland's statement—in both dimensions, "gender wars" are about individuals (one playable character Purna, one rogue misogynist programmer) acting thoughtlessly on their personal emotions. Misogyny is never understood as a widespread oppressive institution, and feminism is denied its status as a methodical tactic of resistance against oppressive institutions. Thus, a more progressive mode of game development involves more than just proofreading the in-game text before retail release; it requires critical reflection on workflow, process, team structure, and game design.

Notes

1. Robert Purchese, "*Dead Island* Developer Techland 'Disturbed' by Feminist Whore Skill," *Eurogamer,* September 8, 2011, http://www.eurogamer.net/articles/2011-09-08-dead-island-developer-techland-disturbed-by-feminist-whore-skill.

2. Brian Crecente, "*Dead Island* Maker Gives Leading Lady a 'Feminist Whore' Skill," *Kotaku,* September 8, 2011, http://kotaku.com/5838387/dead-island-maker-gives-leading-lady-a-feminist-whore-skill.

3. Ibid.

4. Wesley Yin-Poole, "*Dead Island*'s Whopping Five Million Sales Proves New IP Can Succeed at the End of a Console Lifecycle, Publisher Says," *Eurogamer*, February 5, 2013, http://www.eurogamer.net/articles/2013-02-05 -dead-islands-whopping-five-million-sales-proves-new-ip-can-succeed-at -the-end-of-a-console-lifecycle-publisher-says.

5. "*Grand Theft Auto V* on Steam," *Steam*, nd, http://store.steampowered .com/app/271590/.

6. "*Dead Island* on Steam," *Steam*, nd, http://store.steampowered.com /app/91310/.

7. "Quick Question about Feminist Who—I Mean, Gender Wars," *Steam Users' Forums*, September 18, 2011, http://forums.steampowered.com/forums /showthread.php?t=2128730.

8. "*Dead Island* FAQ/Walkthrough by BlueYoshi579," *GameFAQs*, October 6, 2011, http://www.gamefaqs.com/pc/933053-dead-island/faqs/63097.

9. "Modding," *Cheat Happens*, September 13, 2011, http://www .cheathappens.com/show_board2.asp?headID=108494&titleID=17278& onPage=4.

Chapter **12**

Welcome to *My* Fantasy Zone
Bayonetta and Queer Femme Disturbance

AMANDA PHILLIPS

> *I am interested in a broad conceptualization of queer femme as that which exceeds the normative limits of femininity, of the femme slut who refuses to bend to demands for chastity from normative institutions, but also commands the sexual agency to decide not to be sexually available.*
> —Micha Cárdenas, "Blah, Blah, Blah: Ke\$ha Feminism?"

When it debuted in 2009, Platinum Games' *Bayonetta* sparked a frenzy of debate among feminist gamers on the Internet. Described variously as camp queen,[1] masculinist fantasy par excellence,[2] "love letter to femininity,"[3] and failed Lady Gaga,[4] Bayonetta is situated at a divide in the community: What place does sexiness have in the cultural construct of the progressive heroine? The game features an unrealistically proportioned hypersexual witch who hunts down angels using magic powered by her hair, which also serves as her primary means of clothing. The more powerful the attack, the more hair is shifted from covering her body to destroying its target. Bayonetta brutally dispatches her heavenly foes to the bubbly sounds of J-pop, interjecting bondage-themed special attacks between more traditional gun- and swordplay and pistols shooting from her platform heels. Her five-hundred-year-old European spell-casting maneuvers resemble contemporary exotic dance.

On the surface, Bayonetta is the ideal candidate for thinking about the objectification of women in video games, a topic that is best understood by many in terms of Laura Mulvey's theory of the male gaze—or rather, a version of the male gaze that focuses exclusively on its interest in what happens when a straight man looks at a woman rather than the ways in which power and desire become entwined with the complicated technical and cultural apparatuses of cinema.[5] Despite feminist film scholars' thorough critique and reconfiguring of their own theories on the power dynamics of visuality since 1975, contemporary critics remain loyal to this reading of Mulvey's original formulation when discussing representations of female characters in video games through a feminist lens. Yet, while much popular critique holds Bayonetta up as an example of straight male desire run wild, this femme fatale is not typical in her orientation toward heteronormative masculinity or in her relationship to the apparatus of the gaming machine: there is something distinctly queer at her core that disrupts efforts to cast her according to this timeworn trope.

The game follows Bayonetta's quest to reconstruct her memories after being resurrected in the twentieth century, the last survivor of a war between her female clan, the Umbra witches, and the all-male Ithavoll sages that took place centuries ago during the historical witch hunts in early modern Europe. This narrative backdrop is a simplistic invocation of serious questions about gendered power, though the consistently campy execution might be read equally as parody of feminism or critique of patriarchy—and usually it is a combination of the two. The game inverts the war between heaven and hell, placing Bayonetta and the gamer on the side of "evil" against a thinly veiled analogue of the Catholic Church. Most of the action takes place in the Baroque environment of the fictional religious European city-state of Vigrid, while Handelesque choirs announce the arrival of angels (organized according to the Celestial Hierarchy first put forward in the fifth century by Pseudo-Dionysus the Areopagite) to do battle with Bayonetta. The game is segmented into "Chapters" and "Verses" (rather than levels) to add an additional biblical flair to the entire production. Set against the historical violences and prohibitions perpetrated against women and sexual minorities by chaste religious institutions, as well as the Catholic Church's ongoing position as a bastion of colonial, heteropatriarchal power, Bayonetta's sultriness has more purpose than the decontextualized sexiness of most female heroes. In the words of games journalist Chris Dahlen, "her sex is a weapon," and it is aimed squarely at one of the world's most symbolic male-dominated, sexually prohibitive, colonizing institutions.[6]

Bayonetta's weaponized sexuality falls into the category of what Micha Cárdenas calls "femme disturbance," the propensity of femininity to disrupt phallic power structures through its own excess.[7] Femme disturbance, rather than wholly reclaiming a feminine figure for progressive ends, disrupts simplistic notions of agency and resistance to open the way for recognizing how systems might be assailed from within.[8] Fictional figures are important in imagining new ways to confront oppressive regimes, and characters like Bayonetta are often overlooked because they resemble too closely some of mainstream feminism's historically abjected subjects: the stripper, the sex

FIGURE 12.1. Bayonetta struts toward the camera. Screen capture from *Bayonetta*.

worker, the slut. Her body is hypervisible, seemingly designed for a viewer's pleasure. Her hair–clothing appears as a skintight leather catsuit on her body, and she walks with a sassy swing in her hips. Her proportions are unrealistic, her body contorts in improbable ways, and her performance of sexiness sometimes seems un-self-aware, potentially making her the perfect object for the voyeur (see Figure 12.1). Prior to the game's release, its marketing campaign came under fire for encouraging passersby in a Japanese subway station to undress a mural of Bayonetta by taking individual advertisement cards concealing her near-naked body. In the context of a subway system well known for male sexual assault of female passengers, this was rightly condemned as a harassment training mechanism.

However, the visual enticement of misogynist consumers is only one side of Bayonetta's story. In fact, like many feminist film theorists, the game is preoccupied with and skeptical of both the cinematic eye and the straight male gaze. Bayonetta's relationship to visuality is not straightforward. She has the ability to make herself invisible at will by crossing into Purgatorio, a parallel plane of reality in which witches and angels can meet to do battle but into which normal humans cannot see. Human characters in the game world react to Bayonetta's destruction of physical objects and will act startled when she runs by, but they cannot see or touch her. During one cinematic sequence, for example, an investigative journalist named Luka attempts to take a picture of Bayonetta with his camera, only to discover that she cannot be captured on film (see Figure 12.2). She uses invisibility to her advantage particularly against this relentless male pursuer, running circles around him and painting his face with lipstick while he attempts to ascertain her position.

Straight male desire in the game's cut scenes is mediated through the figure of Luka, whose fantasies about Bayonetta are enacted by the cinematic gaze and coincide with his inability "really" to see the world around him. In Chapter 5, for example, Bayonetta launches herself at Luka unexpectedly. They fly through the air. Time slows down. Luka's hand slides across her buttocks. Bayonetta clutches his face to her bosom. They land, Luka on bottom and Bayonetta steadying herself with a sexy flourish, as a falling pillar destroys the platform on which they had been standing. Bayonetta leaps off him without another word to battle the incoming foes that he can't even see. Luka's fantasy of a willing embrace is shattered when it turns out Bayonetta was saving him from danger he was unable to perceive. In Chapter 14, Bayonetta watches for danger as Luka pilots a helicopter. When she commands him to look, his response is a breathless, "Oh, I'm looking . . ." as another fantasy slow-motion sequence focuses on water dripping down Bayonetta's breasts.

Then missiles blow them apart.

Both scenes (and several others like it) parody Luka's inability to see, as he says, "the reality of things." In his blog post about gendered power in *Bayonetta*, William Huber suggests Luka is a stand-in for the male gamer—though Huber's basis for this claim rests largely on his skepticism regarding Bayonetta's function as point of iden- tification in the game world rather than an object purely for view- ing.[9] Luka does refer to characters from unrelated video games as ex-girlfriends, lending credibility to Huber's reading while also play- ing to a fannish desire for Easter eggs, connecting Luka to an out- side world to which only gamers have access. If he does function as a

FIGURE 12.2. Luka attempting to take a photograph of Bayonetta. Screen capture from *Bayonetta*.

gamer surrogate in some ways, however (for male viewers rather than female ones, who from this critical perspective presumably would have no trouble identifying with a female avatar), his status as the punch line to numerous jokes about vision also implicates the male gamer himself within this critique.

From the beginning, however, the narrative codes heterosexual union as deviant and dangerous: Bayonetta is the product of an Umbra Witch mother and a Lumen Sage father, a violation of the gendered clans' separation that plunges the world into war. So many critiques of Bayonetta focus on her relationship with men on- and off-screen to the exclusion of the other female characters in the game: Jeanne, the sister witch who is her primary antagonist until near the game's end, and Cereza, a child who wanders into the line of fire and accompanies Bayonetta through most of her journey. Father Balder, the Lumen Sage at the head of Ithavoll who is also Bayonetta's father, brings overtones of pedophilia and incest to the game when he tries to unite his body with Cereza, whom he reveals to be Bayonetta's childhood self, by luring the girl into his lap. Cereza's role is often critiqued as a means to constrain Bayonetta to the familiar role of mother and caretaker. However, the revelation of the girl's true identity toward the end of the game shifts the meaning of their relationship: protecting the little girl orients Bayonetta toward radical self-care rather than reproductive futurity. Her growing affection for Cereza is actually directed inward, her combat skills directed toward self-actualization.[10]

While Bayonetta does eventually require assistance to survive the endgame, it comes not in the expected form of Luka but in Jeanne, another Umbra Witch with whom Bayonetta is much more evenly matched intellectually, sexually, and in terms of actual power. Their girl-power relationship, and indeed the entire conceit of a separatist clan of powerful warrior women, is the stuff of 1970s lesbian feminist fantasies. They maintain a healthy adversarial respect for one another throughout the early stages of the game, which develops into recognition and deep affection as they recall their history together: childhood friends who grew up and fought alongside each other in the war. The game is bookended by a repeated animation, re-skinned to reflect a change in costume after five hundred years, which has them twirl in the air and match up back to back, descending as Bayonetta shouts, "Just stay close to me!" Though there is never an explicit sexual encounter between the two, neither is there one with Luka, whom Bayonetta taunts and punishes in much the same way as the angels in the game. Indeed, the "Torture" attacks that are often identified as part of the game's sadomasochistic aesthetic are influenced not so much by sexual practice as by actual instruments of torture, like iron maidens and guillotines, meant to invoke the historical witch hunts in Europe. The one notable exception is the bondage horse, which Bayonetta uses to bring the only feminine-bodied angel in the game to an explosive orgasm.

Bayonetta engages queer narrative and aesthetics just as much as she actively refuses heteronormative gestures in the game, but her relationship to queerness exists in more than just these surface signifiers. While the cinematic scenes in the game metaphorically ridicule Luka's gazing male eyes, they also by extension call into question the reality of the events that a camera can show the spectator. The game's stylized cut scenes come in two varieties: those fully animated by a computer, and storyboard sequences in which still images and partially frozen movement take the place of full motion animation. These latter scenes are framed with film sprocket holes, as if the cinematic eye has been overtaken by the procedural camera of game animation, not only relegating cinema to a pastness of narrative visuality but also undermining its reliability to capture the full details of a narrative event. What replaces it is a type of machinic vision unique to video games.

Alexander Galloway discusses the development and impact of gamic vision as it evolves from the cinematic subjective shot, expanding the ability of this point of view to encourage rather than thwart the spectator's identification with the camera's subject.[11] Implicit within this structure is the machine-eye view—a subjective shot from the perspective of the rendering engine responsible for tracking and drawing the portions of game space visible to the gamer in real time. Whereas a film critic might look to the creative decisions of the director behind the camera, a gamic camera may or may not have a human subject framing the shots. Many contemporary commercial games like *Bayonetta* have navigable 3-D spaces that often require a gamic camera to automate the framing process. Watching Bayonetta becomes quite complicated during game play, and the gamic camera has much to do with this. Twitchy combo-driven combat mechanics ensure that Bayonetta as an avatar is usually a blur. The camera only slows to witness her most powerful (though not necessarily most sexual) attacks, and the photo-finish freeze-frames that end a sequence of battles (eliciting much commentary about her status as an object for the camera) often obscure Bayonetta's figure behind an explosion of bloody body parts.

Bayonetta's real-time camera primarily functions to keep the avatar in the middle of the screen and is locked at a distance that prioritizes a wider radius for ease of negotiating the game's combat sequences, which are fast-paced, crowded with moving elements, and often feature enemy combatants who are orders of magnitude larger than Bayonetta herself (see Figure 12.3). While some gamic camera systems allow the user to control both the angle and zoom of the shot, this is not a feature of *Bayonetta*'s scopic regime. This lack of control has been a source of complaint by fans on message boards concerning both personal combat preference and sexual frustration over the inability to view the avatar up close. Indeed, the only way to zoom in on Bayonetta's body during play is to manipulate the system in a way that resembles sexual assault of both avatar and camera: the gamer must position her body in a corner and rotate the camera so that it becomes pinned between avatar and wall and is forced closer to her. Here, the enticement of voyeurism clashes with technological restriction.

What is visible is a complicated matter in video games that is bound up in software procedures like the constant calculation of visual output based on user input or game rules such as the "fog of war" that determines what the gamer is allowed to see based on her previous actions and earned abilities in the game. In *Bayonetta,* an exploit known as the "camera trick" exposes the strange ways in which procedures interact with visuality in the game: if the gamer activates a special power known as "Witch Time" during play and has the gamic camera positioned such that the enemies on-screen are not visible, they will not attack Bayonetta even if they had been actively hostile before triggering the event. These types of interactions, wherein user control over the gaze works on more than simply the visual scene of the game, indicates that in gaming, the gaze can be permeable and recursive. Indeed, just like in pornography or horror, it is in the visual scene that gamers receive the information that transforms the medium into what Carol Clover calls a body genre—only this time, the loop is closed, with the bodily response feeding back into and transforming what happens on the screen via a peripheral device like a game controller.

Brenda Brathwaite's history of sex in video games cites an interview with Atari founder Nolan Bushnell in which he suggests that developers considered the sexual implications of gaming hardware as far back as the arcade joystick.[12] Current mainstream game consoles do not employ peripherals designed exclusively for sex, but they do create moments that I would call sexual analogues, in which controller functions mimic sexual activity. Certain weapons, for example, allow Bayonetta to create and mount a pole around which she twirls, dealing significant damage to the unfortunate audience of this spectacle; the gamer must perform this action by twirling the analog stick on the controller. The game's sexual analogues get really interesting during the Torture attacks that require swift, repetitive, single-button presses in order to max out the power of the attack.

FIGURE 12.3. Bayonetta (center, barely visible on-screen) fighting the enormous Temperantia. Screen capture from *Bayonetta*.

This mechanic is by far the most common in the game, and its sexual implications aren't fully illuminated until a boss battle, when the attack is given the label of "Climax." This sexual analogue, unlike those in other games that mimic the rocking back and forth of penetration (as in Santa Monica Studio's *God of War*) or Simon-like button-pressing sequences that code heterosexual coupling as a complicated but routine sequence of moves (as in Quantic Dream's *Heavy Rain*), the Climax finishers in *Bayonetta* invoke clitoral masturbation, particularly when one considers the common gamer strategy of placing the controller in their own lap and pressing with the index finger rather than the thumb in order to maximize button-pressing speed. If we take the metaphoric potential of the game's sexual analogues seriously, the gamer's pleasure as registered by the body is characterized not by the twisting phallic columns of hair-summoning demons on-screen or suggestive combat moves of the avatar but by the simulation of clitoral stimulation on the controller. *Bayonetta* as a soft-core production certainly induces masturbatory pleasure as its critics claim, but it forces the tactile enactment of that pleasure into a clitoral structure.[13]

This gesture is merely disruptive rather than necessarily progressive in nature, working against the prevalence of phallic structures in video game culture, in soft-core practice, and in cinema. It pushes back from within a binary gender system in which phallus and clitoris are metonyms of cisgendered bodies. *Bayonetta*'s plot and game play go one step further by leading the gamer to destroy an all-male Vatican analogue by systematically dismembering its giant, glittery white angelic guardians. From a scopic regime that entices the consumer oriented toward the exploitation of the male gaze, *Bayonetta* ultimately enlists the gamer in a project that de-privileges and ridicules phallic scopophilia, dismembers the structures of religio-corporate masculinity, literally and figuratively castrates its central figures, and channels masturbatory pleasure at the game's climaxes into a clitoral form. Here, Carol Clover's comments about the dual sadistic and masochistic nature of the gaze are particularly salient: just as horror films use sadism as the sleight of hand to entice audiences into an ultimately masochistic experience, so, too, does *Bayonetta*. Tanner Higgin's primary complaint that *Bayonetta* ul-

timately fails to "make men uncomfortable" about their potential desire for her body neglects to take into account the game's thinly veiled
(and numerous) references to castration, which range in transparency
from sequential bodily dismemberment to bloody tentacle severing
to shooting the penis off a cherub statue.

Clover argues that horror films subvert what she calls "our ultimate gender story," that "sadistic violence is what finally distinguishes male from female," and that masochism has no place in
hegemonic straight masculinity.[14] Her description of the critical response to the violent rape-revenge film *I Spit on Your Grave* is worth
quoting at length:

> *I Spit on Your Grave* provides, for many long stretches of its hour-
> and-a-half narration, as pure a feminine–masochistic jolt as the
> movies have to offer. No such possibility is even hinted at in the
> reviews that led to its condemnation and censorship, however.
> On the contrary, the film was characterized, in tones of outrage
> and in the name of feminism, as the ultimate incitement to male
> sadism, a "vile film for vicarious sex criminals," a "sleazy exploi-
> tation movie" that "makes rapists of us all." But there is some-
> thing off here: something too shrill and totalizing in the claim
> of misogyny, something dishonest in the critical rewritings and
> outright misrepresentations of the plot required to sustain that
> claim, something suspicious about the refusal to entertain even
> in passing the possibility of involvement with the victim's part,
> something perverse about the unwillingness to engage with the
> manifestly feminist dimensions of the script.[15]

What happens in *Bayonetta*'s reception is an echo of this same reaction—a milder version in response to what one might call a milder
text playing out decades later. Feminist critics condemn the way the
game seems to offer her body up to the male gaze without interrogating the ways in which she demonstrably avoids it and turns it on itself.
Chris Dahlen documents the shame and embarrassment professed
by straight male gamers playing the game,[16] echoed in academic
blogs by figures like Tanner Higgin[17] and William Huber;[18] for these
men, she is a grotesque representation of what they are supposed to

find attractive, an object to possess rather than to serve as a point of entry into the game world. Those who write in Bayonetta's defense mark her as a point of identification only for women (and, significantly, queer) gamers.[19]

Here again we see the repetition of a failure to believe in a masculine identification with a feminine character, despite the game's other appeals to "hard-core" (presumed male) gamer set. *Bayonetta,* for all its flirtatious feminine trappings, is a brutally difficult game with game play that focuses on skill and familiarity rather than luck: it is important to master the combat combos and special moves, because basic attacks are not adequate to survive the waves upon waves of angels that the gamer must face. These gamic attributes, which seem to appeal to the masculine video game demographic that values challenge and mastery over technology, nevertheless encourage critics to believe that Bayonetta's body is on offer only as eye candy rather than as an extension of the gamer's own subjectivity into the game world. This failure to believe in cross-gendered identification thoroughly infuses the industry's public statements and gamers' own self-assessments. The "target demographic" of straight white males addressed by researchers like Adrienne Shaw, who notes that expectations of male straightness permeate popular and academic conversations alike, is one of the foundational mythologies on which video games are designed, the reason given for the preponderance of bald white space marines and continued objectification of feminine bodies: you must give the market what it wants to be.[20] When critics and academics alike take for granted that the power fantasies supplied by video games are accessible to all players and yet, except in rare cases, fail to explore the queer and transgender fantasies that attend female-bodied avatars, this seems to point to a repetition of the disavowal that Clover identified decades ago.

It seems no surprise, in light of Clover's work, that the particular woman around which this particular controversy revolves does significant, unreserved violence not simply to men, but to masculinity. But the deeper issue here—that her essence somehow cannot be contained by the camera—gets at the heart of how game studies tries to articulate its object against other media forms like film: if something like a gaze operates in gaming, it is more than a visual field. It is, rather, a matrix of recursive vectors of desire among the elements of a gamic system: human, hardware, software, rules, narrative, and representation. What mediates Bayonetta, then, is not the penetrative cinematic camera described by Laura Mulvey and against which gamers judge her fitness as a feminist icon, but rather a recursive gamic system that kinesthetically entangles the body of the gamer via technological peripherals and the demands of play. Bayonetta's aggressively feminine sexuality reaches beyond the screen to implicate the gamer in its own pleasures, disturbing the narratives we tell about what it means to be a gamer, or a woman, or a slut, or a hero in contemporary times.

Notes

1. Denis Farr, "Bayonetta: Dragging Angels to Hell," *Border House* (blog), February 19, 2010, http://borderhouseblog.com/?p=1562.

2. William Huber, "Sexy Videogameland: If You Run Out of Ammo, You Can Have Mine," *Zang.org* (blog), January 13, 2010, http://zang.org/2010/01/13/sexy-videogameland-if-you-run-out-of-ammo-you-can-have-mine/.

3. Leigh Alexander, "Bayonetta: Empowering or Exploitative?" *Gamepro* (blog), January 6, 2010, http://www.gamepro.com/article/features/213466/bayonetta-empowering-or-exploitative/.

4. Tanner Higgin, "Making Men Uncomfortable: What Bayonetta Should Learn from Gaga," *Gaming the System* (blog), December 2, 2010, http://www.tannerhiggin.com/making-men-uncomfortable-what-bayonetta-should-learn-from-gaga/.

5. Laura Mulvey, "Visual Pleasure and Narrative Cinema," *Screen* 16, no. 3 (1975): 6–18. Mulvey worked within a particular school of feminist theory organized around reformulating psychoanalytic perspectives on power and identity formation, and her take on the scopophilic encounter was useful for describing a prevalent orientation toward the feminine body that resonated with many women's experiences: sexual objectification. Despite the fact that the idea of the male gaze was controversial and contested at the time because of its insistence on a fixed spectator for cinema (and, in fact, Mulvey wrote that it was merely a provocation in "Afterthoughts on 'Visual Pleasure and Narrative Cinema' Inspired by *Duel in the Sun*," *Framework* 15–17 [1981]), it has somehow come to stand in for the more

heterogeneous body of feminist criticism about the gaze that emerged alongside and after the piece. The question of identification with the screen is actually much more nuanced in feminist and queer theory. Competing psychoanalytic perspectives exist, such as Constance Penley, "Feminism, Psychoanalysis, and the Study of Popular Culture," in *Cultural Studies,* ed. Lawrence Grossberg, Cary Nelson, and Paula Treichler (New York: Routledge, 1992), 479–500, which argued for a more complex understanding of cross-gender libidinal identifications. The cinematic gaze itself has been exhaustively explored, critiqued, and dismissed in the literature, from the oppositional gaze that refuses identification with either subject or object of the camera in bell hooks's *Black Looks: Race and Representation* (Boston: South End Press, 1992) to Carol Clover's insistence that film induces visual pleasure through identification with multiple subjects in *Men, Women, and Chain Saws: Gender in the Modern Horror Film* (Princeton, N.J.: Princeton University Press, 1992). Critics have exploded the cinematic gaze and its relation to identity politics to the point that Nick Mirzoeff characterizes the work of the field as operating with "a transverse look or glance—not a gaze, there have been enough gazes already," in "The Subject of Visual Culture," in *The Visual Culture Reader: Second Edition,* ed. Nicholas Mirzoeff (New York: Routledge, 2002), 18.

6. Chris Dahlen, "Her Sex Is a Weapon," *Edge Magazine* (blog), January 13, 2010, http://www.edge-online.com/blogs/the-loser-mechanic.

7. Micha Cárdenas, "Blah, Blah, Blah: Ke$ha Feminism?" *Journal of Popular Music Studies* 24, no. 2 (2012): 178.

8. For a comprehensive collection outlining contemporary feminist concerns about the agency/resistance binary, see Sumi Madhok, Anne Phillips, and Kalpana Wilson, eds., *Gender, Agency, and Coercion* (New York: Palgrave Macmillan, 2013).

9. Huber, "Sexy Videogameland."

10. In fact, in a bizarre temporal twist, when Bayonetta returns Cereza to her own time, she gives her a token handed down from their mother: in that moment, she becomes her own mother.

11. Alexander Galloway, *Gaming: Essays on Algorithmic Culture* (Minneapolis: University of Minnesota Press, 2006).

12. Brenda Brathwaite, *Sex in Video Games* (Boston: Charles River Media, 2007).

13. This gesture should be contrasted with clearly phallic masturbatory controller gestures, such as in Grasshopper Manufacture's *No More Heroes* game, which requires Wii gamers to shake the rod-shaped Wii remote with one hand in order to charge the main character's light sword.

14. Clover, *Men, Women, and Chain Saws,* 226–27. One might contrast this with other critiques of Mulvey's sadistic, scopophilic male gaze. For Gaylyn Studlar, for example, masochism is fundamental to cinematic experience and to male sexuality. See Studlar, "Visual Pleasure and the Masochistic Aesthetic," *Journal of Film and Video* 37, no. 2 (1985): 5–26.

15. Clover, *Men, Women, and Chain Saws,* 228.

16. Dahlen, "Her Sex Is a Weapon."

17. Higgin, "Making Men Uncomfortable."

18. Huber, "Sexy Videogameland."

19. See Alexander, "Bayonetta"; Farr, "Bayonetta"; and Tiff Chow, "Bayonetta: Sexuality as Decoration vs. Celebration," *.tiff* (blog), January 12, 2010, http://tiffchow.typepad.com/tiff/2010/01/bayonetta-sexuality-as-decoration-vs-celebration.html.

20. Adrienne Shaw, "On Not Being a Gamer: Moving beyond the Constructed Audience," *Ada: A Journal of Gender, New Media, and Technology* 2 (2013): http://adanewmedia.org/2013/06/issue2-shaw/. Shaw specifically critiques this construct as detrimental to both the production and the study of video games.

Chapter **13**

Role-Play as Queer Lens
How "ClosetShep" Changed My Vision
of *Mass Effect*

TODD HARPER

Her name was Rosalinde Shepard. She was born on Earth, in a dystopic future where crime and poverty reigned as humankind's journey to the stars heightened economic disparity. The military seemed like a natural choice for her, and in fact she made her career by fighting off an invasion by alien slavers almost single-handedly (while on vacation!). The trajectory of Rosalinde Shepard's career from that point on was of galactic importance. She rose through the ranks to become captain of the SSV *Normandy,* the savior of humanity multiple times over, and the woman who—at the cost of her own life—destroyed the invading Reapers and secured peace for the galaxy for all organic life. A master of both firearms and scientifically granted telekinetic abilities, she was a paragon on and off the battlefield, a true hero.

Now, consider someone else. *His* name is Ephraim Shepard, and in many ways, he's quite different from Rosalinde. Ephraim was from a space colony, a human settlement on a planet far from Earth. Rather than being a war hero, he enlisted after being the sole survivor of an attack on his home by massive, monstrous alien sandworms.

Ephraim was a biotic (the in-game term for someone who possesses the telekinetic-esque abilities mentioned above), though unlike Rosalinde, who started her career as a "Vanguard" (a frontline biotic soldier), Ephraim was a "Sentinel" who focused on biotic and engineering/medical skills rather than combat. And like Rosalinde, Ephraim was a galaxy-saving hero who stood up against the Reapers.

These overlapping yet different portraits represent two approaches I took to playing BioWare's popular *Mass Effect* series of role-playing games (RPGs). Rosalinde Shepard was my initial version of the player-created avatar: a career soldier wielding quips and dubiously explained space magic with equal deadliness. I followed her story across three titles using the series' trademark "carry over" style, where game-play choices in one game can be imported to the next.

Rosalinde is just one flavor in a long tradition of what many call "FemShep": female Commander Shepards. This term—which originated in fandom spaces—is bound up in the gender politics of gaming at large, BioWare's marketing of the *Mass Effect* games, and the relationships of players to games and avatars. The idea of "FemShep" sets her counter to the male, BioWare-presented "default" Shepard, who appears in all types of *Mass Effect* marketing material, with almost no exceptions. Carlen Lavigne has written on how BioWare's packaging and marketing of FemShep for *Mass Effect 3* highlights the complicated relationship between the publisher's perception of her place in the game, and the rhetorical importance she has as an icon for fans—particularly women fans—of the series.[1]

For me, she is also one in a long line of characters I have played in various role-playing games, digital or not. Rosalinde was my avatar when I played the *Mass Effect* games "for fun" and "for myself" rather than for analytical or professional reasons. If the series is about the story of "your" Shepard, then Rosalinde's story is my canon, my "official" Shepard. Of course, my having an "official" Shepard suggests that there are other possibilities, what-ifs, and potential alternate versions. Enter Ephraim.

A key recurring element in not just *Mass Effect* but most BioWare titles is the ability to "romance" a character. The number of romance options increased over the life of the series: three in the first game, six in the second. However, the third and final game represented a significant shift. Not only did the number of options explode to twelve, but for the first time, the game offered same-sex romances for both genders: male Shepards could romance another man, either new character Steve Cortez or series veteran Kaidan Alenko.[2]

Thus, in the summer of 2012, I undertook a play-through of the entire trilogy with one particular what-if in mind: a male Shepard who was a closeted gay man. Playing as Ephraim Shepard, the man I would come to refer to as "ClosetShep," presented an interesting opportunity to examine my game-play choices in a series that presents those choices as being fundamentally important to the experience. In effect, I was retroactively explaining, in narrative form, a primarily mechanical innovation that only manifested itself in the final game of the series. If Shepard could have a gay romance in *Mass Effect 3,* why not in the first two games? What was keeping him from expressing himself? The idea that he was uncertain and in the closet seemed like an attractive explanation, and I was not the only critic to come to that conclusion.[3]

The idea of using a different starting context as an interpretive lens is hardly new, but in this case I was interested to see how the separate context of the closeted, male Shepard would affect a game-play experience that was unlikely to change on its own. For the most part, regardless of the gender of your Shepard, the *Mass Effect* games present you with identical base experiences. Dialogue, events, character reactions: all are mechanically the same. What this play-through really represented was a sense-making experiment. Given the real-life facts—that a cisgendered gay male Shepard having a same-sex romance wasn't possible until *Mass Effect 3*—how could adjusting the lens to "well, he was in the closet" shape how those experiences were consumed and interpreted?

As many queer people will tell you, being in the closet isn't just about hiding your sexuality. It's a context that changes and influences everything that you do, as you put the work into maintaining that facade. The key to playing "Ephraim the closeted Commander Shepard" was to examine the seemingly unimportant choices, the "unrelated" things, which might be different coming from the perspective of a man trying to hide his sexuality and identity from those around him. It's also worth noting that I don't believe this would have worked as an interpretive exercise if it were my first time playing the games. In effect, ClosetShep was possible because of the existence of Rosalinde Shepard (whom I jokingly called "CanonShep" or "RealShep"). Rosalinde's story was a product of my playing the game as if I was "just playing a game," for lack of a better phrasing; put another way, she was the control group for ClosetShep's experiment. As I played, it was her choices and her story to which I constantly compared Ephraim's, her baseline against which he was judged.

It would be difficult to list all the ways these two characters diverged or found concordance over the course of all three games, since that amounted to well over a hundred hours of game play in the end. Certainly, some large-scale choices stand out. Ephraim Shepard went the first two games studiously avoiding romance; in the first game I decided he would be a relentless do-gooder, putting the job before his relationships and himself; comparatively, Rosalinde fell in love with crewmate Kaidan Alenko and found strength in that connection.

Bear in mind, between the first game and *Mass Effect 2*, Shepard effectively "dies" and is resurrected two years later by an organization called Cerberus, and suddenly the (to this point) relatively similar trajectories of these two Shepards shifted. Rosalinde gave up being a Vanguard in favor of retraining as an Adept (a backline fighter focusing on telekinetic powers) and spent the game trying to re-create the life she'd lost; Ephraim gave up being a Sentinel in favor of becoming a Vanguard—a class the game describes as "high risk, high reward"—due to the feeling that he'd lost everything and now had nothing else to lose. Rosalinde became more reflective in her dialogue choices and actions, while Ephraim became reckless, even self-destructive.

One moment in *Mass Effect 2* stands out: a brief reunion with the aforementioned Kaidan Alenko. Cerberus, the organization that you work for in *ME2*, has a reputation established in the first game as ruthless terrorists that Shepard expresses reservations about working for. Kaidan, meanwhile, continues to be enlisted in the Earth Systems Alliance navy, and thus isn't part of your group. When you briefly reencounter him in *ME2*, he's incensed, angry, and hurt regardless of whether you were his romantic partner; having believed Shepard dead for two years, Kaidan feels betrayed that Shepard is now working with the "enemy" after all they've been through to-gether. When I played as Rosalinde, this anger seemed natural considering the love they claim to have shared. Playing as Ephraim, however, the deep notes of betrayal and hurt in Kaidan's dialogue suddenly took on a different tone. Speaking to Rosalinde, Kaidan felt angry, but talking to Ephraim there was a note of confused betrayal that seemed to transcend friendship.

This is important because Kaidan was one of the only options for ClosetShep's eventual coming out in *Mass Effect 3,* and indeed that was the route I took. The road there was rocky. In the opening hours of *Mass Effect 3,* Kaidan is one of a handful of people who escapes Earth alongside Shepard, as the unstoppable alien menace of the Reapers assaults the planet. They head to Mars to retrieve another old friend and, in the process, Kaidan voices continued concerns about Shepard's time with Cerberus. Perhaps worse, by the time the group leaves, he's been seriously—almost mortally—wounded and spends most of the game's first half unconscious in a hospital bed. Eventually, Kaidan recovers and the two are reunited, meeting at a café for dinner to catch up on recent events.

With Rosalinde, the tenor of the scene—reflected in her hesitation and uncertainty, traits uncharacteristic of either Shepard even in their mildest moments—is explained by the fact that the two are obviously in love, and their shared past makes dealing with the situation hard. With Ephraim, on the brink of leaving the closet, this hesitance suddenly feels like words long unspoken, steps long untaken. The context of *Mass Effect 3*'s plot is that civilization as we know it is about to end—and in a matter of weeks, not years or decades. Ephraim Shepard might not have another month to work out whether he wants to share his feelings for Kaidan with him. He might have to do it right now. And when, eventually, Kaidan and Ephraim do reconnect over dinner later in the game, the conversation read from ClosetShep's point of view makes it abundantly clear that Kaidan has had the same reservations, the same thoughts. It's Kaidan who makes the first move, in the end, and when Shepard asks, "You and me, Kaidan?" the latter simply responds, "Yeah. It feels right, doesn't it?"

Interestingly enough, if you're playing as FemShep and don't have an established relationship yet, the dialogue is actually quite different. At first the small talk is the same, but once the issue of the relationship arises there's no hesitance, no sense that he might be rejected. Heterosexual Kaidan is considerably more assertive. There's a note in both scenes that Kaidan has been keeping these feelings bottled up for a long time, but with FemShep all the hesitation, the fear of rejection, the worry that it might not be reciprocated, is gone. A colleague, observing both scenes one after the other, also noted that Kaidan shows actual public, physical affection for FemShep but does not for a male Shepard.

Denis Farr suggests that this specific writing might be an attempt on BioWare's part to explain why this romance, which should realistically have been possible earlier in the *Mass Effect* series, wasn't. He also argues quite effectively that playing a closeted Shepard requires a willing suspension of disbelief concerning the politics of its world; in a universe where a human and an alien can have an unquestioned, unproblematic relationship, why would coming out as gay suddenly involve drama? Who would care? As Farr notes, the game throws out the excuse that Kaidan said nothing because he perceived that Shepard was "so focused on the work," trying again to explain why it wasn't until now that he spoke up. So, in that sense, Kaidan's hesitation might have nothing to do with being "out" at all and everything to do with not knowing whether Shepard felt the same way. Of course, presuming that Kaidan's character is consistent across various options, the FemShep romance puts that into question, too. Because we see only a tiny cross-section of the lives of all these individuals, we have no way of really knowing, and the game doesn't engage the idea of sexuality much, if at all, outside of this specific, romance-oriented context.

Of course, complicating this is the fact that as a character that can be romanced by either gender in *ME3*, Kaidan has what some have called "Schrödinger's sexuality."[4] Like the cat in the box, Kaidan's sexuality exists in a sort of quantum superposition that the player can collapse into observed certainty by choosing to romance him or not. Kaidan's sexuality is defined primarily by his relationship to Shepard, an interesting contrast to the other same-sex male option, Steve Cortez, who is narratively defined as having had a husband who was killed in action. A similar effect happens in BioWare's *Dragon Age 2*, where all but one romance-capable NPC will accept a main character of either gender; as that character's last name is Hawke, some fans of the game refer to those characters as "Hawkesexual." And of course, in all these cases, characters very rarely refer to themselves with labels like "gay" or "lesbian." We have no way of knowing, for example, whether Kaidan identifies as bisexual, a part of the queer spectrum that is heavily effaced in mass media representations.

The ending of *Mass Effect 3* involves a choice between three options: destroying the invading Reapers, controlling them, or causing a chain reaction that fuses organic and cybernetic/synthetic life in the galaxy, bringing the threat of the Reapers to an end but irrevocably changing the face of galactic civilization. All three choices result in Shepard's "death" in some form. Rosalinde, my "canon" play-through, chose to destroy the Reapers, despite knowing that some of her closest companions would also be killed in the process. But for Ephraim the story was different. It's difficult to explain this fully without a lot of wordy, sci-fi jargon-y explanation of the *Mass Effect* universe, but in short, the organic–synthetic fusion option (which fans have dubbed the "synthesis" option) resonated with me more as his choice. Writing in his "voice," I put it thusly on Twitter as I live-tweeted the end of ClosetShep's virtual life: "I don't want to control. I'm tired of destruction. I just want everyone to have a chance to find out who they really are."

Farr had a slightly different read on the situation than I did, but in the end I feel like he reached similar conclusions and felt the same way. He writes:

> Sebastian [Farr's closeted Shepard] saved the universe by deciding to synthesize organic and synthetic life, a deus ex machina that seemed less important as I found myself at a loss for what that meant for his romance with Kaidan. I, as a person, did not particularly find Kaidan compelling. The romance, on the other hand, felt correct for Sebastian, a man who chased his dreams; whether those dreams were of Kaidan Alenko, or of seeing the galactic community come together and end their hostilities. Ultimately, his sacrifice read as someone who felt so undeserving

of that particular love with Kaidan, that he was willing to give himself up. He was willing to sacrifice everything to ensure that other people could continue living without the kind of fear that ruled his life quite firmly for the first two games.[5]

Queering, queer readings, and fan (re)interpretation are nothing new in mass media, and not even really new in video games, particularly in gaming fan culture. Consider Ika Willis[6] arguing that queering in fan work is about more than a simple matter of resisting a dominant, non-queer reading, or Jenny Sundén[7] discussing queer *World of Warcraft* players using queerness as a mode of transgressive play that makes the underlying value systems of the game's world and culture apparent. Certainly, both my own work on how BioWare structures in-game romance options mechanically[8] and Stephen Greer's writing on how in-game affordances affect the ability to "play queer"[9] emphasize the impact that the structure of games as a medium can have on players' ability to queer their consumptive practice.

I wonder, though, if we haven't overlooked the potential usefulness of a kind of "comparative queerness" as a tool for understanding individual players' experiences in actually engaging with and playing in game worlds. When dealing with story-driven content in particular, this rereading of content one has already experienced with a new lens surprised me in what it revealed about the game I was playing. Perhaps more important, it highlighted things about my relationship with the game and the characters I was playing I wouldn't have noticed otherwise.

Rosalinde Shepard is almost certainly an "idealized" me. Her tough, funny, no-nonsense personality represents traits to which I aspire; even her physical appearance plays into ideas of how I wish I were rather than what I am. The choices I made playing as her felt much more consonant with how I expected the *game* to go; I was writing in the character that I felt the story should have.

Ephraim Shepard, on the other hand, felt like a much truer— sometimes uncomfortably so—reflection of who I am, in all probability because I had given him a backstory and motivations that often came from my own experiences as a person. I've never been a tough-as-nails woman space marine, but I've been a closeted gay man who's had to suffer through loss and who is unsure of what his place in the world is. Certainly, some of Ephraim was still idealized; he was a fit borderline superhero who wielded psychic-like powers in outer space, after all. But as a player I was often surprised by what I found myself choosing while playing as Ephraim because it "felt right." Not because it was what I wanted, but because I felt it was consistent.

Annika Waern[10] has discussed the possibility of "bleed" between players and their avatars in RPGs. Interestingly enough, she does so by discussing another BioWare franchise, the *Dragon Age* series. Her conclusion is that in these situations—particularly romances—the boundary between what the player feels and what the character feels becomes blurry. A desire on the part of players to put parts of themselves into the character encourages them to have an emotional reaction to things that happen to their avatar. Speaking anecdotally, I believe that both of my Shepards presented me with moments of bleed, but the tenor of those moments shifted dramatically depending on my starting point.

The question that remains is how this might be applied in frameworks other than story-driven RPGs. It's unlikely, for example, that I could go into a game of *Tetris* with this sort of approach because *Tetris* is highly abstract, but what about sports games? The "create an athlete and follow their career" mode is quite popular in many of these games. Is it possible to apply this sort of queer background reading in those situations? What sort of affordances does the game need to make before this becomes realistic and useful? Consider, for example, that the ClosetShep play-through was heavily inspired and enabled by BioWare's late addition of male same-sex romance options to the *Mass Effect* series. This isn't to say that being able to romance Kaidan from the start would have shut this down; ClosetShep could still ignore him until the final game. However, as Farr notes, the fact that this wasn't the case likely directly led BioWare to make certain production-level decisions about dialogue and presentation that heavily enable this reading. Would this exercise have been as useful without them? It's difficult to say.

One thing is clear, however: taking the time to construct a narrative and then play it out in a game has considerable potential as a tool for queer game analysis. In particular, it seems to have its greatest power when compared against an experience that might be considered the "expected" or "default" one. Just as queer media consumers are often asked to reinterpret a perceived social norm in queer terms, it is possible, and even enlightening, to apply this idea to game content as well.

Notes

1. Carlen Lavigne, "'She's a soldier, not a model': Feminism, FemShep, and the *Mass Effect* Vote," *Journal of Gaming and Virtual Worlds* 7, no. 3 (2015): 317–29.

2. It's important to note that *Mass Effect* titles restrict the player to "male" and "female" as gender options, and the first game's "same-sex option" relies primarily on the heavily female coding of the character Liara T'soni, an alien from a supposedly mono-gender race.

3. See Denis Farr, "With the Galaxy in Flames, My Video Game Hero Finally Came Out of the Closet," *Kotaku*, May 14, 2012, http://kotaku.com /5909937/with-the-galaxy-in-flames-my-video-game-hero-finally-came-out -of-the-closet.

4. See Denis Farr, "*Dragon Age 2*: Schrödinger's Sexuality," *Border House*, January 12, 2012, http://borderhouseblog.com/?p=7507.

5. Farr, "With the Galaxy in Flames."

6. Ika Willis, "Keeping Promises to Queer Children: Making Space (for Mary Sue) at Hogwarts," in *Fan Fiction and Fan Communities in the Age of the Internet,* ed. Karen Hellekson and Kristina Busse (Jefferson, N.C.: McFarland, 2006), 153–70.

7. Jenny Sundén, "Play as Transgression: An Ethnographic Approach to Queer Game Studies," presentation at the Digital Games Research Association annual conference, London, September 1–4, 2009.

8. Todd Harper. "Dragon Gay-ge? Same-Sex Romance Options in Bio-Ware Games," presentation at the Popular Culture Association annual conference, Boston, April 11–14, 2012.

9. Stephen Greer, "Playing Queer: Affordances for Sexuality in *Fable* and *Dragon Age*," *Journal of Gaming and Virtual Worlds* 5, no. 1 (2013): 3–19.

10. Annika Waern, "'I'm in love with someone that doesn't exist!' Bleed in the Context of a Computer Game," *Journal of Gaming and Virtual Worlds* 3, no. 3 (2011): 239–57.

Chapter **14**

Queer(ing) Gaming Technologies
Thinking on Constructions of Normativity
Inscribed in Digital Gaming Hardware

GREGORY L. BAGNALL

According to game theorist Markku Eskelinen, "Writing about games
and gaming in general [is] . . . under-theorized."[1] With this observation in mind, this essay will attend to and point out a significant
paucity found within game scholarship. We could suggest that this
is a more systemic absence plaguing digital humanities writing in
general, the umbrella under which we might place game studies.
That absence is the presently lacking conversation between queerness and gaming and, more specifically, a missing discussion around
how we might, by looking beyond character representations and stories, understand games as digital artifacts bound up with natural-
ized, patriarchal constructions of gender and sexuality. This essay
endeavors to illustrate that gaming technologies are inscribed with
heteronormative constructions of difference, and that they therefore figure as a kind of politic as much as game stories and mechanics do. Moreover, this argument suggests that we, as game scholars
and gamers, should look toward games' material technologies in
order to interrogate the ways that games fundamentally reiterate

binary logics and foreclose on the fullness and complexity of queer expressions of identity.

Material gaming technologies mediate and influence our experiences with games. This approach to thinking about gaming technologies is not unlike the way that digital humanities scholars understand screens. Gaming technologies are informed by the very same dominant, hegemonic, heterosexist paradigms that game scholars, critics, and developers have identified in games themselves. A useful springboard into this point is the platforming maven Lara Croft. The body of work on the design aesthetics governing *Tomb Raider's* eminent treasure hunter represents well the "screen essentialism" coined by Nick Montfort and discussed by Matthew Kirschenbaum as the "digital event on the screen" studied irrespective of the technological mechanisms, like storage devices or computer code, that make it possible.[2] But, additionally, interest in Croft makes clear that gender- and queer-oriented game writing focuses almost exclusively on character designs, storytelling elements, and game-play mechanics and systems.

Lara Croft, though perhaps an idealized, vaguely pornographic "techno-puppet" designed for the heterosexual, male player, is interestingly assessed in Anne-Marie Schleiner's "Does Lara Croft Wear Fake Polygons?" which explains the multifaceted, gendered, and queered positions that Croft, as avatar, occupies.[3] Schleiner describes Croft's queer potentiality: Croft is simultaneously a female Frankenstein's monster, a drag queen, a femme fatale, a potentially positive role model and anti-"bimbo," and a "vehicle for the queer female gaze."[4] Sharon R. Sherman's "Perils of the Princess" similarly treats video games as on-screen texts and discusses their perpetuation of gender stereotypes, as well as female subversions of the "male message" of games and of the genders of the main characters.[5] Although both of these scholarly works betoken the promise palpable in a marriage between gender and sexuality studies and game studies, they also point to this lack of scholarly attention to the materiality of games.

This is not to say that games are incapable of being differently inscribed. In Brendan Keogh's "Just Making Things and Being Alive about It," game developers Porpentine, Mattie Brice, Anna Anthropy, and merritt kopas discuss a burgeoning gaming scene comprising queer and other marginalized developers made possible by tools like Twine, originally designed for hypertext fiction writers.[6] In the feature, Brice discusses her autobiographical *Mainichi* (Japanese for "everyday") and its systems. In the game, Keogh explains, "a seemingly effortless task [like walking between your house and the café] becomes peppered with interruptions as you have to deal with people staring at you, people catcalling you, people misgendering you. The clunky, stop–start face of the Japanese role-playing game genre is used to show just how much effort it takes Brice to get through her daily life."[7] Eventually, because the game endlessly loops, continually returning you, as the player, to the protagonist's bedroom, you are offered the opportunity to repeatedly experiment in making different choices—paying with cash versus credit or walking on a different side of the street—and thus you learn to "change the way you live just to avoid harassment."[8] *Mainichi* conveys, then, through its systems, what Brice "has to deal with in her day-to-day life" as a queer woman.[9] Moreover, this interactive memoir does not offer the faint echo of queerness that we find in Lara Croft; rather, it establishes queerness as an inescapable, essential experience that players live, albeit virtually. Still, despite its compelling, powerful, and important "everyday" experience, *Mainichi* articulates a kind of queerness witnessed in other media: one interrogated by digital representations and, though less common, digital systems.

To both expand on the creative and critical work accomplished by queer developers like Brice and theorists like Schleiner and sidestep the absence, in game writing, of material technologies, I intend to rely on, in the remaining sections of this essay, a mix of game studies and digital humanities scholarship. Specifically valuable to this conversation will be Zach Blas's attention to "queer technology," useful in thinking about how games, if viewed as queer technologies, have the capacity to "mutate and confuse," as well as reproduce, the same heterosexist logics palpable in other technologies, such as in computer communications and the design of and functionary relationship between plugs and outlets.[10] Similarly, Sadie Plant's *Zeros and Ones* explores binary symbolism and numeric representations as conceptual epistemologies tied to, in part, Cartesian duality present in the binary code of zeros and ones, under which zeros are feminine and bear a relationship to the psychoanalytic "lack" of women, conceptually indicating absence, as opposed to ones, which are symbolically masculine and tied to the phallus.[11] Likewise, when we shove a plug into an outlet, we are mimicking penetrative, heterosexual sex acts and myopic gender formulations. Interestingly, this particular design—male/female—is not inherent to the way the device operates; it could be stripped of its implicit gendered power dynamics and recast.

Throughout media criticism, scholars have articulated the various intersections between gender, queerness, and technology. "Technology" has itself been broadly conceived of as anything from bras to cars[12] to the technologically inscribed queer and nonbinary body.[13] But the projects of new media artists like Blas (or Shu Lea Cheang's *Brandon,* or Monica Ong's *Remedies*) construct, through new media, sites for queerness and for questioning and dismantling hegemonic paradigms. By looking more closely at gaming hardware and juxtaposing *Gone Home* with discussions of technologies below, I hope to demonstrate, as these artists do, the importance of looking to normatively gendered game hardware as both informing and mediating digital gaming experiences. This work will reveal new ontological and epistemological possibilities and, subsequently, shift our relationship to games.

The Queer Story of *Gone Home*: Where We Have Been

The Fullbright Company's 2013 first-person adventure *Gone Home,* billed on the game's official website as a "story exploration video game" (http://gonehome.game/), gives voice to a hyper-personal, queer experience told through what Daniel Reynolds's "Letters and the Unseen Woman" describes as an "epistolary architecture," or "the distribution of messages around a game space."[14] The game opens on the porch of a house: in the lower left-hand of the first-person shot rests luggage, tagged for Kaitlin Greenbriar, the player, who has just returned home after spending a year overseas. In front of the camera awaits a stained-glass door. In a note taped to the glass, the player's sister Sam apologies for her absence: "I'm sorry I can't be there to see you, but it is impossible." The sister goes on to explain that she does not want the player to "go digging around trying to find [her]" and that the two will "see each other again someday." The player later discovers that, while they were abroad, Sam met and began dating fellow student Lonnie. Their parents were unable to accept Sam's lesbian relationship, and so Sam and Lonnie ran away together.

Game critic and writer Danielle Riendeau frames the game as a kind of affective mirror, reflecting back to her, primarily through Sam's struggles as a queer youth, specific experiences that "applied to [her]" and are "so heart-wrenchingly real and painfully close to [her] own."[15] Gender, sexuality, and technology scholar Samantha Allen similarly praises *Gone Home* as a cultural and political document. Addressing that which exists outside the "magic circle," it shows itself invested in producing and making apparent "queer experience" and in engaging cultural structures.[16] To this end, the game offers players the opportunity to examine and navigate a dark but seemingly mundane house, a Wunderkammer of sorts, picking up and inspecting a collection of artifacts and determining the secrets they hold regarding Sam and her family. The game designers' decision to juxtapose objects like Bibles with queer and feminist literature like the zine *Grrrl Justice Now: Kicking against the Patriarchy,* which all wait to be discovered by the player, suggests that the game is interested in representing and tackling cultural structures and ideas external to the space of the game. *Gone Home* appears, for critics like Allen, to be an exemplar of the successful marriage of queerness and meaningful cultural play, in which we can see "play" as, Eric Zimmerman writes, "the free space of movement within a more rigid system."[17] Game theorists have likewise attempted to pin down the concept as that which enables players to "take part in generating, embodying, and transforming . . . cultural meanings."[18] As a game-design value, play, like queerness, encourages complexity and unpredictability to exist and blossom in cultural systems, be those digital games or the gender binary. If this is true—if game systems resist or even thrive within cultural structures—let us then look at the oppositional messages encoded in gaming hardware: those values that contradict games' ludic and transformative capacities as offered to us by game play.

Locating Queerness in Technological Materiality: Where We Might Go

Queer technologies are specifically empowering as tools of queer agency. They resist heteronormative culture, the values of which are often designed into hardware. If it is to be categorized as queer, gaming hardware must question and transform patriarchal paradigms. The design and functions of this hardware must enable subversive play strategies. The brand of "queerness" discussed here is one sometimes described by theorists as "detach[ed] . . . from sexual identity" and identified as "more of a posture of opposition than a simple statement about sexuality."[19] We hear in this the rhetorics of noncompliance that reject the discourses of traditional familial life.[20] Gaming hardware might even join games like Brice's *Mainichi* in allowing players to experience facets of queer life. Joli St. Patrick and Avery McDaldno's 2013 Queerness and Games Conference talk "Beyond Representation" outlines many features of queerness and queer life as related to games, including uncertainty, change, fluidity, and complicated multilayeredness.[21]

Given that most gaming interactions are performed on screens through controllers, and keeping in mind what kinds of interface devices are commonly used to communicate our desires and enact agency in gaming environments, input devices seem to occupy a position of consequence among gaming hardware and technologies and can communicate these experiences, like uncertainty or change. A wealth of the play actions afforded to us by gaming systems are explored or executed by input devices like joysticks and controllers (voice commands are an exception). When they use existing hardware to play nearly all console games and many computer games, gamers are forced to enact heteropolitics. In attempting to control a character or the camera, invariably players utilize the joystick. Joysticks determine the agency players have over the world and over their character: their ability to move and interact with objects and other characters. As such, while game play may be able to critique cultural systems, it is undermined by the contradictory logics of controllers. As the prime navigational mechanism and explorative tool of nearly all console games, we must not underestimate the importance of game controllers. As Blas advises, "Attempts to formulate a queer technology implicates the urgency in carving out a queer freedom in hi-tech culture and providing the queer community with discursive/ practical tools for activism, resistance, and empowerment."[22]

For games, formulating a queer technology means starting to offer alternatives to the prescriptive heterosexual ideology reflected in hardware. A productive area where we might begin such an undertaking is with controllers. Input devices, like gamepads that feature at least one analog stick (PlayStation's standard DualShock 3 or 4 or Xbox's standard controllers utilize two), map games and gamers to the still-thriving phallocentric logics and perpetuate the conflation of hardware and masculinity (as opposed to software and femininity).[23] As a variation of a joystick, analog sticks might be considered as one possibility among many. In short, we must reimagine gaming hardware in order to problematize such ideologies. To do so, we might begin to wonder the following: How would game experiences be altered if controllers no longer assigned in-game agency to phalluses? Furthermore, how could game controls communicate queer experiences—like, say, uncertainty? We might explore this, for instance, by creating a controller designed to, after each play session concludes, offer the player or the developer the option to remap its controls. For instance, instead of "X" always controlling, say, the character's ability to jump, it would be perpetually reassigned to other buttons. This reproduces the idea of uncertainty and decentralizes control, while also orienting players toward their own disempowerment.

Thus, just as differently structured games facilitate different kinds of gaming experiences, this essay finds that restructured or redesigned gaming technologies will meaningfully affect our play experiences in ways largely untouched. While I do not mean to say that we should entirely do away with present-day controller design aesthetics, I do think we could explore different options, which would allow us to retain the fluid mobility afforded by our dual phallus–joysticks while still disavowing their unfortunate investment in heteronormativity and disempowering cultural systems. We might even initially look to, at least for some digital games, the viability of remodeling preexisting alternatives like the more gender-neutral directional pad, a move that symbolizes for me a gestural reinterpretation of the main source of our agency as players.

Notes

1. Markku Eskelinen, "Towards Computer Games Studies," in *First Person: New Media as Story, Performance, and Game,* ed. Noah Wardrip-Fruin and Pat Harrigan (Cambridge, Mass.: MIT Press, 2004), 36.

2. Nick Montfort, "Continuous Paper: The Early Materiality and Workings of Electronic Literature," 2004, http://www.nickm.com/writing/essays /continuous_paper_mla.html; Matthew Kirschenbaum, *Mechanisms: New Media and the Forensic Imagination* (Cambridge, Mass.: MIT Press, 2008).

3. Anne-Marie Schleiner, "Does Lara Croft Wear Fake Polygons?" *Leonardo* 34, no. 3 (2001): 221–26.

4. Ibid., 225.

5. Sharon R. Sherman, "Perils of the Princess," *Western Folklore* 56, nos. 3–4 (1997): 245.

6. Brendan Keogh, "Just Making Things and Being Alive about It: The Queer Games Scene," *Polygon,* May 26, 2013, http://www.polygon.com/features/2013 /5/24/4341042/the-queer-games-scene.

7. Ibid.

8. Ibid.

9. Ibid.

10. Through his ENgenderingGenderChangers, useable products that are presently sold in boutiques in California, Blas explores in material technologies the relationship between queerness and technology; see Zach Blas, "Queer Technologies: Automating Perverse Possibilities," December 3, 2014, http://www.queertechnologies.info; and Zach Blas, "What Is Queer Technology?" 2006, http://www.zachblas.info/publications_materials /whatisqueertechnology_zachblas_2006.pdf.

11. Sadie Plant, *Zeros and Ones: Digital Women and the New Technoculture* (London: Fourth Estate, 1997).

12. Nina E. Lerman, Ruth Oldenziel, and Arwen P. Mohun, eds., *Gender and Technology: A Reader* (Baltimore: Johns Hopkins University Press, 2003).

13. A good starting point for delving into this conversation/debate is Susan Stryker's "Transsexuality: The Postmodern Body and/as Technology," in *The Cybercultures Reader,* ed. David Bell and Barbara M. Kennedy (London: Routledge, 2000), 588–97; and legal theorist Dean Spade's "Mutilating Gender," in *The Transgender Studies Reader,* ed. Susan Stryker and Stephen Whittle (New York: Routledge, 2006), 315–32.

14. Daniel Reynolds, "Letters and the Unseen Woman: Epistolary Architecture in Three Recent Video Games," *Film Quarterly* 68, no. 1 (2014):

48. Incidentally, it may be worth noting that a more recent example of this phenomenon—that is, of somewhat myopically praising queer game stories and characters—might be the conversation swelling up around BioWare's 2014 *Dragon Age: Inquisition,* which has been lauded for its inclusion of the minor character Krem, a trans man. Unfortunately, though, Krem is voiced by a ciswoman, a casting choice that puts *Inquisition* in the company of other media using cisgender actors to speak for and tell the stories of trans* and gender nonbinary people. Some recent examples include Jared Leto as Rayon in the 2013 film *Dallas Buyers Club* and Walton Goggins as Venus in the 2012 season of the TV program *Sons of Anarchy.*

15. Danielle Riendeau, "Opinion: Finding Someone Like Me in *Gone Home,*" *Polygon,* August 19, 2013, http://www.polygon.com/2013/8/19/4627606/opinion-finding-someone-like-me-in-gone-home.

16. Samantha Allen, "Closing the Gap between Queer and Mainstream Games," *Polygon,* April 2, 2014, http://www.polygon.com/2014/4/2/5549878/closing-the-gap-between-queer-and-mainstream-games.

17. Eric Zimmerman, "Narrative, Interactivity, Play, and Games," in *First Person: New Media as Story, Performance, and Game,* ed. Noah Wardrip-Fruin and Pat Harrigan (Cambridge, Mass.: MIT Press, 2004), 159.

18. Katie Salen and Eric Zimmerman, eds., *Rules of Play: Game Design Fundamentals* (Cambridge, Mass.: MIT Press, 2004), 510.

19. Judith Halberstam, *In a Queer Time and Place: Transgender Bodies, Subcultural Lives* (New York: New York University Press, 2005), 1; L. A. Kauffman, "Radical Change: The Left Attacks Identity Politics," *Village Voice,* June 30, 1992.

20. This is made apparent in *Gone Home,* insofar as Sam rejects the hypocrisy of her suburban nuclear family, choosing instead to run away with her girlfriend.

21. Joli St. Patrick and Avery McDaldno, "Beyond Representation," *Buried without Ceremony,* November 25, 2014, http://buriedwithoutceremony.com/beyond-representation/.

22. Zach Blas, "What Is Queer Technology?" 2006, http://www.zachblas.info/publications_materials/whatisqueertechnology_zachblas_2006.pdf.

23. Wendy Hui Kyong Chun, *Programmed Visions: Software and Memory* (Cambridge, Mass.: MIT Press, 2011).

Chapter **15**

On *Gone Home*

MERRITT KOPAS

I dream of empty houses.

I think it's a common dream: returning to childhood homes to find them empty and abandoned, exploring them and finding they've shifted and changed in your absence, even as they retain an eerie familiarity. It's cliché. Like, of course things change and of course you can never go home again, and maybe it's because I lived in a lot of different places growing up, but this kind of dream has been a permanent fixture in the landscape of my sleep.

Gone Home is about exploring an empty house—one that you never lived in, but one that's full of familiar things. It's about space and absence and leaving and most obviously it's about a love relationship between girls. It's a game about a lot of other things, too, and there are a lot of other narratives going on. But I'm going to talk about why *Gone Home* was important to me, and a lot of that has to do with the simple fact that this is a video game about girls in love.

This is a video game. About girls in love. That shouldn't be exceptional in and of itself, but it is. And because it's a video game about a big empty house and because it's a story about girls in love, anyone who has any familiarity with either of those genres is going in expecting the worst to happen. Because seriously, setting a lesbian love story in a creepy old mansion is the perfect confluence of terrible. So from the start you're thinking, okay, ghosts. Or suicide. Or probably both.

So you're moving through the house, and you're finding these audio journals from your little sister, Sam, telling you all about this girl she's met named Lonnie and how cool she is. And you're kind of on edge because the lights are flickering and every once in a while the house creaks in the storm and you don't know what's going to come first, the beginnings of a lesbian tragedy suicide sequence or something jumping out at you from a dark corner.

And then there's this scene in a bathroom on the second floor. I'd entered the room from the hallway coming out of Sam's bedroom, having just read a few ominous-sounding notes from her. In the bathroom you turn on the light and immediately notice that there's blood in the bathtub, and your heart races because this is a video game and you're exploring an empty house on a dark and stormy night and nobody is around for some reason and you're just waiting for it to turn out that, surprise(!), everyone is dead.

Let's be honest here: if you have been playing video games for any length of time and you see a red splatter in a bathtub there's no way you're assuming it's anything other than blood.

So you edge closer and you pick up a bottle next to the bathtub and read the label: "red right hand." It's hair dye. And you realize that this isn't a game that's interested in evoking the limited range of emotions most video games are content to deal with, and that maybe it's even playing with your "games literacy," which is a polite way of saying your internalization of the awful tropes that have come to dominate our understandings of what video games are supposed to do.

And then you put the bottle down, and you trigger one of Sam's audio diaries.

I started choking up almost as soon as I started playing the game. When I got to this entry, "Dealing with Roots"—in which Sam describes the intimacy of helping Lonnie dye her hair—I started bawling.

Look, I am a trans woman who is not done grieving her childhood. My family moved around a lot when I was a kid. I have kind of weird and important associations with the Pacific Northwest, having lived out here for the past four years and it having been the first place I've lived as a queer woman. And I only discovered riot grrl a couple of years ago. I wish I'd had access to it in that childhood I'm still dealing with.

I know I'm bringing a lot of my own stuff to this game. I know my experience of it is being shaped by my history, even more because the player character is a kind of cipher with no real spatial storytelling to indicate much of substance about her relationships to any of the other characters in the game.

I know all that, and honestly? I don't really fucking care, because this is a game that feels like it was made for me, and that's rare and important and at the end of the day—especially in a medium that caters overwhelmingly to straight boys—universality can suck it.

So I'd been thinking this around halfway through the game—this feels like it's for me, and maybe this is just a really powerful personal story and nothing bad or video-gamey is going to happen after all—and then I found Sam's story, "Heaven at the Edge of the World."

Around the house you find these stories Sam's written throughout her life. The situations are always different, but the characters are always the same: Captain Allegra and her loyal first mate. Late in the game you find one of these stories inside a secret panel, within a folder labeled "Private: do not read!" It's a story Sam wrote in '92, a few years before meeting Lonnie. In the story, Amazons have captured Captain Allegra's first mate. The captain rushes to save him but arrives moments too late; the Amazon queen has dropped the first mate into a vat from which she emerges as a woman. "She is one of us now," the Amazon queen gloats. "She is ours."

Then: "Allegra glared into the queen's eyes and said: 'That's the love of my life. And you can't have her.'"

How many fucking ridiculous scenarios like this did I dream up as a kid? I mean, it's obviously not the same setup, because in Sam's case the story is a way to queer the straight narrative she's grown up with, to keep these characters she's obviously so invested in, but to make them more relevant to her life. So the first mate, the love of the captain's life, becomes a woman and Allegra doesn't skip a beat, seamlessly switching pronouns as if it were really right all along that the first mate be a woman. Fuck. More tears.

In the same compartment you grab the second half of the combination to open Sam's locker. Inside you find a picture of Lonnie and get another audio message. Sam describes her first kiss with Lonnie. And you're just like, this is really a game that is just going to let two girls be in love with each other, and that isn't selling a doomed love narrative or male-gazey lesbian titillation. This is just about exuberant, awkward, amazing love.

So what about Katie, the character through which you're learning all this, moving around the house?

Really, Katie is an absence in the game. She's been absent for a year and is mostly absent from the house, because when you move away, even if it's just for a while, people need to get on with their lives, and when you're not a part of their daily routines then they don't build up as much evidence of your existence. Obviously Katie doesn't have a room in the house, having been out of the country when the family moved. Her stuff is tucked away in the basement, the guest room, and the closets. That means that she's mostly outside of the game's story, because the space doesn't have any real stories to tell about someone who has never lived in it.

Katie isn't so much a character in *Gone Home.* She's the camera. And for someone like me who never really felt present as a kid, who always felt like she was observing other people and never really observing herself—her own feelings, her own body—that's kind of perfect.

Here's the thing, though: I don't want to be Katie anymore. I want to be Sam. I want to be present in my youth. I want a riot grrl romance. I want to make zines and go to girl-band gigs and dye my (girl)friend's hair.

But I can't have that, not in the way that part of me still desperately wants it: it's not the '90s, I'm not a teenage girl, and neither of those things is ever, ever going to change. That's something I'm still dealing with. But ultimately *Gone Home* left me hopeful rather than grieving. Hopeful about storytelling and games, and hopeful about my own experiences. Because obviously we can't go back home, into our pasts, and change things—like Katie, all we can do is observe, witness, turn things over in our heads until they make a kind of sense that we can work with. But we can write new stories, ones where girls in love don't die tragic deaths and where big empty houses are scary but ultimately safe and where you can have a teenage girl romance at twenty-five, or thirty-five, or whenever you want to.

Part IV QUEER FAILURES IN GAMES

Chapter **16**

The Trouble with Communities

ADRIENNE SHAW

Communities are nice. I try to be a careful writer, but I feel comfortable making that a universalizing statement. I think it is uncontroversial to say that it is nice to feel part of a community. If I were to ask a random room of people what feelings being part of a community generates, most would offer affects of the warm and fuzzy variety. Being part of a community can give us strength, grounding, and a place simply to "be." Yet communities are also contentious and limiting. Communities are never as inclusive as intended or as easily defined as they appear from the outside. In this chapter, I address these seemingly contradictory experiences of community-ness and discuss how they shape work around queer gaming and queer game development. I argue that an understanding of communities as multiple and overlapping, as intersectional and coalitional, is crucial to making real queer game design, queer game culture, and queer game studies a reality.

In talking about community, I want to make a distinction between community and culture. Raymond Williams famously asserts that "culture is one of the two or three most complicated words in the English language," noting that it is used in radically different ways in various academic fields.[1] He does not offer a similar qualifier for community. He does state that community is a complex term and that there is a tension between "on the one hand the sense of direct common concern; on the other hand the materialization of various forms of common organization, which may or may not adequately express this."[2] That is to say, with culture the difficulty in studying it has to do with specifying the object of study; what do we mean, what are we looking at, when we describe "game culture," for example?[3] With community, though, the difficulty is that some use it to describe, to use Williams's description, "an existing set of relationships" while others use it to "describe an alternative set of relationships."[4]

Community then describes either what is or what we wish might be. That means, for example, we can use the term to describe a particular online queer game player community (as I do below) by identifying what about it makes it produce those feelings of community-ness. On the other hand, we can speak optimistically about how a queer gaming community might be embodied in events like GaymerX, Different Games, and the Queerness and Games Conference, as described elsewhere in this volume. In either case, though, we still have the sense that community means something specific, and something that is particularly good to have. Indeed, Williams argues that what is unique to the word "is that unlike all other terms of social organization . . . [community] seems never to be used unfavourably."[5] Again, communities are lovely things to be a part of; and yet communities are also often contentious. Moreover, and seemingly counter to their pleasantness, communities are often produced through conflict. Indeed, their ability to offer us safe spaces presumes that there are other spaces where our safety is not guaranteed. Fascinatingly, though, the niceness of community does not go away even at a time when being a member of a community makes one a target of harassment or if harassment is precisely what pushed a community together.[6]

In late 2014, people associated with or simply emboldened by the #GamerGate movement began to take friendships, and even acquaintanceships, with people who had turned a critical (often feminist) lens on games as a sign of wrongdoing, collusion, conspiracy, or just generally a plot to destroy games and their fans.[7] People writing about games designed by people they personally knew, in most cases indie games by marginalized designers, became evidence of unethical journalistic practices rather than a sign of close-knit professional communities. Academic organizations, citation practices, and promoting work by like-minded colleagues became vilified. So-called redline drawings, or Microsoft Paint graphics drawing lines between screencaps of tweets, blog posts, pictures, and website copy, abounded on sites like reddit, 4chan, 8chan, and imgur and were widely shared in #GamerGate circles as damning evidence of collusion. As a personal example, on my book's Amazon page, a brief five-star review by Lisa Nakamura, who also officially reviewed the book for the University of Minnesota Press, is followed by a three-star review stating "Just so people know, the only other review of this book is by Adrienne Shaw's buddy, so take her 5-star recommendation with a handful of salt. Full disclosure. #GamerGate."[8] This accusation is supported with a screencap of a tweet exchange between me and Dr. Nakamura, where I thank her for giving my book a shout-out in a keynote. That she is a well-respected scholar in my field and her support of my work, in our industry, is not in fact made suspect by the fact that we have met and keep in touch online, does not matter when run through the Internet conspiracy machine. Freelance journalists giving press to games by marginalized independent designers along with academics in the same field promoting one another's work are equally suspect. Community becomes a conspiracy when viewed as being formed around attacking gamer culture, which is how some #GamerGate supporters view those they describe as "social justice warriors." It seems impossible for them to accept that the communities they have targeted simply formed around a different relationship to video games.

Personally, one of the best outcomes of #GamerGate, despite its weaponizing of friendships, was that I felt my sense of connection to a feminist and queer gaming community grow tenfold. I felt a part of something with which I had previously just felt an affinity and tangential connection. I made new friends and I came to know casual acquaintances much better. Despite the "chilling effect" it had on many people, #GamerGate pushed us together in a way that forged stronger bonds between us.[9] I suspect that people who took part in #GamerGate felt something similar, as they, too, forged a community in the face of changing definitions of game culture and media backlash against the activities of some of the movement's more vocal and vicious members. This is not meant to justify the support that those who were not doxxing, swatting, threatening, or harassing offered to those who were, but merely to point out that how communities form is consistent regardless of what that community might be.[10]

The above examples illustrate one of the things I think is particularly fascinating about communities: they become strong through hardship. I mean that particularly in a way that emphasizes that communities are not simply formed around shared identifiers or group membership. Rather, we recognize what our community is, often and unfortunately, when something tragic happens. This feels particularly true as I write this in the weeks following the #BlackLivesMatter protests that were precipitated by the acquittal of the police officers who murdered Eric Garner and Michael Brown. This certainly struck a chord with what the media is calling "the black community," but I think more rightly it struck a chord with what we might call, less sound bite–ingly, the communities of people who believe in racial justice in the United States. How can something that feels so wonderful—community—come so consistently from such dark places?

More than that, once the moment of "danger," for lack of a better word, passes, many of us are aware of the tensions that can arise in communities, as differences manifest in ways that run counter to communal claims that "we" all agree or that "we" are all the same.[11] Related to this, from the outside it is easy to see groups and communities as singular in a way that belies internal conflicts. When people speak of the LGBTQ community, the trans* community,[12] the black community, the Latinx community, the Asian community, and so on, they often presume that all people who can be hailed as part of those groups belong to those communities and that those communities speak for everyone within those groups. Yet this belies the fact that communities are multiple, often overlapping, spaces that are never meant to speak for "social groups" as a whole. Rather, they are formed around similar, historically specific goals and experiences. Remembering that allows us to work through, without ignoring, those tensions. It also offers a slightly different way for talking about why communities matter, as I explore below with an example from my own research.

In 2007 I conducted a cyber-ethnography of an online LGBTQ gaming site.[13] At that point in time, much of the research on queer communities had focused on physical spaces.[14] Starting in the early 2000s, and following the rise of Internet studies more generally, researchers began to acknowledge and examine the creation of online communities, queer and otherwise.[15] The creation of online communities was often analogous to the development of queer communities. As Bronski has demonstrated, historically the marginality of queerness produced queer communities, particularly in urban centers.[16] Similarly, Bird argues, "Internet communities, like place-based communities, do not just happen. They develop in response to particular circumstances and to the needs of a particular set of individuals."[17] Individuals need safe spaces, particularly when those individuals do not conform to dominant norms.[18] Moreover, individuals can inhabit multiple online and offline communities, even within a single site, simultaneously.

In my 2007 study, two of the ways in which the gaymer community was defined as a gay gaming community in particular, in addition to discussions of gaming, was the presence of sexual banter (predominately gay male–centric) and the discussion of homophobia.[19] Although the prevalence of sexually explicit discussions was a point of controversy in one thread, several interviewees mentioned the freedom of talking about their sexuality as a major benefit of the site. Moreover, being able to discuss experiences of homophobia with others was important.[20] This formation of community around identity also played a key role in the creation of subcommunities within the site. Members grouped together based on massively multiplayer online games, console types, game preferences, other interests, age/maturity level, and nationality and gender to some extent. These groups would talk online, play games together online, meet in person, or have conversations around discussion threads. Speaking to the multiplicity of communities, even within this one relatively small online community there were many communities.

Similarly, the marginalization of gaymers from both the gay or queer and gaming communities is what drew people to the site. Many of the people I spoke to, regardless of their sexual or gender identity, felt that they found in this space a community that offered a reprieve from what they felt was an anti-gaming sentiment in their LGBTQ networks and the homophobia they experienced in online gaming spaces.[21] For many of them, the main reason for being on the site was that it was a "safe space" where they felt less pressure to censor their gaymer identities, which they experienced as a hybrid or intersectional identity that was not defined by being "gay" so much as appreciating a gay sensibility and queer worldview. It was a place where, as one interviewee put it, "I feel like I can be myself with queer community . . . where I really have to watch my footing sometimes with some of the players that I come into contact with . . . Playing first person shooters as a female is hard enough . . . without having to tell the boys that I have a girlfriend too." As one of the few active female members of the site, this interviewee did not always feel perfectly represented by dominant discussions in the forums. She did, however, feel that the community gave her space to be herself. Communities are not simply about finding commonalities that eclipse difference; they are about finding camaraderie despite difference.

As I've said before, communities do produce good feelings. For those who agreed to be interviewed, which was already limited by people active enough on the site to respond to my interview requests and see the particular threads I posted, the site was a largely positive space. Yet the dominant language of the site was English, the main users were predominantly self-identified as homosexual and cisgendered males, and keeping up with the conversations required being invested in and following mainstream game culture. Many people I spoke with noted that bisexual and transgender members were few and far between, chalking that up to being a trend in mainstream U.S. LGBTQ communities more generally. Moreover, site members as well as journalists used this and other online LGBTQ gamer groups as evidence of a burgeoning gay gamer market.[22] The rhetoric used for this purpose was much the same as that used to sell a gay market to mainstream U.S. advertisers in the 1990s, focusing on a largely untrue assumption that gay men had larger amounts of disposable income than did other demographics.[23] There are many problems with this construction of a gay gamer market, but two in particular stand out to me: (1) assuming this was a new market implied that gay men had never been part of video game culture before; and (2) assuming that good representation of gay men requires an identifiable gay gaymer market. In sum, much as queer activism helped demonstrate an existence of a queer (or really just gay) community that in turn could be marketed to, the "discovery" of queer (or really just gay) gamer communities set the stage for targeting a queer (or really just gay) gamer market.[24]

Later, in the 2010s, more and more people became aware of queer game designers and theorists like Anna Anthropy, merritt kopas, and Mattie Brice (to name just a few). I say "became aware of" because much of the discourse in 2012 to 2013 spoke of queer designers as a new phenomenon, erasing decades of queer game history. Moreover, conversations about their work started to raise questions about what queer game design would look like in a way that felt as proscriptive as asking what a queer games community should look like. Some of those conversations have been approached with more nuance by several contributors to this volume. However, news stories in particular began to describe this as a queer indie game "scene," glossing over differences and tensions in the many different goals of people who identify as queer designers.

What happens when we stop talking about gaymer communities as a site for articulating what LGBTQ gamers want? What new avenues of inquiry are available when we stop describing queer game designers as a scene? Well, we start to acknowledge the incongruities and tensions within and among communities. The trouble with communities is not that they are not inclusive; no community can be all things to all people. The trouble with communities is that too often we speak as though the goal is to create one great community rather than providing space for multiple communities to coexist. Community building is not a zero-sum game; it is not a competition. Having multiple game cultures does not inherently displace others. Individuals can live in, be in, and thrive in multiple communities simultaneously. Multiple communities can exist without taking away from one another. They form in moments of conflict, but why they are important is so much bigger than that. For me, embracing the multiplicity of communities and building coalitions across them can allow us to have open conversations about things that are problematic in game design, texts, communities, cultures, and studies. Looking at communities this way requires understanding that the goal of creating inclusive spaces is about much more than avoiding hurt feelings. We need talk about the limits of games communities— all of them—including the limits of the queer games communities, as more than "an existing set of relationships" and think creatively about how we might create "an alternative set of relationships."[25]

Notes

1. Raymond Williams, *Keywords: A Vocabulary of Culture and Society,* rev. ed. (New York: Oxford University Press, [1976] 1983), 87.

2. Ibid., 76.

3. Discussed in Adrienne Shaw, "What Is Video Game Culture? Cultural Studies and Game Studies," *Games and Culture* 5, no. 4 (2010): 403–24.

4. Williams, *Keywords,* 76.

5. Ibid.

6. This, of course, is a reference to the late 2014 online movement called #GamerGate. In the interest of space I will not attempt to summarize the events. A more detailed account is available in Shira Chess and Adrienne Shaw, "A Conspiracy of Fishes, or, How We Learned to Stop Worrying about GamerGate and Embrace Hegemonic Masculinity," *Journal of Broadcasting and Electronic Media* 59, no. 1 (2015): 208–20.

7. According to Robert Cathcart, speaking rhetorically, a movement requires that "there must be one or more actors who, perceiving that the 'good order' (the established system) is in reality a faulty order full of absurdity and injustice, cry out through various symbolic acts that true communication, justice, salvation cannot be achieved unless there is an immediate corrective applied to the established order." Robert S. Cathcart, "New Approaches to the Study of Movements: Defining Movement Rhetorically," *Western Speech* 36, no. 2 (1972): 87. Regardless of whether one agrees with #GamerGate's description of itself as oppressed, it is important to acknowledge that #GamerGaters often describe themselves as a part of a movement.

8. "*Gaming at the Edge* Customer Reviews," *Amazon,* nd, http://www
.amazon.com/Gaming-Edge-Sexuality-Margins-Culture/dp/0816693161.

9. I use the term "chilling effect" in the same sense Mario Rodriguez
does to describe how surveillance practices in online spaces serve to limit
when people feel free to speak. His example is the NSA PRISM program's
effect on Internet users, but I think it shares useful corollaries with the
threat of harassment faced by anyone who publicly criticized #GamerGate.
See Mario Rodríguez, "A Chilling Effect? Privacy and Surveillance Post-
PRISM," *Orlando Sentinel,* June 19, 2013, http://articles.orlandosentinel
.com/2013-06-19/news/os-ed-nsa-privacy-facebook-061913-20130618_1
_prism-julian-assange-chilling-effect.

10. Doxxing refers to a document dump, or posting a large amount of
personal information about a person online including addresses, phone
numbers, pictures, and tax records. Swatting refers to calling the police to
raid a person's home on the false report that they are going to harm someone else.

11. But one example of this is explored in Susan Krieger, *The Mirror Dance*
(Philadelphia: Temple University Press, 1983).

12. Which, if we are to believe news coverage, is apparently distinct from
the LGBTQ community. This is an unsurprising artifact of discourse, because when most people use LGBTQ they often just mean gay. Rarely does
anyone outside the queer community use the term queer community, which
is interesting if unsurprising.

13. Adrienne Shaw, "Talking to Gaymers: Questioning Identity, Community, and Media Representation," *Westminster Papers in Communication and
Culture* 9, no. 1 (2012): 69–89.

14. Brett Beemyn, ed., *Creating a Place for Ourselves* (New York: Routledge,
1997); Gordon Brent Ingram, Anne-Marie Bouthillette, and Yolanda Retter,
eds., *Queers in Space: Communities, Public Places, Sites of Resistance* (Seattle:
Bay Press, 1997); Moira Kenny, *Mapping Gay L.A.: The Intersection of Place
and Politics* (Philadelphia: Temple University Press, 2001); James McCourt,
Queer Street: Rise and Fall of an American Culture, 1947–1985 (New York: Norton, 2004); Eric C. Wat, *The Making of a Gay Asian Community: An Oral History of Pre-AIDS Los Angeles* (Lanham, Md.: Rowman and Littlefield, 2002).

15. Mary Bryson, "When Jill Jacks In: Queer Women and the Net," *Femi-
nist Media Studies* 4, no. 3 (2004): 239–54; John Edward Campbell, *Getting It
On Online: Cyberspace, Gay Male Sexuality, and Embodied Identity* (New York:
Harrington Park Press, 2004); Denise Carter, "Living in Virtual Communi-
ties: An Ethnography of Human Relationship in Cyberspace," *Information,
Communication, and Society* 8, no. 2 (2005): 148–67; Mark McLelland and

Nanette Gottlieb, eds., *Japanese Cyberculture* (London: Routledge, 2003); David Porter, ed., *Internet Culture* (New York: Routledge, 1997); Katie J. Ward, "Cyber-ethnography and the Emergence of the Virtually New Community," *Journal of Information Technology* 14, no. 1 (1999): 95–105.

16. Michael Bronski, *Culture Clash: The Making of Gay Sensibility* (Boston: South End Press, 1984), 193.

17. S. Elizabeth Bird, *The Audience and Everyday Life: Living in a Media World* (New York: Routledge, 2003), 74.

18. Emma Renold, "'Other' Boys: Negotiating Non-hegemonic Masculinities in the Primary School," *Gender and Education* 16, no. 2 (2004): 247–66.

19. "Gaymer" has been a contentious term, and even in 2007 when my study was conducted. Some felt it hailed a gay male gamer, rather than a broader LGBTQ gamer, identity. On the site, however, the term was used by everyone including heterosexual, bisexual, lesbian, and trans* members who did not identify as gay specifically. It was a way of embracing a gay sensibility, rather than gay sexual identity. More on the evolution of this term is available in Adrienne Shaw, "Circles, Charmed, and Magic: Queering Game Studies," *QED: A Journal in Queer Worldmaking* 2, no. 2 (2015): 64–97.

20. Similar phenomena are seen in Campbell, *Getting It On*; and Ward, "Cyber-ethnography."

21. This included gay cismale participants, but also lesbian, bisexual, transgender, queer, and one heterosexual cismale participant.

22. Research by Jason Rockwood in 2006 and Paul Nowak in 2009, and press on their results, focus on producing and defining a "gay gamer" audience in the hopes that they can then be appealed to by the video game industry. See Alexander Sliwinski, "Gay Gamer Survey Results with Large Hetero Inclusion," *Joystiq*, February 26, 2007, http://www.joystiq.com/2007/02/26/gay-gamer-survey-results-with-large-hetero-inclusion/; Mike Fahey, "What Do Gay Gamers Want from Their Games?" *Kotaku*, October 8, 2009, http://kotaku.com/5377127/what-do-gay-gamers-want-from-their-games.

23. For a discussion of the rise of the gay market see Katherine Sender, *Business, Not Politics: The Making of the Gay Market* (New York: Columbia University Press, 2004). She describes, among other things, how this rhetoric ignored the age, race, and gender dimensions of income inequality, and focuses specifically on urban, normative, middle- to upper-class, gay, white males as their exemplar. It was also an image of an ideal market created largely by gay marketers to help make a case for gay visibility in the 1990s.

24. Ibid.

25. Williams, *Keywords*, 76.

Chapter **17**

"Play Like a Girl"
Gender Expression, Sexual Identity, and Complex Expectations in a Female-Oriented Gaming Community

GABRIELA T. RICHARD

*Yeah, we guys have some ego issues regarding the fact that you're tak-
ing over everything that defines us and gives us identity. You're enforcing an evolution that in best case would take millenia and expecting us
to adapt in a few hundred years. I saw the video of your subtle leader,
Amber Dalton, as she attempted to convince people it wasn't about
proving you're better than us guys, yet your little clan here is allgirls?
It's hypocricy, and it's all about the women getting the priviledges of the
men (and* NOT *the other way round) than it has to do with equality.
Well, that and winning over guys to wave your little clan banner around
[their] faces [to] claim that they lost because you're girls. Otherwise,
the genderbased clanname would be completely pointless, right? It's all
about making men feel bad about their own gender, and when they do,
you yell they're the sexists, to make them feel even worse, and justifying
what you do. Me, on the other hand, I'm too smart to be fooled into such
delusions. Meh, you're just another feminist movement, and I hope I get
the chance to frag the superiority complex out of you someday, especially your precious leader. It would just be one out of an endless and
unstoppable ocean of girl gamer clans, but boy, would it rock my world.*
—Banned forum user, 2006

The quote above is illustrative of the extreme end of the kind of hostility directed at female game players more generally, and at Pandora's Mighty Soldiers (PMS) more specifically.[1] PMS is an all-female gaming community (known as a "clan" in the gaming space) cofounded by Amber Dalton (aka Athena Twin PMS) and her twin sister, Amy Brady (aka Athena PMS or Valkyrie FD), along with other female "gamers."[2] Historically, 2006 was a great year for the clan: they had won major sponsorships, they (rather than "booth babes")[3] were hired by Microsoft to promote Microsoft products during the Electronic Entertainment Expo, and they were featured throughout print and TV media (including on MTV). While the above critique is not likely to be expressed openly or completely in most online or offline circumstances, it helps to illuminate the concern expressed by mostly heterosexual male players in the digital gaming world: a sense of gender identity tied to gaming (as part of "everything that defines us [males] and gives us [males] identity"); the use of evolution to justify differences between the proposed binary construction of the genders ("you're enforcing an evolution . . . and expecting us [males] to adapt"); a fear of emasculation at the hands of females who are perceived to be invading the gaming space ("winning over guys to wave your little clan banner around . . . [and] claim that [males] lost because you're girls"); a concern over the loss of privilege associated with being male ("it's all about the women getting the [privileges] of the men"); and the desire to use violence to defend male identity and space ("I hope I get the chance to frag the superiority complex out of you [women] someday").

In fact, while comments like this one may appear to be on the extreme end of the spectrum of gender-based criticism, similar rhetoric can be found across the Internet. Websites like *Return of Kings* have grown increasingly popular as places where critical male users congregate to categorize and police heteronormative and hierarchical constructions of masculinity.[4] For example, *Return of Kings* boasts several articles aimed at regulating acceptable male behavior, constructing "real" men as "alphas," and men who support women or female equality in male-dominated spaces (or otherwise deviate from this rigidly constructed form of masculine heterosexual normativity) as "betas" or "omegas," intentionally derogatory terms. One of the site's notable articles declares that women have ruined video games in several key ways: (1) by promoting inclusivity through the design of diverse and queer characters, (2) writing critical gaming journalism articles without "actual meaningful game content," and (3) pretending to be gamers to attract men with few romantic options, who are termed "the thirstiest betas in existence."[5]

Gendered Expectations, Heteronormativity, and a Female-Supportive Gaming Community

Computing and gaming have long been regarded as a culture in which "initial socialization" is important for confidence, skill, and identification, and in which men are largely considered the intended audience.[6] Kimmel, studying young and (primarily) white, heterosexual male culture, found that key spaces and activities, including gaming, have become increasingly claimed for male-dominance bonding as these same men have perceived a rise in gender equality and political correctness in mainstream culture.[7] Bertozzi has further illustrated that female players in male-dominated, competitive play spaces disrupt male "standards of civility, their . . . self definition as male, and culturally sanctioned expressions of sexual desire."[8] Overarching discourse, as transmitted through the media, paints women competing in these spaces as "unwitting pawns of feminist ideology, which places them in an arena in which they are certain to be hurt," and where punishment is "somehow deserved" when a woman is "where she [does not] belong," even if the act involves gender-based violence and hostility outside the game space.[9] Similarly, Sundén found that female and queer players disrupted the fantasy of the "ideal player—a player who is symbolically male and straight."[10] Women disrupted this notion simply by being female, and queer men disrupted it by supporting inclusivity or deviating from heterosexuality.

It is partly due to this kind of pervasive hostility that the PMS clan felt the need to enforce its all-female policy, even after allowing men to join its linked, yet separate, brother clan, H2O, in 2005.[11] While the clan operated under the name "Psychotic Man Slayerz" from 1998 to 2002, it changed its name to "Pandora's Mighty Soldiers" soon after its formal debut in 2002.[12] Though male players expressed interest in joining the clan on several occasions, it wasn't until a few years later that men were allowed to join H2O formally, and then only through a vetting process, by which a female member would sponsor them (though they can now join independently).[13] Furthermore, even though anyone can join the clan's public forums, only members who have passed the multiple-week recruitment process can view private forums (including additional private forums separated by gender) and play regularly with members during sanctioned practices (a requirement to remain an active member). The clan supports play across multiple gaming platforms, including consoles and the PC, and across multiple game genres with team competitive or cooperative play, such as first-person shooters, massive multiplayer online role-playing games (MMORPGs), multiplayer battle arenas (MOBAs), real-time strategy games, racing games, and even open sandbox games (e.g., *Minecraft*). PMS clan members play in small groups called divisions, which focus on a certain game or franchise on a certain platform (e.g., the *World of Warcraft* PC division or the *Call of Duty* Xbox division), and most divisions are single-sex.[14]

In my own experience as a female player and ethnographer in both a single-sex and co-ed division of the PMS clan, I found that instances of emphasis on (or even divisions centered on) co-ed play often had the unintended consequence of de-emphasizing female play and participation and reinforcing male play, as men often came to the clan with more experience and confidence, having received greater social support for their inclusion in gaming activities.[15] Members, however, can play with any players in the PMS|H2O community, across gender, during their own time, and even create competitive tournament teams with members of the opposite sex. However, both of these activities do not count toward maintaining active member status, and must be done in addition to practice hours.

For female players who want to remain sexually desirable to male players, cross-gender competition creates a dissonance where "females who dare to compete and win at the same level as males often find it necessary to emphasize the fact that they remain sexually 'female,'" and thus they are protective of "their status as sexually viable."[16] Despite the clan's emphasis on sportsmanship, particularly the requirement to avoid "smack talk" and to always say "good game" (regardless of whether opposing mostly male teams outside the clan say it in return), I found that female PMS players tended to adopt male-defined gamer speak online. In other words, hypermasculine attitudes and aggressiveness was highly valued in all-female game spaces as long as it stopped short of harassment and unsportsman-like behavior. Conversely, while we were required to adopt a strict dress code (no full or partial nudity could be shown online or dur-ing professional gaming events), female players tended—and were sometimes even encouraged—to dress feminine and make ourselves pleasing to the male heterosexual gaze, particularly when we played in places where we would be seen. The PMS clan was led by women who were very sexually attractive by Western normative standards, and who were navigating and negotiating their own approval in the male-dominated space. While I do not believe that the PMS leader-ship focused solely on self-promotion, or that it was their intent to fully endorse these norms of beauty (and there were plenty of mem-bers who didn't fit the stereotype of female beauty), those that were more "feminine" and sexually desirable seemed to have better lever-age when it came to attending gaming industry events as clan repre-sentatives, being recommended for industry work through clan con-nections, and moving up in leadership roles.[17]

As others have shown, when women adopt heteronormative mas-culine behaviors, it may seem empowering or counter-hegemonic. However, it actually does little to change existing power structures. Cassell and Jenkins reflect how "when girls take over games that have been traditionally male, the norm is not questioned."[18] LeBlanc argues that women in male-dominated domains are expected to be "tough, like the guys, but . . . also . . . pretty and sexually available" though not "overly promiscuous."[19] However, male-oriented sexual desirability is a fragile form of acceptance and approval for women in hypermasculinized spaces. Arguments over the "fake geek girl," put forth by men and women alike, propose that there is a way to measure female authenticity that relates to attractiveness and sex appeal.[20] Female gamers are "marked out as 'fake' by default, [hav-ing] to prove themselves innocent."[21]

Problematizing the Gender Binary and Heteronormativity

The gender binary is a pervasive and limiting construction of desire and sexuality. As expressed by Butler, the binary "conception of gen-der presuppose[s] not only a causal relation among sex, gender and desire, but suggests as well that desire reflects or expresses gender and that gender reflects or expresses desire."[22] Butler goes on to explain how drag "*implicitly reveals the imitative structures of gender itself,*" as opposed to its fixed nature.[23] Foucault famously argued that the categorization of the "homosexual" created a new structure in which individuals were now fundamentally defined for their acts, as opposed to being individuals who participate in and enjoy certain acts.[24] Namaste further asserts that "heterosexuality needs homosexuality for its own definition: a macho homophobic male can define himself as 'straight' only in opposition to that which he is not—an effeminate gay man."[25] The fear of emasculation, and the need for asserting heterosexuality as part of an assumed authentic masculinity, keeps men unable to explore sexual desires, perform alternative gender constructions, or even express deep emotions and feelings.[26] This problematizes the acceptance of not only homosexuality but also identities and sexualities that do not adhere to or in fact disrupt the gender binary.[27]

Homosexuality in the clan was neither explicitly supported nor unsupported. However, the clan's focus on respectable gaming restricted the use of homophobic, racist, and sexist language. As a result, many gay and lesbian gamers felt a sense of "friendliness" from the clan. In 2011, with the inclusion of more "out" gaymers in the clan, there appeared to be even more open support, in public and private forums, for gay members.[28] An example of this can be seen in this request, made on a PMS forum in 2012, from a former H2O member: "OK so I'm a gay guy who likes to play video games, sue me . . . I'm trying to find some other gay/gayfriendly players to play with . . . It would be nice just play with people without words like 'homo' and 'f**' getting thrown around." A high-ranking H2O general, who was out and at the forefront of promoting more openness, soon responded, "Greeting fellow gay gamer! I have found this to be a very friendly community . . . [and] respectful and tolerant . . . I have been a member of a few other gay gaming communities and they seem to always turn into a hookup service, which just kinda creeps me out. If you ever want to play some games just hit me up ☺."

Nevertheless, this friendliness didn't seem to correspond to the numbers of "out" gaymers in H2O (nine were counted in 2012). The constraints to "coming out" could in part be explained by the clan's policies related to limiting personal drama. Throughout the forums, division discussions, and play, a common theme involved keeping one's relationship drama to one's self. In fact, as exemplified through the handbook, relationships between clan members were strongly discouraged.[29] Unfortunately, the variability in how these rules were enforced, depending on the division or gaming platform leadership, had a direct effect on perceptions of inclusivity. Not all leaders or generals exhibited similar levels of acceptance, awareness, or understanding, and, at times, certain behavior would be policed only if it made a particular member uncomfortable. In late 2007 a forum thread was started by an "out" lesbian clan member who angrily addressed what she considered discriminatory behavior: the deletion of an earlier thread in which she had mentioned being gay. She titled her new thread "So basically can I not speak of being a lesbian???" In it, she wrote, "Cause that is what it is coming out to be on these forums because we can no longer speak about something as natural as boobs and sexual preferences. I'm a lesbian and I'm proud to be it!!! . . . Being a lesbian I find this totally against our constitutional rights." Two former H2O leaders responded. "You have no rights in a private forum other than what the administration gives you," said one. The other more pointedly defended the rationale for the removal: "The topic was 'boobs' not really appropriate for a giant and popular clan site that is PMS. If a higher up came in, or even a sponsor, and saw that, they might and could possibly be offended. That's why it was removed. There was no discriminating against sexuality."

However, the lesbian clan member was adamant in proclaiming that "it wasn't just about the fact it was talking about boobs." She wrote, "Did you not see the lesbian talk that was also put in there??? That is another reason it was removed." While I was not privy to the original post, the response in which the H2O leader rationalized that the post might offend members and sponsors resonated with a general tension I had noted between "coming out" and expressing sexual preferences in the clan. Several similar situations arose in personal communication between me and other lesbian gamers in the space. Eventually, as if to rectify the situation, a thread for "lesbians" was started in the private, female-only section for members, where individuals could discuss and debate experiences, preferences, and even come out to each other. However, the fact that this space was available only behind the scenes—out of view from sponsors, nonmembers, and men—raised interesting questions about where and for whom clan members could express their sexuality, as well as how the clan was constructing and reacting to assumptions of female sexual expression.

While expressing sexuality was an often confusing and potentially contentious process for many PMS members, those who identified themselves as non-cisgender had the most difficulty managing whether and where they belonged. During the course of my multi-year ethnography, I discovered several threads where potential recruits who identified as transgender or non-cis attempted to apply to the clan but were confused about how the clan would categorize them and whether they would be welcomed. Many of these threads, unfortunately, have since been removed, but their documentation helps to illustrate a changing trend within the community. Consider, for example, the following 2011 thread in which a trans gamer[30] asks to join the clan:

> Inquiring Recruit: Hiya, I'm new here, I've had a look around the forums but couldn't really see an answer to this, are transgender girls welcome in PMS? It says PMS is for females, H2O for males, what about people who are trans/gender queer, are they allowed to apply for their chosen gender clan? Thank you

> PMS General: Hi [name removed]. Please see our handbook [link] this should answer all of your questions

> Inquiring Recruit: Hiya, thanks for the link, I found: Female is defined as a person with the female sexual organs at the time of membership. I guess that answers my question. There are people living fulltime as women who cant afford surgery, some who live in countries where surgery is illegal. ☹ I really hope you'll reconsider your policy one day. Thank you.

H2O Former Division Leader: hey [name removed], your still able to join H2O if you like, we have had transgender members in the past and when it comes the time that you chose to have your surgery you are able to switch over with no issues. The clan doesn't discriminate on sexual preference or life choices so your more than welcome to join us if you like.

Inquiring Recruit: Thanks for your kind reply [name removed], but H2O is for guys and I'm not a guy :/ It's ok

Though the community allowed transgender membership, it was regulated within a narrow view of biology. The rationale for these transphobic policies may have come partially from the clan's experiences with and concerns over impersonation in a space where women's legitimacy and acceptance was already fragile and highly regulated. Alternatively, the clan may have feared being mocked. However, by the time a new potential recruit presented the forums with a similar request about a year later, the situation had changed:

Inquiring Recruit: Im not trying to cause problems but I firmly believe I belong in PMS after all I live every day as a woman and have had 2 count them 2 surgeries . . . anyways lol not ranting or anything. However my [boyfriend] who is the H2O member is really upset with some information he got saying I may not be recognized as a woman even after all my efforts . . . rather then him get upset and since im well trained in being emotionally hurt over this I am aiming to find out myself since I dont want him to leave the clan . . . since he kinda had you all first.

H2O Member: The rule can in some instances be overwritten, ive seen it both ways, its . . . more of an effort but it can be done, [de]pending what system you are on I would find who the generals are and then get in contact with them, Ive seen preop on xbox . . . I also maybe suggest messaging [the PMS General] about this as she is whom i contacted when I was poking around asking questions . . .

> Inquiring Recruit: well I just got in contact with a wonderful per-
> son . . . the general I believe and yes . . . I have placed [an applica-
> tion]. Hopefully Ill get a final decision and thank you all for being
> so nice.

As illustrated through this exchange, and as juxtaposed with the previous exchange, trans and non-cis identity and acceptance in this history of PMS is highly contextual. In the end, the inquiring recruit in the second exchange was able to join the clan. On the one hand, a case could be made that, between the two forum threads, the clan had moved toward a more nuanced view of gender binaries. On the other hand, the clan's acceptance of the second potential recruit could also have been due to her gender reassignment surgeries or to her relationship with a current male member (through whom she may have gained access to a backdoor vetting process to which others were not privy).

Even within queer theory, debates around trans identity have been long-standing. As proposed by Stryker, "'transgender' increasingly functions as the site that contains all gender trouble, against which both homosexuality and heterosexuality are understood as stable and normative categories of personhood."[31] Transgender identities problematize and disrupt the very notion of gender as biology, raising a unique set of issues around gender, hierarchical notions of power, and performativity. Many trans-identified individuals must navigate this arena alone. As a result, it is perhaps no surprise that, while lesbian, gay and bisexual gamers were eventually able to gain acceptance in the clan, the terms of acceptance for trans gamers remained somewhat opaque. Despite the acceptance of some trans gamers into the clan, as of writing this in 2014 the policy that only applicants with female sexual organs are considered "women" (and vice versa for men) remained the same, but a redesign of the policy in 2016 made considerable strides, updating the policy to state that "female is defined as a person born as or living as a female at the time of membership, and likewise for H2O Clan," a historical movement in an inclusive direction.

Conclusion

Expectations of gender, sexuality, and performativity are prevalent and largely cultural constructs that invade and regulate many domains, not just gaming. However, the propensity for gaming to be claimed as a place for masculine, heterosexual dominance-bonding and expression presents challenges for everyone involved, regardless of sexual identity: male gender identity is, in many ways, just as highly policed and fragile as female gender identity. Nonetheless, female gender identity requires special consideration as gaming becomes increasingly popular and constructions of authenticity collide with femininity. In light of the antifeminist backlash of #GamerGate, which was instigated in part by groups and individuals associated with places like the *Return of Kings* website, the kinds of support fostered in identity-supportive communities is needed more than ever.[32] However, these communities have limitations as well. Even within safe spaces for gender identity, sexuality has been shown to be subjected to larger cultural norms. Trans gamers, standing in juxtaposition to normative constructions of both gender and sexuality, experience specific challenges in spaces constructed in opposition to hypermasculinity. In some ways, the argument can be made that, until there is greater acceptance for gender diversity in the larger culture, subcultures will continue to wrestle with conflicting expectations. However, counter-communities within subcultures offer unique affordances for pushing boundaries and rebelling against hierarchy, and they allow members to form and foster skills, confidence, and networks that begin to level the playing field.[33]

Notes

All quotations from online users are reproduced as they appear on the original sites, including errors in spelling, punctuation, and grammar.

1. Up until 2016, "Play like a girl, Play with girls" was part of the original slogan on the logo for PMS Clan (http://www.pmsclan.com/). However, once their website was updated, only the logo for PMS and H2O remained.

2. The term "gamers" has come under fire in recent times because of its exclusionary nature. For example, a recent Pew Research Center study (available at http://www.pewinternet.org/2015/12/15/attitudes-about-video -games/) found that, while women play games as much as men, they are less likely to adopt the "gamer" label. Researchers, such as Adrienne Shaw, have long critiqued the "gamer" label as not being inclusive of those who play games. See Adrienne Shaw, "On Not Becoming Gamers: Moving beyond the Constructed Audience," *Ada: A Journal of Gender, New Media, and Technology* 1, no. 2 (2013): http://adanewmedia.org/2013/06/issue2-shaw/.

3. "Booth babes" is a term used to describe attractive models and other individuals (frequently also "cosplayers," a term used for fans that dress like fantasy characters) hired to promote digital games and other products to consumers, usually at trade shows. They have been critiqued for often being scantly clad and often hired for their looks, as opposed to their product knowledge.

4. *Return of Kings* (http://www.returnofkings.com/) was originally thought to be satire, but it is actually quite explicit in its description as a "blog for heterosexual, masculine men" and "meant for a small but vocal collection of men in America today who believe men should be masculine and women should be feminine." The site's "About" section (http://www .returnofkings.com/about) goes on to claim that men and women are bio-logically different, hence the need for this kind of policing. They further state that the site acts as "a safe space on the web for those men who don't agree with the direction that Western culture is headed" and that "women and homosexuals are prohibited from commenting here. They will be im-mediately banned, and anyone who replies to them will also be banned. This includes replying in any thread that they started." The site hosts a collection of articles on the ills of feminism, males who deviate from heteronorma-tive constructions of gender, homosexuality, and "transsexuals," as well as articles about how to exploit women.

5. "3 Ways Women Have Ruined Video Games," *Return of Kings,* Decem-ber 9, 2013, http://www.returnofkings.com/21204/3-ways-women-have -ruined-video-games. The article claims that women propose diversity ef-forts while men do the "real" work of designing "physics engines," without which there would be no money to "subsidize feminist outreach programs."

6. Sara Kiesler, Lee Sproull, and Jacquelynne S. Eccles, "Pool Halls, Chips, and War Games: Women in the Culture of Computing," *Psychology of Women Quarterly* 9, no. 4 (1985): 451–62.

7. Michael S. Kimmel, *Guyland: The Perilous World Where Boys Become Men* (New York: HarperCollins, 2008).

8. Elena Bertozzi, "'You Play Like a Girl!' Cross-Gender Competition and the Uneven Playing Field," *Convergence: The International Journal of Research into New Media Technologies* 14, no. 4 (2008): 474.

9. Ibid., 477.

10. Jenny Sundén, "Play as Transgression: An Ethnographic Approach to Queer Game Cultures," in *Proceedings of DiGRA 2009: Breaking New Ground* (Brunel University, U.K., 2009), 3.

11. "Pandora's Mighty Soldiers (PMS) Handbook," nd, http://www.pmsclan.com/forum/showthread.php?t=30905.

12. Justine Cassell and Henry Jenkins, "Chess for Girls? Feminism and Computer Games," in *From Barbie to Mortal Kombat: Gender and Computer Games,* ed. Justine Cassell and Henry Jenkins (Cambridge, Mass.: MIT Press, 1998), 2–37; "Pandora's Mighty Soldiers (PMS) About Us," nd, http://www.pmsclan.com/page.php?page=About%20Us.

13. An interesting fact learned during the ethnography, through PMS clan leadership, was that the name H2O was explicitly derived from men being interested in joining in the early days and being told they could be the "water boys" for the women playing in tournaments. Once their sincerity was noted, they were able to join by being vetted by female members and assigned as "their" H2O, denoting that those female members had taken responsibility for overseeing the men's adherence to the clan's mission. See "Pandora's Mighty Soldiers (PMS) Handbook."

14. Divisions in the PMS clan are represented by games supported by membership of more than eight to ten individuals who regularly attend practices. However, since there are only a handful of co-ed divisions (in part because the process to remain co-ed requires less than eight members of one gender), most play and participation is limited to single-sex divisions.

15. Gabriela T. Richard, "Supporting Visibility and Resilience in Play: Gender-Supportive Online Gaming Communities as a Model of Identity and Confidence Building in Play and Learning," in *Identity and Leadership in Virtual Communities,* ed. Dona J. Hickey and Joe Essid (Hershey, Pa.: IGI Global, 2014), 170–86; Gabriela T. Richard, "Understanding Gender, Context, and Video Game Culture for the Development of Equitable Digital Games as Learning Environments" (PhD diss., New York University, 2014).

16. Bertozzi, "'You Play Like a Girl!'" 479.

17. Richard, "Understanding Gender, Context, and Video Game Culture."

18. Cassell and Jenkins, "Chess for Girls?" 35.

19. Lauraine Leblanc, *Pretty in Punk: Girls' Gender Resistance in a Boys' Subculture* (New Brunswick, N.J.: Rutgers University Press, 1999), 130.

20. Famously, one front-end developer and blogger for CNN proposed

that fake geek girls were "a '6' in the 'real world,' but when they put on a Batman shirt and head to the local fandom convention du jour, they instantly become a '9'" by "parad[ing] around a group of boys notorious for being outcasts." See Joe Peacock, "Booth Babes Need Not Apply," *Geek Out! CNN Blog*, July 24, 2012, http://geekout.blogs.cnn.com/2012/07/24/booth-babes-need -not-apply. However, popular memes that try to distinguish between the "real" and fake geek girl often depict the authentic geek as serious or goofy and unattractive, and the fake geek as hypersexualized or attempting to use sexual desirability or availability to her benefit (e.g., posing with game controllers in a sexy manner).

21. Daniel Nye Griffiths, "'Fake Geek Girls': How Geek Gatekeeping Is Bad for Business," *Forbes*, July 26, 2012, http://www.forbes.com/sites /danielnyegriffiths/2012/07/26/fake-geek-girls-gamer-edition/.

22. Judith Butler, *Gender Trouble: Feminism and the Subversion of Identity* (New York: Routledge, 1999), 30.

23. Ibid., 175.

24. Michel Foucault, *The History of Sexuality, Volume 1: An Introduction*, trans. Robert Hurley (New York: Pantheon, 1978).

25. Ki Namaste, "The Politics of Inside/Out: Queer Theory, Poststructuralism, and a Sociological Approach to Sexuality," *Sociological Theory* 12, no. 2 (1994): 222.

26. Gust A. Yep, "The Violence of Heteronormativity in Communication Studies: Notes on Injury, Healing, and Queer World-Making," *Journal of Homosexuality* 45, nos. 2–4 (2003): 11–59.

27. Michael S. Kimmel, "Masculinity as Homophobia: Fear, Shame, and Silence in the Construction of Gender Identity," in *Race, Class, and Gender in the United States: An Integrated Study*, ed. Paula S. Rothenberg (New York: Worth, 2004), 81–93.

28. "Gaymers" is a popularized term used to denote LGBT gamers, as exemplified by GaymerX (http://gaymerx.com/), a large, LGBT-oriented and inclusive gaming convention.

29. "Pandora's Mighty Soldiers (PMS) Handbook."

30. Following the lead of "gaymer," I am using "trans gamer" to denote transgendered players.

31. Susan Stryker, "Transgender Studies: Queer Theory's Evil Twin," *GLQ: A Journal of Lesbian and Gay Studies* 10, no. 2 (2004): 212–15.

32. For more information on how #GamerGate started and its main targets—women in gaming, game criticism, and design—see Nick Wingfield, "Feminist Critics of Video Games Facing Threats in 'GamerGate' Campaign," *New York Times*, October 15, 2014, http://www.nytimes.com/2014/10/16

/technology/gamergate-women-video-game-threats-anita-sarkeesian .html. For a cultural analysis of why there has been such a vitriolic backlash against individuals perceived to be against game culture, see Katherine Cross, "The Nightmare Is Over," in this volume.

33. Richard, "Understanding Gender, Context, and Video Game Culture."

Chapter **18**

The Nightmare Is Over

KATHERINE CROSS

Former *GameSpot* editor Carolyn Petit, speaking with me on a panel at 2014's GaymerX2 convention in San Francisco, recounted a private message she received in response to a review of the video game *Gone Home*: "I got this message from a reader and it was pretty well worded, and well thought out . . . but what he was saying is, essentially, 'Well, Carolyn, you shouldn't have given *Gone Home* such a high score because if game designers see games like *Gone Home* getting so much acclaim then we're not going to have traditional games anymore!'" Time and again, this leitmotif of gamer speak arises: the idea that someone, somewhere is going to take your games away: a "terror dream" that sees us reliving the paternalist past and lashing out at all criticism in hopes of keeping the grasping hands of the censor at bay.

They're Not Coming for Us

Autumn Nicole Bradley, the writer and game designer, discussed this idea with me as we went through our histories as gamers; a conversation became a theory that corralled the facts and events of the last few years into an explanation for one of the signal phenomena of gamer culture. Why do we treat most criticism or change as a coming apocalypse? And why do so many gamers seem to treat games made by and/or about queer people as destructive invasion?

Journalist Susan Faludi coined the psychosocial metaphor of "the terror dream" in her eponymous 2007 volume published by Metropolitan Books. It describes a buried, nightmarish memory, rising to the surface periodically to control our actions whenever our taken-for-granted world seems to be under threat. "The nightmare confounds order," Faludi argues, "[and] alerts the sleeper the wished-for narrative isn't holding." She uses this to frame an eloquent discussion of how the United States reacted to the tragedy of 9/11 and how a muscular jingoism and misogyny were really the frightened reflexes of a country revisiting past humiliations.

Faludi tells the story of how an attractive, unifying cultural mythology can turn violent at the sign of a perceived threat, a collective nightmare that inspires terrified reactions—either to real threats or to shadows.

For many gamers, especially men, that "wished-for narrative" of a grand cultural mythos is a tale of triumph against censorious parents, violent nerd-hating bullies, and puritanical politicos who wanted to take away their beloved hobby—a tale in which a boys' club prevailed and gamers could indulge the womanizing power fantasies of strength and valor that "real life" had denied them.

I spoke with Mitch Gitelman, studio director of Harebrained Schemes (of *Shadowrun Returns* fame), for the original *Polygon* article on which this essay is based. His thoughts on the matter as an industry veteran remain worthwhile. He believes that the historical narrative that downplays the contributions of female and queer gamers constitutes an exclusionary "nostalgia for something that shouldn't exist." "Games haven't been reflective of reality throughout their history," he argues. Instead, having been created by men for men, they were a "natural reflection of male fantasy" that sheltered two generations of young men who often felt put upon by a world that wanted to take it all away from them.[1]

Lost to Moral Panic

To this day, gamers are revisiting a buried experience, reinscribing and reinterring it every time the "take our games away" discussion comes up. But what experience?

"Gamers' feeling that something is going to be taken away from them is not entirely a fantasy," Gitelman reminds us. From Jack Chick to Jack Thompson, from Senator Joe Lieberman to governments around the world, it has seemed at times that there really are grasping bullies around every corner trying to take games away. The censor even emerged in the person of our own parents, as often as not.

But now, of course, Mom doesn't want to take our games away. She wants to *play* them. And in so doing, many male gamers fear, she will ruin the experience forever—never mind that women have been here from the earliest days of gaming, as players, artists, developers, and designers.

Such gamers see our virtual world as a fragile and ephemeral one, perpetually under threat from outside forces. For the many gamers who lived through the '80s and '90s, growing up at a time when video games and *Dungeons & Dragons* were being scapegoated for mass shootings, suicide, and Satanism, the experience left a psychic scar that expresses itself as a violent reflex at the first sign of criticism.

If we are defending gaming from the slings and arrows of "outsiders," then, in a society that retains prejudicial stereotypes about women and LGBT people, those people, too, will be construed as invaders whose criticisms, or even just their very *presence,* herald the end of gaming as we know it. To give ground to feminist criticism, for instance, is seen too often as analogous to supporting a government ban. Games about LGBTQ people are seen as the flagships of this invasion; *Gone Home* is popularly criticized in many quarters by gamers who are convinced that its accolades are a form of affirmative action bestowed on the title simply because it tells the story of a lesbian couple.

What is unique about the criticism directed at *Gone Home* is that its most inveterate critics cannot help but cite its lesbian characters in their criticism. One customer review on GOG.com is headlined "Cheap Social Justice Disguised as Horror." The reviewer says, "Since this game was made by social justice warrior hipsters from Portland, it's presented as a BEAUTIFUL LIFE EXPERIENCE where lesbians are perfect magical pixies. The lesbian angle doesn't even factor into the story. The girls face no prejudice or social exclusion. Would have been the exact same story with a straight couple, then people would rightfully call the kids out for being idiots." Another commenter on the same site writes in their review, "Your sister is homosexual and run off with her girlfriend, yes that is the whole plot of the game. . . . Who cares? It's boooooooring! How can anyone says that the story is a master piece, it is just a f*** love story, it blows my mind."

Still another review adds, "I'm not going to say much in regards to the ostensible heartfelt teenage love story going on in this 'game.' I'm not even going to talk about the marital disorder going on with the protagonist's parents—something 99.99% of reviews have over-looked in favour of the ooh-aah lesbian candyland."

Such reviews are typical fare. Again and again one sees the same themes come up. The argument that the story would have been iden-tical with heterosexual protagonists is taken as gospel, even though the characters *do* face opprobrium and uncertainty over their ro-mance that would not have befallen a straight couple, and at least one of the game's subplots would make no sense if the central couple had been straight. But that is really beside the point. To many of these angry gamers, *Gone Home* is not really a game and deserves no praise from gaming outlets; the fact that it was critically acclaimed is prima facie proof to them of a social justice conspiracy that unfairly extols queer people merely because they're queer. This in turn leads to anxiety that a creeping force is due to take all of male gaming's beloved, real, un-queer games away from them.

In this fight, so far as these gamers are concerned, no quarter can be given; all discursive space for compromise and evolution is col-lapsed into suffocation by crushing fear.

The A/political Helix of Rage

Even outside of these openly "political" issues, this terror dream sur-faces. The outrage over *Mass Effect 3*'s ending, for instance, was in some ways the apotheosis of this trend. Valid artistic criticisms of what could fairly be called an unduly minimalist ending quickly spiraled out of control into angry campaigns with furious declarations that the game's developer, BioWare, was ruining role-playing games and gaming as a whole, and that the simplistic color choice of the ending foretold the stultification of gaming.

The advert for downloadable content that appeared after *Mass Effect*'s credits only stoked the outraged fear that the end of gaming was nigh, and that games were being reduced to lazy, uncreative, simple pay-to-play machines for "QQing [crying] casuals."

Each of these blow-ups reveals a tangle of anxieties that weave in and out politics, legitimate concerns, and paranoid prejudices and fears. Disarticulating this helix of rage, which is sometimes highly politically charged, and other times obsessed with putatively apolitical issues, is never easy.

Dragon Age 2, for instance, was also not above genuine artistic criticism, with repetitive level design and a story climax that undermined core characters and premises, but the sheer hatred for the game among many gamers was a supernova that defied all description. Their hatred became a kind of reflexive outrage disconnected from any and all critique. It inflected the online harassment of former BioWare writer Jennifer Hepler, which culminated in threats against her family. It also laced into homophobic anger at the game's inclusive romance options and led to the infamous rant from forum user Bastal, who lamented that "the straight male gamer" was no longer at the center of design decisions.

Above and beyond any reasonable critiques to be made of the design of *Dragon Age 2,* it was the target of such attacks simply because it was an avatar of uncomfortable changes. Rather than being on a hero's journey, Hawke was at the mercy of events; Isabela was a woman of color; men flirted with your male character. In so many ways, *DA2* constituted the existential challenge that often arouses the terror dream, inspiring a hatred for everything it seemed to represent.

Unreasoning terror of this sort, which explodes in every direction, makes for an inhospitable critical climate. It gives developers a lot of chaff to sort through on forums and social media while searching for constructive criticism that helps them do better work, and it silences whole communities of gamers and designers who have good-faith reasons for wanting to take gaming in a different direction.

As gamers, we will have to learn how to develop a critical community that does not mistake acidic rage and hatred for the kind of productive passion that has so often led to great games. When every effort at change is seen as Jack Thompson redux, we remain bedeviled by the ghosts of censors past. We end up hamstringing the maturation of our own beloved virtual worlds.

Harebrained Schemes' Gitelman ended our conversation by sounding a hopeful note: "The next generation of game developers grew up in a different time. What the older guys might see as progressive or new is just common sense to them. Plus, more and more developers are women and minorities. Change is happening, and it's going in the right direction. You're just going to see more and more of that as time goes on."

Outsider/Insider

To be sure, we face myriad challenges, particularly from the swelling corporatization of gaming and its budget-busting consolidation and influence peddling. But the threat is not coming from people like me who want to see better-written games that tell richer stories, and who believe that one of many ways to do this is to diversify the populations on whom those stories focus. Nor is it coming from prominent women gamers, or activists fighting against maladies like online harassment. Nor, indeed, can it be said to come from games studies scholars who research the medium and sometimes offer prescriptions based on their theories.

What these groups do have in common, however, is that they often portend or advocate for *change and criticism,* which have become mistaken for destruction by too many gamers.

Often, gamers have been trained, both by marketers and by real-life events from the 1990s and early 2000s, to believe that the threat is coming from *without.* In 2008, Electronic Arts infamously staged astroturf protests of its *own* game, *Dante's Inferno,* hoping to make it appear as if Christians were calling for the game to be banned. Marketers have long promoted the idea that gamer love must be a reactive thing, forever under outside threat. Protecting against these threats or opposing them has become part of the very practice of *being a gamer* in too many spaces. Even when looking at games like *Mass Effect 3,* whose real or perceived failings were obvious products of the gaming industry, gamers interpret whatever they dislike (in this case, the abbreviated ending) as an artifact of outside influence corroding the old clubhouse.

Similarly, criticisms made by feminist gamers are too often seen as external to gamer culture. Popular mythology from certain corners of the gaming community holds that no activist women cared about gaming before 2007—even though discussions of sexism, in both the industry and in games themselves, can be found even in trade publications from the early 1990s.

The terror dream demands an *external* invasion, however, to justify itself and its aggressive reactions. This is why feminist critics are immediately presumed to be outsiders to gaming. In turn, this presumption feeds the sense that games are being threatened. It analogizes internal critiques, or even benign outsider critiques, to the brimstone-laden bromides of genuine censors and fundamentalists.

Ending sexism should not be seen as akin to ending gaming as an enterprise. "No one is going to take your military shooters away!" pled Carolyn Petit, and I can hardly find better words. Many of us may be tired of the same military shooters dominating budgets, headlines, and the attention of the gaming community, but that doesn't mean we want to eliminate them, only that we want to make room for greater diversity of play and players. More people to play, more games to play, more ways to win: it's all rather benign, even boring.

To quote Faludi talking about American militarism, "We dreamed ourselves into a penny-dreadful plot that had little to do with the actual world in which we must live." Her words apply equally to those parts of gamer culture where gamers stand on hypervigilant alert for the bogeymen who are coming to take their games away for good.

The reaction to retailer Target pulling *Grand Theft Auto V* from its shelves in Australia in late 2014 makes plain that too many young gamers are still clamoring to be the heroic anticensorship warrior-cum-martyr against rapacious outsiders. The fact that Target pulled the game in response to a petition from sex worker rights activists only cemented the association between activist women and the destruction of gaming in the minds of these young gamers.

Yet the furor came and went, and *GTAV* sells as well as it ever did. Australians (who, it should be noted, depend far less on stores like Target than suburban Americans do) were not wanting for places to buy the game. The apocalypse that launched a thousand outraged e-mails and petitions seemed more like a teacup squall in the end.

The terror dream of games being stolen away represents our shared heritage as gamers of a certain generation who have survived a turbulent and uncertain era. But we have to realize that we gamers are actually *winning* the censorship battle. Our medium is not going anywhere. It is here to stay, as surely as painting, poetry, sculpture, or photography. Though gaming may change, adapt, and fractally effloresce over time, there will always be video games.

The nightmare is over, and it's time for us to wake up.

Notes

1. This mentality has a long and vicissitudinal history too complex to explore properly here, but I have made an effort elsewhere in *Lean Out: The Struggle for Gender Equality in Tech and Start-Up Culture* (published by O/R Books), edited by Elissa Shevinsky, in my essay "Fictive Ethnicity and Nerds." In brief, I argue that white male nerds have built an exclusionary culture as a way of making meaning of shared experiences of bullying in secondary school and preventing those traumas from being repeated. This vision casts feminists and women more generally as outsiders playing the role of "bullies" or "cheerleaders," and justifies attacks against them in response. Put another way, for many young men at the barricades of nerd culture, high school never ended.

Chapter **19**

Queer Gaming
Gaming, Hacking, and Going Turbo

JACK HALBERSTAM

Who Wants to Play Video Games?

In this essay I seek out the fertile overlap between animation and video gaming in terms of thinking about what queer potential hides in the realm of play. While digital worlds draw from both the elongated possibilities of animated bodies and the pliability of coded realities, we might consider the bendiness and shiftiness of both genres in terms of a queer orientation to reality that requires improvisation, physical stretching, and a recoded sense of being. Queer subjects constantly recode and, within limits, rebuild the worlds they enter. Since the world as we know it was not designed for queer subjects, then queer subjects have to hack straight narratives and insert their own algorithms for time, space, life, and desire.

Many scholars have written at length about the philosophy of play and its importance to art, to experimental thought, and to irrational human endeavor.[1] Play, in many gaming contexts, both releases players from the restrictions of everyday reality but also encourages them to think in terms of parallel worlds, extended realities, and frivolous pursuits. Indeed, we could consider the realm of video games in terms of what Joseph Roach has named as the process of *surrogation*.[2] Surrogation, which can also be thought of in terms of the relation between player and avatar, means for Roach the ways in which performance and play can bring certain "hidden transcripts" from past, present, and future to the fore. In this respect, we might think of gaming as a world where we don't just try to change *what* we think, but *how* we think. Change in the realm of the game is not just narrative shifts in terms of characters—not simply adding gay, lesbian, or trans characters—it is change at the level of codes or algorithms.

Rather than just hunting for LGBT characters in the worlds of gaming, we want to seek out queer forms, queer beings, queer modes of play. Take the character BMO from the animated television series *Adventure Time*: in one episode, s/he asks Jake and Finn to play video games with him. The game is *Conversation Parade* in which, using console technology, text on a screen, and a joystick, BMO has the radical idea that s/he wants to engage her human friends in conversations about themes like "the stars in the sky." When the bozos do not respond well, BMO shuts down. Here the concept of "engagement" or "conversation" becomes part of gaming and even represents a queer iteration of gaming. And in this instance, queer casting is certainly part of the impact of BMO: *Adventure Time*'s BMO is a computer/game console modeled on a hybrid of an early Macintosh computer and a Game Boy. BMO is neither male nor female, or rather they switch gender depending on the context in the narrative. They accompany the two friends Finn and Jake on various adventures serving as a game console, a VCR, an alarm clock, a flashlight, a toaster, and so on. BMO brilliantly captures one way of thinking about queerness in terms of function or practice rather than essence and being.

In my previous work on animation, I made the argument that CGI changed the face of animation, not simply because we shifted from 2D to 3D—since apparently most spectators do not register this shift when immersed in the film—but because the shift from analog to digital, from linear to fractal, made other stories, relations, and outcomes possible.[3] If previously, animated worlds had often featured larger animals chasing smaller ones across a still landscape (e.g., Tom and Jerry, Coyote and Road Runner, Sylvester and

Tweety), after *Toy Story* (Pixar, 1995, dir. John Lasseter) the world of objects took on a new dimension that forced us to reckon with what Haraway described many years ago as the surprising liveliness of our gadget companions. New stories in which animated creatures rose up against humans became the norm in animated films for children, from *Chicken Run* to *Monsters Inc.,* and so the archetypal story of the uncanny vividness of the creatures with whom we share the world has been upgraded for a new era of machinic fantasy. While nineteenth-century stories of lively toys by E. T. A. Hoffmann and others captured the fears aroused by a new age of industrial machines, *Toy Story* reworks that narrative for a digital age. Hoffman's stories are full of robotic dolls ("The Sandman") and dancing Christmas toys ("Nutcracker and Mouse King") that lure humans into a fantasy of lively object worlds, but the Pixar films and other CGI animation, in contrast, often play with the idea of entire universes that underpin ours. In *Monsters Inc.,* the monsters that frighten children by night are scared of the children by day. In *Robots,* a world of animated metallic robots struggles to outlive shifts in technological innovation that threaten to render them outmoded. And in *Toy Story,* the toys vie for the attention of the human who owns them / plays with them. The magic that, in the earlier productions, enchanted children and drew them into alternative realities now becomes the magic of technology, the wizardry of CGI, and the waning of any sense of the real. And it is often the magic of animation that draws young users into immersive game environments, too.

What is new about the stories that emerge from shifts in the mode of imagination from industrial to digital, from nuts and bolts in the world of lively toys to codes and algorithms in gaming worlds of intelligent avatars? And how does queer theory help us to rethink the concept of gaming, the notions of success and failure that inhere to gaming, and the relations between the player and the surrogate figure that represents the player in the game?

I believe the question of what contribution gaming might offer to queer theory requires rethinking the concept of the game, the purpose of the game, the differentials within the game between winning and losing, and the modes of identification and desire that any given game requires. And of course, we are also interested in what queer theory has to offer gaming in terms of a critique of the normative, the predictable, the stable, and the thinkable, and an embrace of the ludic and the loopy. All in all, we want to know under what conditions change can happen and does happen and what evidence it leaves and where. As theorists like Bruno Latour remind us, we often think ourselves into corners by dividing spheres of human life from one another and then naturalizing these divisions to the point that we actually believe them to be real and true.[4] Similarly, we have a tendency to stick with identity categories that we ourselves constructed and we use them to describe complex forms of life even when our embodiments, relations, intimacies, and social forms far exceed the range of those categories. So, can we also write new code for the new complexities of our worlds?

My earliest experience with gaming worlds was way back when *Sim City* first came out and I loved the idea of building a city on my own terms. I had great hopes for my own private Idaho: I imagined a city that never sleeps, where the wealth is shared, the resources are many, and the problems few. It was to be the virtual enactment of urban Zapatismo, a queer utopia, a new socialism, a paradise on earth. No doubt despite my warm and fuzzy anarchist dream, I also liked the idea of playing God, being master of my domain, and dictating reality to my Sim citizens! Well, inevitably, my Sim city was in flames almost before I had built my first neighborhood. I kept raising taxes and my citizens were not happy. I learned the hard way that good ideas on paper don't always translate into real or virtual results, and that the worlds we make are limited mostly by our ability to imagine anything different from what we already know.

Building on my own experience and feeling limited in the game by the multiple regulations that function in the real, we could ask how much "free" space there is ever in a game to change the rules of the game. And in a related question, Is there space within the game to "go wild"? A few more questions along those lines include:

1. Under what conditions can "new life" be imagined, inhabited, and enacted?
2. Where does change occur—at the level of code, environment, action, actor, imagination, relation, interaction?

3. How and when and where does heteronormativity function within any given game? When we talk about norms, are we talking about normative play, normative conception, or normative outcomes?

4. Finally, what are the possibilities for extending our understanding of queerness through games? Can the ludic offer us possibilities for thinking change that are not available in serious environments? What are the relations between the queer, the wild, and the ludic?

Wrecking/Fixing

So let's begin with an animated film about gaming that actually deals with many of the big questions about queerness and algorithms. And again, I want to access gaming through animation if only because animation is so much a part of the gaming environments and makes up a large part of their allure to children.

Wreck-It Ralph (Disney, 2012, dir. Rich Moore) is a cute film about the nature of good and evil, the definition of glitches, and the meaning of community, games, mobility, love, and loss. The basic conceit of *Wreck-It Ralph* evolves out of gaming logic: Ralph is a character in a game, situated in an arcade among other games, and his function in his game is to destroy buildings while the human/player works as quickly as possible, through an avatar named Fix-It Felix, to build up what Ralph has decimated. Within the game and among the game's characters, Felix, predictably, wins acclaim and love for his role as fixer and Ralph, equally predictably, is the game's bad guy. He is hated because he destroys for the sake of destroying, and he must learn to live with his definitional negativity. With the help of a Bad Guys Anonymous group, Ralph reconciles to the idea that you cannot change the game, and that bad guys can never be good.

In a hilarious scene where the bad guys meet and mull over the roles to which they have been assigned, the group tells Ralph that he has to accept himself and accept the role he has been given in his game: "You can't mess with the program, Ralph!" The bad guys also warn him not to "go turbo" and to fill his function in the logic of the game. While Ralph denies he is "going turbo," he also asks, "Is it turbo to want a friend or a medal or a piece of pie every once in a while?" What Ralph resists here is not simply being the bad guy but the way in which the bad guy, despite the fact that the game requires him and could not function without him, is denied any of the rewards. The game, in other words, requires both failure and negativity but it only rewards success and positivity.

Like *Toy Story,* this movie's mise-en-scène is not the day world when kids fill the arcades and play the games, but the night world of "after hours," when the characters slip through the wires to visit one another in different game environments, or else they stay put and socialize in their own game worlds. In Ralph's home turf, he is banished every night to a local dump where he must sleep among the rubble of the worlds he has destroyed and the others that have yet to be built. He is a kind of Nietzsche-like figure whose role as destroyer is constitutive of the newness to come.

Before I go further into the plot summary, it bears pointing out that the story is both highly conventional and highly innovative. It is conventional in that it imagines a world where objects come to life, and when they do they lose their status as other and seem to be just like us. It is conventional in that good and evil are set up in dialectical relations. It is conventional in its quest narrative wherein one character seeks redemption, another learns to embrace those less fortunate than himself, and still more characters are lost and saved, ruined and remade. And, on the road to ruin and mayhem, a good time and lots of life lessons are gained by one and all. Finally, it is jarringly formulaic in its hetero pairings that match Ralph (John C. Reilly) up with a glitch girl (Sarah Silverman) in a game called *Sugar Rush* and Felix (voiced by the very gay Jack McBrayer) with a tough female soldier, Sergeant Calhoun (voiced by the very gay Jane Lynch), from a first-person shooter game titled *Hero's Duty.*

But the film transcends expectations in a few ways that may be significant as we struggle to move our notions of change, queerness, and transformation beyond a quest for recognizable gay/lesbian/ trans characters on the one hand and humanitarian and nonviolent scripts on the other. And it does so mostly by scrambling the relations between good and evil, managing to animate a class critique of the distribution of good and evil across characters (Felix is born to be good: his father gave him a magic hammer / silver spoon; Ralph is born to be bad), and by recognizing that the glitch in the matrix, far from representing the evil of disorder and the site of failure, actually presents opportunities for unpredictable and improvised modes of transformative opportunity.

Queer Codes / Queer Tech

Before we turn to the "glitch" as a queer ghost in the machine, let's think about queer codes. Zach Blas has made artwork based on his idea of "queer code," and he collaborates with Micha Cárdenas to imagine and even create queer technologies that can connect queer bodies across time and space.[5] Cárdenas develops "wearable technology" that allows its bearers to access and connect with each other in public spaces, and Blas has developed the concept of "gay bombs" or activist weapons. These bombs are detonating concepts that can be dropped into discourse to create explosive reactions. They scramble history, recode the rubrics of sexuality (inclusive/ exclusive, zero/one, having/lacking, legitimate/illegitimate) and hinge on hacking into hetero-normative code to rewire realities. To theorize, Blas notes, citing Galloway and Thacker, "means writing code." And so queer theory is queer code, it breaks codes, recodes, hacks codes, drags codes.

This queer theory of queer technology invites us to think about ideologies and practices of being in terms of a new lexicon: subject/ object/abject might be now replaced with multitudes/swarms/viruses or users/players/hackers. And if rules are protocols, power morphs into control and relation becomes connection or even connectivity, then clearly what we once thought of as revolt, resistance, and rebellion now demands its own update. The computer game's inherent orientation toward winning, for example, can be and has been reimagined as a series of encounters, procedures, progressions within which, eventually, one may access a new level, but one rarely accesses anything like winning.

My book *The Queer Art of Failure,* without resorting to this new lexicon of being as playing, did recognize that social systems established around winning defined in terms of wealth, health, possessions, longevity, mobility, and access surely produce a community of people who must reside in failure in terms of their poverty, illness, ephemerality, stasis, and lack of access. Jesper Juul, in *The Art of Failure,* has observed that we surely play games in part to experience failure rather than avoid it and that this experience allows us to experiment with failure; any game developer, in other words, must develop systems that are balanced between being complex and being navigable.[6] When playing a game, one would become quickly bored by only winning or only losing and so players must fail in the game before they succeed. Play must deliver a sense of accomplishment upon winning, which means that inevitably failure must be possible at all times. Whether video games are any different in this respect from any other game I cannot say, but I remain interested in the idea that we experiment with failure in video games and that failure must be a precursor to winning if the game is to be deemed acceptably deep and challenging. In a world where we have tried to fix the game so that winners and losers become distinct populations with little overlap among their membership, a world where the losers can be winners and the winners can lose becomes appealing in a new way.

Failure is indeed an art, but for me it has been important to stress the "queerness" of the art of failure, the art of failing that depends on the resilience and fortitude of abject subjects or rejected people who turn their failure into style, to quote Quentin Crisp.[7] And this is where we return to the notion of queer code: if hetero-normativity sets up a code for blending into one's society that will be offset by a number of non-norms who fail to achieve those norms, then queer codes represent strategies to rewrite the notion of achievement altogether and to exploit the normative code in order to produce transformative possibilities, often through the act of failing. Some new games have tried to build on such insights about queerness: and so, a game or visual novel like *Analogue,* for example, or *Analogue: A Hate Story,* invites players to enter a world in the twenty-fifth century when a Korean capsule has been found drifting in space. The avatar boards the capsule and finds a series of documents and ships' log that allow the player to piece together what has happened. The narrative fragments finally cohere to tell of a patriarchal and sexist world, modeled on the medieval Joseon dynasty that has self-destructed. The player must discern what happened by navigating documents with the help of two AIs who are at war with each other and inherently unreliable as guides for the protagonist. This is an interesting game for its investigation of the coding of misogyny and for the casting of misogyny as the cause of internal collapse. It is also queer in the way it forces the "player" to collaborate with and manipulate AIs as it navigates the archive of social breakdown. Other queer games include *Gone Home*—a narrative game in which a young woman returns home to find her family gone—which is feminist in that it eschews violence for other kinds of affective experiences and proposes that the video game might be a site less to win by killing than to rethink the concept of losing/winning as the point of the video game altogether.

But other games released between 2010 and 2014 challenge the frame of the game by blending high concept with high aesthetic values. Games like *Thomas Was Alone* (2010) by Mike Bithell and *Braid* (2010) by Jonathan Blow also try to engage philosophical questions about friendship, camaraderie, and the possibilities of cooperation. And a game like *Monument Valley* (2013) by Ustwo produces puzzle scenarios that are also painterly and visually rich environments.

In *Thomas Was Alone,* for example, a series of rectangles and squares of different sizes and with different functions attempt to advance through treacherous terrain by learning what they are good at (jumping, bouncing, creating platforms, etc.) and by figuring out how to combine their skills with the skills of others. No rectangle can move through the system alone. The game, while not complicated, is imaginative and full of whimsy and melancholy. The shapes represent AIs that have been released and animated by a glitch in a computer system. As two-dimensional objects, the shapes all feel that there is another world, just out of reach, and they journey through different levels, expressing hopes and fears, dismay and exhilaration, love and loneliness.

Thomas Was Alone and these other games often read, on the surface, as very conventional plots with unconventional visual components. *Monument Valley* and *Braid,* for example, are both games that involve the rescue of a princess. And *Thomas Was Alone* opposes the loneliness of its major protagonist to the togetherness and heterosexual union of two of the shapes. But at the same time, in all of these games, the world inside the game is authenticated by a glitch, a mistake, a bug that allows for the electronic creatures to emerge or advance, shape-shift or achieve bliss.

Going Turbo

Ultimately, these games tell stories, some new, some old, with new outcomes, some different, some utopian, others catastrophic. How can we think about changing the code itself? To answer that question, we will return to *Thomas Was Alone* and *Monument Valley* via *Wreck-It Ralph*.

Ralph also finds an alternative path by virtue of a glitch. He looks for a way out of his structural positioning as wreckage by wandering out of his game world and into another one in the arcade to try to gain a medal in a first-person shooter game *Hero's Duty*. His goal is to win a medal, return as a hero, and win the trust and respect of his game world community. But when Ralph enters *Hero's Duty* he quickly finds out that the hero is not really heroic; he is just willing to sacrifice his buddies for his own medal. The revelation that heroism is a fixed outcome rather than an improvised performance of courage and self-sacrificing empathy gives Ralph the insight he needs to refuse the logic of his own game. As he turns to leave *Hero's Duty*, however, he draws out a vicious virus and a tough female soldier who chase him to the edge of that world. Ralph escapes to *Sugar Rush*, a world where cars race through a sweet terrain of treats and candy canes.

In *Sugar Rush*, Ralph meets Vanellope. Vanellope was once a great driver but the evil king of *Sugar Rush* has unplugged her from the game's central brain so that she appears as a "glitch" in the matrix rather than a real character. As a glitch, she cannot race and she becomes an outcast against whom the other game characters come to define themselves as fast, good, true, and sweet. Well, to cut a long story short, Ralph's journey has introduced a virus into *Sugar Rush* and the game, like Ralph's game, gets shut down and is under the threat of being totally destroyed. Ralph and Felix and the female soldier and Vanellope join forces against the evil king and defeat the virus and bring *Sugar Rush* back to life. The collaborative efforts to save these game worlds allow Ralph to see the good in Felix, who can fix what he can break; Vanellope recognizes that she was made a glitch, not born a glitch, and she argues for a different form of community and even for the power of the glitch; and the evil king, who had "gone turbo" and tried to change the game to his advantage by fixing it so that only he would win, has been vanquished and destroyed. By the end of the game, everyone is back in their places but everything has changed.

Embracing the Glitch

Even as *Wreck-It Ralph* seems critical of the good/bad logic of destructive Ralph versus creative Felix, it also recognizes that we cannot live without such dialectics and so, while we cannot make binary oppositions disappear, we can make community dependent on the recognition of all parts of the matrix rather than the valorization of some parts over others. We can also embrace the glitch, tear down as much as we build up, and, every once in a while, go well and truly turbo.

But how do games themselves embrace the glitch? The games I mentioned above, the melancholic *Thomas Was Alone* and the whimsical *Monument Valley* both conceive of their mise-en-scènes in terms of glitchy sequences of events that have either produced sentient AIs, in the case of *Thomas,* or staged a journey through "impossible architecture," in the case of *Monument Valley.* The princess, Ida, in *Monument Valley* is also on a quest for forgiveness, although we are not told what she must be forgiven for, and as she completes stages she is met by a genie to whom she gives gifts and receives wisdom in return.

Both of these games were critiqued in mainstream circles for being "too easy" or not competitive enough, and many reviewers added a note in their commentary on the game about how quickly they had passed through the various levels. But to approach these games only with a sense of competitive judgment or to play them against a clock is to miss their entire orientation. Both the world of *Thomas* and his geometric pals and the journey of Ida through the "sacred geometry"

offer qualitatively different experiences than immersion in a shooting game. What they offer is *wonder*, an immersive experience in
melancholia, a queer sense of time and space, and an immersion in
alternative dimensions that exceed and confound one's expectations
about virtual realities, affect, and potential.

Ida is a princess without a prince, a kingdom, or a future, and
Thomas is an AI who aspires to become an architect in order to re-
make the world that he and the others inhabit. As they search for
exit routes, the shapes in *Thomas Was Alone* also search for portals
to new worlds. The utopian potential of both games is embedded in
their movement without purpose, their aspiration without ambi-
tion, and their acceptance of the frailty of others. Both Thomas and
Ida proceed by means of multiple failures, and they seek to neither
exit the game nor wholly embrace it.

Monument Valley in particular, with its gorgeous visuals, its impossible architecture, and its staging of futility, forgiveness, and loss
can easily be read as an animated world. But as a game, it locates the
player in a very different relation to the visual than a film would.
In *Monument Valley* the player is drawn into a wondrous relation to
time and space, made to feel the slight victories of defeating gravity
and walking on walls, and must identify with the small, the insig-
nificant, the lost. And in *Thomas,* the player returns to a universe
that is not much more complicated than early games like *Pong,* which
allowed users to manipulate a "ball" with a rectangular paddle. But
the difference between those early ball games and *Thomas* lies again
in the relation to time, space, and failure. The only thing you learn in
Thomas is that to advance, you must cooperate; to exit you must work
with others; to change structures, you must dream.

Queer gaming appears in these games as a barely visible tension
between the will to advance and succeed and the recognition of other
goals. It resides in the good-enough princess—the female character
not in search of a male mate—and the neurotic and cheerful squares
who confront their limitations by joining forces with others who
have different skills. These worlds challenge us as players not in
terms of the speed with which we move through them but in relation
to our altered sense of time, space, awareness, and transformation.

Notes

1. See Ludwig Wittgenstein, *Philosophical Investigations,* trans. G. E. M. Anscombe (New York: Wiley-Blackwell, 2009); Roger Caillois, *Man, Play, and Games* (Urbana: University of Illinois Press, 2001); Johan Huizinga, *Homo-Ludens: A Study of the Play Element in Culture* (New York: Martino Fine Books, [1955] 2014); Ian Bogost, *How to Do Things with Video Games* (Minneapolis: University of Minnesota Press, 2011).

2. Joseph Roach, *Cities of the Dead: Circum-Atlantic Performance* (New York: Columbia University Press, 1996).

3. See my "Animating Revolt and Revolting Animation" in *The Queer Art of Failure* (Durham, N.C.: Duke University Press, 2011).

4. See Bruno Latour, *We Have Never Been Modern* (Cambridge, Mass.: Harvard University Press, 1993).

5. For more on Zach Blas's work see http://www.zachblas.info/.

6. Jesper Juul, *The Art of Failure: An Essay on the Pain of Playing Video Games* (Cambridge, Mass.: MIT Press, 2013).

7. Quentin Crisp, *The Naked Civil Servant* (London: Penguin, 1977), 177.

Chapter **20**

The Arts of Failure
Jack Halberstam in Conversation with Jesper Juul

MODERATED BY BONNIE RUBERG

"The Arts of Failure" session took place in October 2013 as part of the inaugural Queerness and Games Conference (QGCon). The QGCon organizers placed Halberstam and Juul in dialogue in order to explore the crossovers between their respective work theorizing failure—in both the context of games and the context of queer theory. Volume coeditor Bonnie Ruberg served as moderator. The floor was also opened to audience questions in the latter half of the session.

RUBERG: We are thrilled to have Jack Halberstam and Jesper Juul with us here. Jack is one of the most influential queer theorists working today. He is a professor at the University of Southern California and the author most recently of *The Queer Art of Failure* and *Gaga Feminism: Sex, Gender, and the End of Normal*. Jesper is one of our most influential contemporary games studies thinkers. He's currently a professor at the Royal Danish Academy of Art, and author of books like *Half-Real, The Casual Revolution,* and, most recently, *The Art of Failure*. From the similarities between the titles of Jack and Jesper's books on failure you can tell why we wanted to put these two scholars in dialogue. Despite the overlaps in their interests, Jack and Jesper have never previously spoken. Jesper's book doesn't mention Jack's. Jack's doesn't mention video games. Yet it seemed natural to explore the ways the two texts speak to each other. I'll start by giving both Jack and Jesper a few moments to introduce themselves.

HALBERSTAM: My book, which followed some of the same argumentative strands that Jesper's did, was interested in the logic of success and failure, and the way that logic constrains us to a very normative viewpoint, such that different social circumstances produce different outcomes: success or failure. So my big claim is that someone might actually want to fail, because they're so dissatisfied with a particular social context. Take the social context of capitalism, for example. If winning the game of capitalism means accumulating wealth, then it may well be that anticapitalists want to fail at that game in order to produce other ways of thinking about money, other ways of thinking about relationships through property, or possession, or whatever it may be. But if you move to the realm of heterosexuality and heteronormativity, the queer becomes the failure logic. In a homophobic logic, the queer fails to be straight, literally. The butch fails to be a woman. The sissy boy fails to be a man. The queer adult fails to get married and have children. They all fail in their socially prescribed role. There are two responses you can have to that. One is to try and play the game as it's been written, to say, "I'm sorry, I didn't realize. I will now get married and have children, and then maybe you will accept me as a success on your terms." Or you refuse the game. You say, "Actually, that outcome is not what I desire." You rewrite the game, and in the process you accept what we call failure. So, that acceptance in failure, that investment in failure, that excitement about failure, is the queer art of failure.

JUUL: My book has lots of similarities and lots of differences from Jack's. It really came from the personal experience of being a sore loser at video games. I was playing all these games, and I'd be unhappy when I played them. I felt like I was returning to games that made me unhappy, and I wondered why that was. At the same time, there's also a cultural movement around failure, a kind of self-help book attitude that says, "Actually, failing is great. Investment companies should fail fast," and all that stuff. I think that's very superficial, because failure also does hurt most of the time. I tried to look at this in a historical, aesthetical way and to look at what's called the paradox of tragedy: why we watch tragic cinema, or read tragic novels, or go to horror cinema even though it makes us uncomfortable or deeply unhappy. I looked at various historical answers to that question, but none of them quite resolved or answered it. So I tried to ask whether failure in games was in some fundamental way different from failure in nongame contexts. One of the examples I had is "gamification": the idea that you can use game structures to, say, educate students or run a company. My conclusion on this is that you can actually look at the 2008 financial crisis and say that, in a way, it was caused by making companies too much like games. You had these clear incentive structures, and if someone just approved a lot of loans, they would get huge bonuses. Then, of course, lots of companies collapsed. You can see that one of the problems is having something important that uses a gamelike structure—whereas, if you play an actual game, you have the option of denying that it's important to you. You can always say, "It's a stupid game." Games, in a way, make these kinds of arguments within themselves. The problem is, if you try to apply this approach elsewhere, you can't say, "I think this performance ratio or this score on my report card is stupid," because you would be fired or you would fail. So it's not true that there's no safe space within games. The idea of the safe space is actually pretty important, because it gives us the opportunity to deny that we care about failure. To me, that's the art of failure in video games: the opportunity for denial, even if we lie to ourselves or to other people.

RUBERG: I wonder if we can triangulate your respective positions on "the art of failure." Jesper is talking about failure in games. Jack is talking about failure in life. What happens when we bring these ideas together? Do we create a queer art of failing at video games?

HALBERSTAM: There are a lot of moments in Jesper's *Art of Failure* that are implicitly queer. It's a really great book for schematizing all the ways you might experience failure in games, and then you can extrapolate from there into other contexts. One category Jesper uses in the introduction is ahedonism. Ahedonism is the idea that humans aren't only oriented around pleasure. This idea that you want to play to win, and that only winning will do, is not simply wrong about games, it's wrong about the human. That feels to me to be a very queer insight. We could also call this a certain type of negativity, which is part of who we are.

JUUL: One similarity between the two books is a certain reluctance to only do a relabeling, to say, "Actually what we thought was failure was success, so just flip it around." What's interesting when you ask this question of games, for example if you're playing single-player games, is that people do strange things a lot of the time. They don't necessarily play for the goal, or they goof around in various ways. Then the question is: What would queer playing entail? Would it mean having a game that allows you to do non-goal-oriented things? But are you supposed to follow the game's logic or reject it? It's a hard question, because games have so many variations on the theme of failure.

HALBERSTAM: Already at this conference lots of people have been thinking through the connection between queerness and games. There's the level of character, and the way in which characters, even when you can choose different genders for them, are mostly all modeled on the heroic, lone male. Then there's something we could call orientation within the game. This might mean using a queer phenomenological approach, for example. Are we oriented in the game? Are we disoriented?

I was just watching the movie *Gravity,* and when you're watching it, especially in 3-D, you really feel like you're in a video game. You're being spun around wildly in space; you're in an antigravity context, and you're trying to propel yourself toward an object, and you may or may not make it. What is it about that experience of disorientation—which might make you nauseous, or might make you completely lose where you are in the game—that's still pleasurable? That's not necessarily connected to ahedonism, but to distinctly other forms of pleasure, not just goal-oriented, pleasure-filled, success-oriented pleasure. In fact, it might deliver you to a place of desolation or being lost, but we pursue it nonetheless. I think that's part of the appeal of this set of interests in failure. It's an irrational side of human impulse that can't be explained away by who will get this many points or who will access the next level. People repeat levels over and over and over and over again, so there's a sort of Freudian pleasure in repetition. I think both Jesper and I are opening up different ways of understanding pleasure. So, to go back to the question, queerness in games goes way beyond the character that you're playing.

RUBERG: Jesper, your book talks so much about the pain of failing at games, but it doesn't address the pleasure of failing at games. It begins to seem like masochism is an unspeakable word. What is the place of masochism in both of your thoughts on failure?

JUUL: I use the line of "pleasure spiked with pain"; that's the closest I come to talking about masochism. There's something fundamental there. I think it's very common, if you're frustrated with the game, not to lower the level of difficulty, but to keep banging your head against it—even though it's futile and you don't really expect to get any farther. It's something that also occurs in education, the idea of self-defeating behavior. If they are about to take a test or give a talk, people do strange things. You stay up all night or get drunk, then if you fail the test the next morning you don't feel so bad about it, because it's not that you're stupid, you're just hung over. Sometimes we seek out failure because, by directly seeking it out, we lessen it; we find a kind of enjoyment of it. I think the worry is that you make this a habit. You should always try to think about what really is in your own personal best interest, and not just aestheticize always being hung over when you take tests, for example, even though there's some enjoyment in that.

HALBERSTAM: The masochism question is a good one. I was also thinking about this when I was reading Jesper's book. One of the examples that comes up in the book is horror films. If we go watch horror films, we know that we're going to be shocked and terrified, and yet we go nonetheless. They don't deliver pleasure in the conventional format. The queer understanding of the horror film that's been articulated by a whole range of queer theorists is that maybe people are longing for other modes of identification. We presume that we only want to identify with the heroic male, but in fact, as Carol Clover's work has shown, lots of young men watching horror films also want to be able to identify with the victim, because it affords them a certain kind of masochistic pleasure to not always be in control. That masochistic pleasure was never considered to be part of a horror film's pleasure-scape, because we assume that we want to avoid masochistic scenarios. Bonnie, your work takes us into this territory, too. You're thinking about why we might want to desire our own unbecoming, the ways in which we desire to be undone. In Jesper's book, if you play the game and you win, you're kind of done. So masochism has been built into all of these experiences in ways that reveal some of the less obvious and less linear aspects of our pleasure centers.

RUBERG: Jack, you and I were talking about agency yesterday, and I put my foot in my mouth by saying, "I'd summarize your 'art of failure' as being about the agency of embracing self-destruction." You said, "Be careful of the word 'agency.'" I wonder how agency fits into this discussion. I do hear it in the way you both describe failure and choosing to fail.

JUUL: In my book, I'm talking about playing games that you yourself have selected. There is a kind of switch between the moment you choose to play a game and the moment you start playing it. When you start playing you are pressured to accept the logic of the game. I think I assume less agency than Jack does. In a way, what I'm saying is that even if you want to decide that you don't care about a particular failure in the game, it's not necessarily something you can control. It might have social consequences even though we might want to deny those consequences, or we might consider them irrelevant, or we might sometimes be betrayed by our own emotions. Failure in a game is subjective, but it doesn't mean that we can actually control it.

HALBERSTAM: Even though I'm talking about the embrace of failure, I'm not suggesting that it's always under our control. In fact, I'm not countering the idea that it's *not* in our control by asking that it *be* in our control. I'm pushing in the direction of undoing. I think that my book is invested in counterintuitive strategies that counteract the logic of failure without offering a new form of agency. I think that what's interesting when you enter the territory of unbecoming, you lose vocabulary, because the vocabulary available to us is much more an active doing/playing vocabulary, which makes sense given our political trajectories. So, when our political trajectory is to not become, or to not complete or to not gain, we only have these negative models. We don't have the full suite of words that we might need to explain these other forms of human experience. That's because they are counterintuitive. What I really appreciate about Jesper's book and the conversation that it opens up is the idea of a counterintuitive mode of playing that takes us to a completely different level, where we're not simply thinking about moving through the game, acquiring points, building strength, getting our health up, and completing, we're actually repeating, spinning, falling, failing, disappearing—all of these other things that offer another kind of pleasure.

AUDIENCE (KATHRYN BOND STOCKTON): Thinking about these two books together, two words that seem important to me are "accumulation" and "delay." In Jesper's work, as I understand it, inside the game there's this temporal moment, whereas Jack was talking about the long arc of these things. Like, if Jack and I were to think of ourselves in childhood failing to be boys, if someone said, "It's great, embrace that!" we'd say, "No way." But in the long arc of things, it became a great and wonderful thing. It's actually the accumulation of loss, of anti-capital, the accumulation of all these experiences over these games that adds up. In life, I don't want to fail at any particular moment: giving a talk, teaching a class, et cetera. But sometimes in the long arc of the accumulation of loss something builds through that that you then retrospectively understand as this tremendous benefit and generative aspect of failure. In *Fight Club,* the whole point is to go out and lose a fight. You really can't understand *Fight Club* without some understanding of Georges Bataille. It's this great film about masculinity, but you have to remember that the point is to lose a fight. By no version of masculinity that we generally know is that true.

HALBERSTAM: This reminds me of a line from a Julian Barnes novel, *The Sense of an Ending.* He says, when we think about profit, we think about gaining resources. Resources accumulate over time, they add up, but he says maybe loss also accumulates over time. But again, we don't know how to measure the thing that we've lost, because it's always in that negative register. So we have to think about both the fact that two negatives can make a positive (that is, over time failure could produce a different outcome than you might expect: some self-motivation or the becoming of something else entirely) and the fact that we need to reckon with what it means to accumulate loss over time. That's a model of history. It's a model of being. It's a critique of capital. It's a way of thinking about being in relationship to losing that might be useful here. What are these games that we're supposed to lose, when losing doesn't necessarily mean the elimination of the player? What other models of losing would be enticing or interesting or not interesting? I don't just mean this as a nice little tidy model of giving yourself up for others, a sacrifice message. Maybe we can think of some more complex reasons to design games where the only outcome is losing.

JUUL: I think that's a great point. There are certain preestablished models for failing. On paper they seem like failure, but they're actually great things. The prescribed versions seem safe and worthwhile, but that's not how you want to actually see it happen.

HALBERSTAM: Jesper, you gave the example of corporations that turn failure into self-help. What we learned in the last financial crisis is that those bad mortgages were designed to fail. They weren't designed to succeed. They certainly weren't designed to be an avenue to success. The person who gets the loan will fail, at which point the insurance company kicks in. So there's failure built in. We have to find a way around that logic, too, otherwise you just keep yourself hemmed into a normative structure, where it will always win and you will always lose. At the same time, I'm thinking about the radical theory of indebtedness as a different form of community. It's not just a community where we all support one another, but where we recognize mutual indebtedness that we owe—not that we gain, but that we owe. Failure doesn't necessarily open us up to freedom, but to degrees of freedom. When you read Jesper's book, you have this sense that there are little tiny pockets, these moments that open up in a game, but that they never give you the wide open feeling of freedom, which of course is just a fantasy anyway. There are moments where the game has shifted, or your loss has revealed something else. Maybe this notion of freedom is as good as we're going to get.

AUDIENCE (ADRIENNE SHAW): Chris Paul, at Seattle University, writes about the myth of meritocracy in games—this idea that anyone can succeed in games, as long as you set the level right for you—and how that belies the history of how people get involved in games in the first place. You can't just pick up any old game and suddenly succeed at it. It's a kind of hegemony, this idea that if you try hard you can succeed, and if you didn't you just didn't try hard enough, as opposed to the idea that the game is not set up for you. Hearing you both talk, I wonder if there is some connection between failure and meritocracy you might speak to.

JUUL: It's interesting, because that has changed a lot over time in video games. In my book, I have this quote from a British game developer who talks about how, in the 1980s when he made games, game designers weren't even expected to be able to complete the games they made themselves. They just assumed that eventually somebody would do it. These days I think that games come with a much stronger promise that you will be able to finish them than they used to. Some people feel that that's bad. I think that demonstrates one of the things that's hard to pin down about games. Is it boring that everyone can complete a game, or is inclusivity a good thing? It can be both at the same time. It's hard to say what the answer should be.

"The Arts of Failure" session concluded with a recap of the threads and themes that emerged in the conversation between Halberstam and Juul. Importantly, both speakers had argued for reimaging the notion of goals in games and for opening up alternative ways of understanding pleasure as a function of play. Also notable was their focus on ideas of loss as accumulation, disorientation, and the potential for a queer phenomenology in video games.

Chapter **21**

"I Wouldn't Even Know the Real Me Myself"
Queering Failure in *Metal Gear Solid 2*

JORDAN YOUNGBLOOD

This essay seeks to build on the recent work on video game failure established by Jesper Juul in his 2013 book *The Art of Failure: An Essay on the Pain of Playing Video Games,* marking gaming as a medium uniquely driven by and constructed through failure. Namely, Juul addresses how (and why) players subject themselves to the process of losing to, getting frustrated at, and ultimately overcoming the various systems and rulesets of games. However, Juul's reading of failure is driven primarily by viewing it as a game-play mechanic to be overcome. He relegates its thematic utilization mostly to the tragic element of forcing the player to witness the death of her protagonist outside of her specific control.[1] In defining failure in games primarily as a temporary negative affective experience predominantly characterized by loss at both the narrative and ludic levels, we lose the larger potentiality of failure defined by Jack Halberstam in his *The Queer Art of Failure* as a way of achieving "more creative, more cooperative, more surprising ways of being in the world."[2] While Halberstam never mentions games specifically, if we take his nascent work on low theory—a model of inquiry that examines texts such as CGI children's movies, stoner comedies, and other nontraditional cultural texts for their "strange and anticapitalist logics of being and acting and knowing"—and begin to apply it to understanding the distinct role of failure specifically within games, we gain a new means of finding what Halberstam terms the "covert and overt queer worlds" within media, which can also be applied to Juul's concepts of failure in gaming.[3]

In essence, I offer failure as an expansion to the analytical model put forth in Mia Consalvo and Nathan Dutton's 2006 article "Game Analysis: Developing a Methodological Toolkit for the Qualitative Study of Games." Citing the fact that the majority of gaming articles that undertook critical analysis of games offered little insight into their techniques "other than the assumption that they were played and carefully thought about by the author," Consalvo and Dutton establish a four-part analytical model that steps through such concepts as the inventory of objects within the game, the interface presented to the player for engaging with a digital world, the interactions allowed between characters and objects, and a final, rather sprawling category deemed "Gameplay Log." Consalvo and Dutton define the "Gameplay Log" as "the overall 'world' of the game and the emergent gameplay that can come into being . . . [including] such things as emergent behavior or situations, the larger game world or system, and intertextuality as it is constituted with the game."[4] It is seen as the "coherence" category, meant to tie together potentially disparate findings in the previous three categories. By contrast, let us attempt to deploy failure as a usefully *incoherent* means of finding coherence, a thematic tie that weaves together game play and narrative not to bring about player improvement but to unsettle her worldview.

To do this, I focus here on a text repeatedly marked by failure: the 2001 game *Metal Gear Solid 2: Sons of Liberty* (hereafter *MGS2*) for the PlayStation 2 console, published by Konami and developed by Kojima Productions. In particular, I want to look at how the player character of Raiden becomes a locus of failure. He is a character designed in part to be a vessel of acceptable player loss, one who endures the tribulations of numerous heteronormative systems, which both enact violence on him and fail to properly incorporate him. Within both the story line and the game-play mechanics, he is habitually situated as "other," unsuccessful, naïve, and ultimately subjected to a series of events that disrupt the categories of masculine behavior and nationalized identity. Raiden's failure is not limited to discrete instances, as *MGS2*'s story line and game-play scenario regularly subject both Raiden and the player to sequences of powerlessness and defeat. Ultimately, these sequences are not "overcome" but rather woven into a more disruptive consideration of player agency, societal expectations, and the "reality" identity. Raiden, then, becomes a sort of case study for what a more robust definition of analyzing game failure can provide, and the level at which these "covert and overt queer worlds" exist within even high-budget games from major publishers.

In defining game failure, Juul breaks down various experiences of failure in different games, ultimately determining that the process of failing is a carefully constructed balance between winning and losing which "forces us to reconsider what we are doing, to learn."[5] This language of "learning," of a productive end, is crucial to Juul's overall project. To fail is a discrete, specific event, eventually—or ideally—overcome by the player figuring out how to defeat the given challenge. This is even the case in games that have story lines where the protagonist fails, as the player must have shown proficiency in leading the game's plot to that moment; as Juul puts it, this is the "successful player and unsuccessful protagonist" setup, where "the player is happy to have successfully overcome failure and played the game to completion, but where (this being a tragedy) the protagonist is correspondingly *un*happy."[6] In his model, a proper playable experience of game failure must inevitably bring about the happiness and the wholeness of the player in the end; games are ultimately safe spaces where we "can struggle with our failures and flaws. This illusive space of games is to be protected, but it must come with license to be just a little angry, and more than a little frustrated, when we fail."[7] For Juul, the question is always *when* the specific act of failing occurs. This sets up the idea of an inevitable "after," when success returns.

Juul's concept of games as safe spaces to fail and inevitably succeed—even in the act of the main character losing—is one that could be usefully reimagined through Halberstam's work on failure in other cultural mediums. In *The Queer Art of Failure,* Halberstam constructs an entire reevaluation of failure that rejects it as purely a speed bump toward mastery and suggests that queer theory embrace the chance "to fail, to make a mess, to fuck shit up, to be loud, unruly, impolite, to breed resentment, to bash back, to speak up and out, to disrupt, assassinate, shock, and annihilate."[8] Halberstam's is a text built around turning the language so often used to ridicule queer life: a "failure" of adhering to social norms and achieving expectations of success. Rather than a dreaded process, failure serves as a way of being that confronts norms of human behavior, subverts the narrative of "growing up," and destabilizes systems of hierarchical knowledge like the university, reproduction, and anthropocentrism, among others: an experience that can "poke holes in the toxic positivity of contemporary life."[9] The role of low theory within this model is identifying unexpected and often overlooked texts that represent "failures." It is not a process meant to solidify but rather to unhinge, reading failure as not just a particular conquered moment within a text but a repeatedly subversive undercurrent.

To explore the possibilities of reading these undercurrents within games, I turn now to *MGS2.* As is apt for a chapter about failure, to even begin to explain the overarching *Metal Gear Solid* plotline is itself a recipe for disaster. Notorious for its repeated double twists, identity confusions, and timeline-leaping plot structure, Hideo Kojima's series about an American agent code-named Solid Snake and his adventures saving the world has become almost as famous for its wildly ambitious storytelling conceits as its game-play mechanisms. While 1998's *Metal Gear Solid* focuses entirely around Solid, *MGS2* splits its attention between two protagonists: Solid and a brand-new character named "Raiden," a young soldier trained primarily through computer simulation. However, Raiden's appearance was a decidedly unexpected one in 2001, due to the fact that his presence wasn't announced prior to the game's release and that he *completely* replaces Solid as a playable option once he appears.

An outraged fan base had to come to terms with the fact that the titular hero of the series had been removed from their control. Compared to the cigarette-smoking, gruff-voiced, absurdly phallic Solid Snake, Raiden is naïve, repeatedly mistaken, and decidedly less masculine in appearance. Rob Gallagher, in his own reading of sexuality in the *Metal Gear* series, notes how player complaints about Raiden "repeatedly took the form of homophobic slurs, which drew on the tradition of associating queer sexualities with impersonation, repetition, sterility, and inauthenticity."[10] Such readings did not simply come from the fans, however; depicted as slender, smooth-featured, and with long blond hair, Raiden is repeatedly suggested throughout the narrative to fail to be a "proper" man. He is first introduced *as* "Snake," only to remove his mask and have his blond hair cascade out in the sunlight—a betrayal of expectations that marks the player reactions Gallagher discusses. Numerous references are made to his hair possibly being a wig, and one particular scene opens with the president grabbing Raiden's crotch to verify his identity, saying with a stunned tone, "You're . . . a man?"

These apparent failures of living up to gendered expectations are layered into how Raiden was initially designed in terms of game play: as a lesser reflection of Snake that allowed players to experience failure without feeling they, *too*, hadn't lived up to being a tough, manly dude. Kojima made this explicit in a 2012 interview with the British Academy of Film and Television Arts, where he explained Raiden's origins:

> If you recall, back in the days of *Metal Gear Solid 2*, when Raiden was the main character in a stealth game he wasn't all that popular. And originally the reason I did that was because if you're playing this legendary character like Solid Snake and you're a new player playing the game and you die it just doesn't make sense storywise. Why would this legendary, super-powerful character die in the first few moments of the game? And so that's why I created Raiden, so Snake was kind of like the character that you look up to, he was the hero, but Raiden was the new guy and new players could play Raiden and it would make sense that they weren't the ultimate bad-ass.[11]

To use Kojima's logic, Raiden was designed to be a less intimidating, more acceptable place to fail. Raiden at once affirms the apparent superiority of the masculine construction of Solid Snake as "hero" while giving new players a playable character that doesn't exert the same pressure to uphold "badassness" in their own play. Badasses, apparently, do not fail like Raidens do; what would not make "narrative sense" on a grizzled veteran suddenly becomes feasible when inflicted on his feminized counterpart.

Yet I do not want to argue that Raiden exists solely as a laughing stock, or a sort of emasculated whipping boy meant purely to prop up Solid Snake as a "real" man. As Gallagher notes, even Solid Snake's own masculinity is a slippery construct, given that his presence in *MGS2* means he failed to stay with the woman he saved in the first game.[12] In fact, the apparently "solid" ground of gender identity and sexuality in *MGS2* is habitually shown to be incoherent, laden with mistakes, and prone to queerly resonant disruption. The first boss in the game is a woman with close-cropped hair and hairy armpits whom Solid Snake assumes to be a man at first, and is later found out to take on the role of a ninja played by a man in the first game; a primary antagonist is named "Vamp" not because of a fixation on blood, but because he is bisexual; even Emma, the game's most prominent damsel in distress, is primarily interested not in Raiden but in her stepbrother, Otacon—who abandoned her in part because he was carrying on an affair with his stepmother. The game is laden with nontraditional sexualities and gender performances, and Raiden is placed center stage as the most prominent manifestation of them.

By not only aligning him with these larger disruptive patterns of gender and sexual identity performance but also deliberately placing the player in his shoes, *MGS2* utilizes Raiden's queerness to create a perceptible rift in the game's structure, pointing to its constructed nature within a narrative that is ostensibly all about the importance of personal freedom and the ways in which the fear of "failure" is deployed as a means of establishing boundaries for behavior and identity. Raiden's story line is built primarily around this very question of control and agency, as he is revealed to be a test dummy originally put through a series of VR test missions that were re-creations of Solid Snake's past. His behavior and attitude are constructed in the image of a masculine hero, and like the player, his expectations of the mission are built entirely out of having run repeatedly through simulations of the events of the first game. Even the format and style of the game's interface is decidedly reminiscent of the first game, with Raiden utilizing a small radar map at the top right corner of the screen to help discern enemy location, visibility, and room layout. This map seems to offer on the screen-by-screen level a sense of orientation, allowing the player to feel in control of knowing where various bodies are and how to escape past them. Yet such moment-to-moment control does not extend to Raiden; on a narrative level, he is repeatedly lied to, deceived, manipulated, and abused by the various factions within the game's story line. Raiden does not *win* so much as *endure* the game, and this experience carries over to the player as well. As Tanner Higgin notes, "The player is supposed to be confused and frustrated by the narrative's delivery. She is not only told she is being controlled but she is meant to feel and intuit it."[13] Instead of Juul's model of increasing mastery, even the best players of *MGS2* may discover themselves lacking any real control over the game, no matter how well they can navigate the playable scenarios.

Indeed, Higgin's comments on how Raiden is "revealed as a gamer who generates valuable simulation data with each press of the button for the surveilling game technology" affirm *MGS2*'s efforts to have the player recognize something of herself in Raiden—and it is not the illusion of control.[14] The player, like Raiden, is essentially a trained reflection of past actions who wields limited power—and by the end of the game, even Solid Snake is left tied up, captured, and largely at the mercy of fate. Much of *MGS2* revolves around ripping down the idea of an "original," leaving instead a series of actions that add up to an identity; in one conversation between Raiden and his girlfriend / mission partner Rose, who contacts him periodically throughout the game, she directly questions him about the "real you" of his identity. His reply—"I wouldn't even know the real me myself"—is a decidedly Butlerian evaluation of how player, character, and social conditioning collide into a mishmash of "real" selves. All the efforts to ground the narrative in a "natural" foundation of performance and identity turn into an ever more tenuous grasp for both player and character on what constitutes such foundations to begin with; an exasperated call from Raiden to Rose late in the game claiming that the whole mission feels "like a nightmare you can't wake up from" is met with a rather stark reminder of the "real" world's own terrors: "Raiden, this is real. And that's why you won't wake up." His failure to become Solid Snake echoes the nightmarish impossibility of any performance ever truly "becoming" the model it follows.

In the midst of this nightmarish repetition, one particular distorted reflection of the first game has a decidedly queer resonance, in terms of both game play and narrative structure. Late in the game, Raiden is captured and placed in a torture device, where he is interrogated about the purpose of his mission. The sequence is a deliberate throwback to a scene in the first *Metal Gear Solid,* where Solid Snake is also captured and strapped into a similar device. Yet a few elements are decidedly different. In the first game, the sequence serves as a test of Solid Snake's manhood and is directly linked to the survival of his love interest, Meryl. The player must tap a button in rapid succession in order to endure being electrocuted; at any time, she may press a button to submit, but this ensures Meryl will die at the end of the game. Meryl is essentially marked off as a reward for properly "winning" the sequence, and Solid Snake's later reaction to finding her dead is largely a reflection of both his own masculine agency and the player's apparent skill level at enduring the button-mashing challenge.[15] As he says while grieving in front of her corpse in the "submit" path, "I gave in to my pain. I sold your life to save my own. I'm a loser . . . I'm not the hero you thought I was." Being a loser, a failure, means being cut off from a "heroic" title and the reward that comes along with it.

In *MGS2,* however, there is no "win" or "lose" scenario meant to affirm or shame a particular style of play. Instead, the sequence revolves entirely around powerlessness. Unlike Solid Snake, who gets to keep his pants on in the machine, Raiden is stripped naked, beaten, and choked with a large phallic tentacle until he is left on the table largely without questions to answer; as one character notes, "I doubt he knows anything of interest." It is on this table, too, that his "true" history is revealed: rather than an innocent American boy, Raiden was a child soldier from Liberia known as "Jack the Ripper," forced to kill as a child and later growing up to psychically block out the traumatic memories of his youth. Having been stripped bare both mentally and physically, the newly exposed Raiden is forced to navi-

gate the next section of the game naked while running around holding his genitals. The usual control mechanics of punching, shooting,
and evading are compressed down to a rather awkward cartwheel,
and if his enemies locate Raiden, he will very likely die quickly in a
gunfight as he is unarmed.

Rather than a conquering narrative of heteronormative male victory, with the "loser" left to feel guilty, *MGS2* turns its torture scene
into an open invocation of masochism. With Raiden at his most
overtly eroticized and vulnerable, both physically and emotionally,
the player must confront the reality of lacking full control—even
if they must eventually shore up this exposure by restoring Raiden
back to the "wholeness" of his costume. And as with masochism, this
apparent pain is not without pleasure as well; the player is habitually
welcomed to look at and observe Raiden's exposed body, and even
use it as a desirable object for enemies to look at. If the player manages to lure a guard back to the torture chamber and act as if Raiden
is still properly locked within the device, the guard will take a glance
down at Raiden's genitals and remark "Wish *I* had that" before walking away—a decidedly homoerotic double entendre of penis envy
and erotic possession that openly taunts the player with what they
may potentially want to see, to "have," as well, since what the guard
can see is covered up by a soda can in the player's view. Teased at
every corner and left hanging, so to speak, the player must make
something out of their powerlessness while waiting for the game to
eventually hand the illusion of control back to them—a rather notable twist on the usual narrative of a player gaining more control as
the game comes to an end.

However, *MGS2* even disrupts this "restoration," as the one aspect
that has kept Raiden largely linked to a heteronormative image—his
relationship with Rose—is subsequently stripped away post-torture.
In one of the game's most powerfully queer moments, a startling
heart-to-heart between Raiden and Rose reveals an unexpected
resonance: their relationship is a direct correlation to the game's
other systems of control, and was nothing more than an artificial
assemblage of sexual expectations he was "meant" to feel. She is, in
fact, a spy meant to inspire him to keep moving through the game's
narrative and monitor his performance; her role as the mission data

collector—that is, the game's save files—holds particular resonance in light of this, suggesting both her control over Raiden's game-play history throughout each level and his personal history through being linked to her. Once again, the "real"—history, memory, even something as apparently natural as attraction—is collapsed, as she tells him, "I reinvented myself to suit your tastes. Hairstyle, clothes, the way I move, things I talked about . . . You say you love the color of my hair, my eyes. They're not even real." Raiden's eventual response, claiming that the relationship "was just a game, not the real thing," is at once a clear metatextual reference to their love being "just" virtual within the game's code while also peeling back the constructed artificiality of seemingly "natural" sexual connections between individuals.

If Raiden earlier realized he "wouldn't even know the real me myself," here he articulates the even further distortion and inaccessibility of a "real me" through its adaptation and adherence to the expectation of another person's "real" self: "I was trying to be someone I wasn't by loving what wasn't real." Even Kojima's specific choice of names—Jack and Rose being the doomed, idealized lovers of James Cameron's 1997 blockbuster film *Titanic*—once again points to the always-already fictionalized, unreal nature of heteronormative relationships that attempt to hide their own construction. Raiden's queer failure to "grow up" from his past as Jack the Ripper and "win" a proper masculine role in fact exposes an even deeper destabilization: a system that, in failing to properly incorporate him, ends up exposing the tenuous gamed structure of virtual gendered rules that govern bodies both inside and outside digital worlds. Whereas Juul argues that "much of the positive effect of failure comes from the fact that we can learn to escape from it, feeling more competent than we did before," *MGS2* disrupts the whole idea of escape altogether and turns failure into the result of an endlessly nested Foucauldian series of controlling systems that are suddenly made manifest to both Raiden and the player.[16]

Thus it is unsurprising the game's previous symbol of order and discipline, Raiden's military commander (and father figure to Solid Snake in the previous game), known as the Colonel, begins to come unhinged as these systems become visible in the game's plotline, issuing him an unexpected command: "Raiden, turn the game console off right now! The mission is a failure! Cut the power right now!"[17] While the commander wants to keep this as a singular incident, *a* failure that concludes when the simulation ends, I would argue *MGS2*'s mission *is* failure: failure of histories, failure of "natural" relationships, and even the failure of a game to "end" and the real world to begin. Despite the Colonel reassuring the Raiden/player hybrid, "Don't worry, it's a game! It's a game just like usual," the damage has already been done, and the boundaries between player and game openly subverted. Gallagher, in his overall analysis of the series, notes that the *Metal Gear* protagonists often "fail at failure"; they save the day despite themselves, stumbling into victory.[18] Yet the traces of those failures, even if reconfigured into a seeming victory, remain visible, and the ability to discern these traces as not merely game-play obstacles or tragic footnotes in the midst of player success provides us an understanding of *MGS2* that does indeed contain queer worlds within. Other such worlds exist within gaming, and playing with an eye for failure may lead us to stumble on them— with no desire to get back out and "succeed."

Notes

1. Jesper Juul, *The Art of Failure: An Essay on the Pain of Playing Video Games* (Cambridge, Mass.: MIT Press, 2013).

2. Jack (Judith) Halberstam, *The Queer Art of Failure* (Durham, N.C.: Duke University Press, 2011), 2–3.

3. Ibid., 21.

4. Mia Consalvo and Nathan Dutton, "Game Analysis: Developing a Methodological Toolkit for the Qualitative Study of Games," *Game Studies* 6, no. 1 (2006): http://gamestudies.org/0601/articles/consalvo_dutton.

5. Juul, *Art of Failure,* 122.

6. Ibid., 93.

7. Ibid., 124.

8. Halberstam, *Queer Art of Failure,* 110.

9. Ibid., 3.

10. Rob Gallagher, "No Sex Please, We Are Finite State Machines: On the

Melancholy Sexlessness of the Video Game," *Games and Culture* 7, no. 6 (2012): 406.

11. "Hideo Kojima: 25 Years of *Metal Gear Solid*," *GamesIndustry International*, October 1, 2012, http://www.gamesindustry.biz/articles/2012-10 -01-hideo-kojima-25-years-of-metal-gear-solid.

12. Gallagher, "No Sex Please," 406.

13. Tanner Higgin, "'Turn Off the Game Console Right Now!': War, Subjectivity, and Control in *Metal Gear Solid 2*," in *Joystick Soldiers: The Politics of Play in Military Video Games*, edited by Nina B. Huntemann and Matthew Thomas Payne (New York: Routledge, 2010), 253.

14. Ibid., 255.

15. The game also takes pains to remind the player to do this task "honestly"; the torturer, Revolver Ocelot, notes that if the player uses a turbo controller to make the button pressing easier to complete, "he'll know." The gesture is in fact a bluff, but it once again enforces the game's suggestion that individual prowess is valued above all.

16. Juul, *Art of Failure*, 45.

17. The Colonel's connection to Foucault and power is heightened by a later line in the game, where it is revealed that he is in fact a computer simulation developed in part by Raiden's own mind: "GW was most likely stimulating cortical activity in the dormant part of your brain through signal manipulation of your own nanomachines. The Colonel is in part your own creation, cobbled together from expectation and experience." He is a self-created system of control, ensuring the player follows directions even without a "real" commander giving the orders.

18. Gallagher, "No Sex Please," 406.

Part V   QUEER FUTURES FOR GAMES

Chapter **22**

If Queer Children Were a Video Game

KATHRYN BOND STOCKTON

Video Games: (No) Promo Homo

Does the domain of video games promote the values of "homosexuality"? Broadly "yes," and narrowly "no." This is not a matter of sexual sameness. This is an issue of expanding strangeness, tying the idea and practice of gaming (video, digital gaming) to queerness—in the sense of strangeness—a queerness deeply tethered to children, who are us.[1]

Fellow gamers of the digital age, don't kid yourselves. I am a queer child and so are you, whoever you are, however you were raised.[2] And we're getting fat—without getting heavy. You and I are *virtually* spreading sideways, not growing up but getting horizontalized by our love of lateral growth, as we indulge in alluring virtualities: things that are actual "in effect not in fact." (Literature, cinema, and of course gaming.) Indeed, from my childhood, I have kept alive a playful, fantasmatic, virtual pastime. (View it as the inverse of *Angry Birds*: not shooting figures but giving rise to them.) I like to call it "Femmes at the Mall." You know what I do: hit a shopping center and imagine that every appealing woman who presents as feminine is a femme lesbian, until proven otherwise. Since I never test them, they are not disproven. And, therefore, due to this generous practice, the world is virtually full of lesbians, thanks to me.

Thanks have not arrived. As our culture cozies up to gayness, making a space for same-sex worship of babies and marriage, gaming highlights two queer fires that are burning brightly, two queer fires that lick around the child, that queer the child, that heat adult and child—not, however, to everyone's delight. These flames can be called *lateralization* and *jouissance*. Or, to simplify: growing sideways (lateralization) and painful over-pleasure (jouissance). (Jouissance, in fact, is the pleasure in excess associated with sexual orgasm's "little death": a pleasure that is pushing into joyful pain.)[3] Or, to jump the gun with an equation you'd never, ever guess:

Queer Child + Big Toe = Candy ~ Gaming

Try to puzzle that. Indeed, we will. But let me state my thesis on the way to this puzzle (how could an essay on gaming lack puzzles?). The queer child shows how adult/child lateralization does not equate with sameness. Not with sexual sameness, as I've stated, and not with adult/child equalization. (Our legal system, at the very least, prevents these categories from becoming equalized.) Rather, adult/child lateralization, or adult/child sideways relations, as I prefer to call them, intensifies children as our radical self-differentiations, our differentiating from *our selves*, or so it feels, in the "childish" pursuit of jouissance, which can come through gaming. Let me start explaining by returning to gayness.

Lateralization, jouissance: before the rise of gaming, as we know it now, "homosexuality" was accused of both. Gays were profoundly lateralized; were said to suffer "arrested development," being "ill in much the same way a dwarf is ill": or, as a psychoanalyst said, "most homosexuals do not feel like adults; rather they see themselves as children or as adolescents," sexually *extending* beyond copulation (if you know what I mean) or *lingering* at midpoints along the way, producing sideways movements or delays.[4] Even more perversely, grown homosexuals didn't birth children, it was assumed, but surely seduced them, making child seduction, which was a dangerous lateralization, their stock in trade. All these assumptions, funny enough, fed the public imagination of gay life as a wild hedonism, truly over-pleasure, painful in its excess.[5] Thus, as I'm rather fond of saying: no one—not even right-wing wing nuts—has been deeming queerness unnatural. They've deemed it *hyper*-natural—everybody's going gay, if we let them—because it's seemed like seductive cheating to live our lives (childish, child-free, soaked in pleasure).

I repeat these accusations, which sound almost quaint, at least in our land, in our own time, because they are sliding, have slid, onto gaming. Gaming is the new "homosexuality," strange to say? Gaming is the new dangerous hedonism? The new domain of later-alization and jouissance? I take as an index two different pieces of sophisticated journalism (so it would seem) from *The Atlantic* (April 2013) and the *New York Times* (April 2012). In the *Times* piece, titled complainingly "Just One More Game . . . How Time-Wasting Video Games Escaped the Arcade, Jumped into Our Pockets and Took Over Our Lives," the author boldly confesses his bewilderment over his attraction to wasteful "stupid games" such as *Tetris, Bejeweled,* and *Drop7.*

"You could say," he says, "that video games and I went through adolescence together," after which he gave them up, becoming "more or less happy and productive." Then came the iPhone during adult-hood, due to which "my inner 13-year-old reasserted himself," as he moved from chess ("the PBS of time-wasters") into *Bix, MiZoo, Tiny Wings,* "designed to be played . . . by any level of player." Lateraliza-tion. Moreover, he writes, "[I was playing] when I should have been doing dishes, bathing my children, conversing with relatives. . . . The game was an anesthetic, an escape pod, a snorkel, a Xanax, [and] a dental hygienist with whom to exchange soothingly meaning-less banter before going under the pneumatic drill of Life." And he spread this "virus" (his word) to other friends, even to his wife. The article ends with the author consulting *Drop7*'s creator, Frank Lantz, who also directs NYU's Game Center. *Unlike* the author, Lantz sees these games as some kind of "hinge" between the mathematical and the spiritual, holding us, in the author's words, "between conscious problem-solving and pure intoxication." Or in Lantz's words, they're "like heroin that is abstracted or compressed or stylized": "It gives you a window into your brain that doesn't crush your brain." In fact, the piece ends, reaches its climax, reaching for a word that stops shy of "crushing." Lantz describes his own heroin-like connection to poker: "Somehow teetering on the edge was part of the fun for me. It was like a tightrope walk between this transcendently beautiful and cerebral thing . . . at the same time it was pure self-destruction."[6] Lantz says no word exists in English for this combination. Then he says it's "game"—the article's last word. Many queer theorists would say it's "jouissance." I say it's "big toe." Maybe even "candy."

Which takes us to the other kind of article I've seen, also driven by adult fantasies of normal productivity and not wasting time. This piece is titled "The Touch-Screen Generation: What's This Technology Doing to Toddlers' Brains?" The title could have been, might as well be, "Are We Giving Heroin to Touch-Screen Kids?" Lateralization and jouissance together haunt this query. Are we making children too much like us, this piece worries—making them drugged-out, pleasure-seeking hounds, and therefore too adult in their wasteful bliss? (Give yourself a moment to absorb these contradictions. We who are too childish, when it comes to games, are making kids adult in allowing childish pleasure.) Consider the complaints of a worried father, himself a reporter for the *Wall Street Journal,* who describes his toddler joyfully "zoning out" with the iPad: "He'd gone to this state where you'd call his name and he wouldn't respond . . . or you could snap your fingers in front of his face"; the dad removed the iPad from the child's life, "even though [the iPad] was the only thing that [held] the boy's attention for long periods, and . . . spark[ed] an interest in numbers and letters."[7] Another contradiction emerges from these comments and sticks to the article. Namely, this: in naming these kids "the touch-screen generation," the author is revealing a countervailing worry that these children do *not* reproduce us. In fact, this common move—of tagging generations with some new label (the Millennials, Generation X, etc.)—is a recognition that those who reproduce differentiate themselves from themselves through these estrangements (of the generations), making "reproduction" a striking misnomer for those bundles of queerness called children.

Still, this piece requires our surprise over what's growing apart on our sides. This is a cadre of children—really, infants—who view iPads as "so many open boxes of candy." (Hold that thought.) Or, as the essay's author puts it, "Kids, who once could be counted on only to chew on a square of aluminum, are now engaging with it in increasingly sophisticated ways"; "American childhood has undergone a somewhat alarming transformation in a very short time." We might wonder, isn't it always transforming alarmingly, according to "adults"? Indeed, right on cue is what you would expect: "American parents are becoming more, not less, wary of what [technology] [is] doing to their children." Hence, "our modern fear . . . that every minute of enrichment lost or mindless entertainment indulged will add up to some permanent handicap in the future."[8] Is sophistication *or* mindless entertainment seducing willing children? Which do parents fear?

Actually, protection talk—we must protect our children from this or that seduction—shows we actually fear our *children*. The author confesses, "I must admit, it was eerie to see a child still in diapers so competent and intent, as if he were forecasting his own adulthood. Technically, I was the owner of the iPad, but in some ontological way, it felt much more his than mine." Or as Marc Prensky, education and technology writer, has put it, "the war is over, the natives won"— "the digital natives," his term for children. And if parents ("digital immigrants") are desperate to deem certain games "education," it may be in defense against the jouissance that makes children harder to control. Apps like *Toca Tea Party* and *Toca Hair Salon*—that indulge the joys of spilling and cutting—are "not about beauty," says the author, "but . . . subversion" and are wildly popular (downloaded more than a million times in the first week). The upshot is this: the author ends up giving in on lateralization *and* jouissance, on the logic "I like" "high quality fun," "shouldn't they?"[9] This is mild wording for what the piece has raised, matched by the author's forcing a Norman Rockwell reference in her last sentence to put to bed the issues her essay doesn't solve.

What is our reply to "Video Games: (No) Promo Homo"? A simple equation:

Queer Child + Big Toe = Candy ~ Gaming

Children Show Big Toe

Perhaps we need to unpack the joy of destruction more decidedly, even playfully. Candy and gaming require we do so. Here, the big toe enters the scene. According to the thinking of Georges Bataille, the big toe, specifically, is the most human part of the body. What the apes don't have; what allows us to stand erect, with our heads toward the clouds but our feet in the mud. It's what shows us that "human life entails . . . a back and forth movement from refuse to the ideal and the ideal to refuse."[10] On the night I receive the Nobel Prize in Literature, I have the runs. My own body wars against my dignity. And makes me crave extremity, which can feel like ecstasy. Just think of Icarus.

Many children know the myth of Icarus and his father, Daedalus. In order to enable their escape from capture on the island of Crete, Daedalus designed for them feathery wings, held together by wax. And though he warned his child not to fly too close to the sun, lest the sun melt the wax, Icarus, filled with the thrill of flying, flew too close and fell from the sky. Presumably, we are told this myth about a youth, especially in our youth, so as to cultivate a sense of moderation. Listen to your parents: don't fly high. Bataille sees a different point. He sees the need to embrace both acts: the flying and the falling. Here we may recall Frank Lantz lauding gaming's tightrope, involving something transcendently beautiful and purely self-destructive. Bataille would further emphasize: Extremity is within you. It's not "out there" in gaming. There's no escaping your own big toe.

This ecstatic state relates to how Bataille backs nonproductivity, which he links to luxury. He understands it as pleasurable loss. His strange essays, aptly named *Visions of Excess,* are gnarled contemplations on extreme pleasure and debasement; they are queer theory before queer theory. With his cryptic titles—"Mouth," "Rotten Sun," "The Big Toe," "Solar Anus"; with his yokings of extreme expenditures to the force of political rebellions, comparing a volcano, which he deems an anus, to the "scandalous eruption" of workers fighting against their masters; with his fixation on an ape's bottom, saying to us, "There is no child who has not . . . admired . . . these filthy protuberances, dazzlingly colored excremental skulls . . . going from shocking pink to an extraordinarily horrible . . . violet"; with this kind of ferment, Bataille stands against what he calls "the principle of classical utility": taking one's "pleasure" in "moderate form" (which he scorns) while one aims at the "acquisition," "conservation," and "reproduction" of goods and life (which he scorns).[11] By contrast, Bataille prefers any outlay of money or energy or even life itself that *defies* the ends of production: he affirms wastings such as "luxury," "artistic productions," "competitive games," so-called "perverse sexual activity," and the bleeding body of Christ (he was raised a Catholic).[12] What a lineup, one might say. Moreover, for Bataille, the ultimate question thus becomes: Who has the *power* to lose and destroy, ecstatically, defiantly? (In one idiom, the U.S. government and very rich people have the power to lose . . .) With his slant on Marx, Bataille scorns the bourgeoisie for using their bastardized destructions—their conspicuous consumptions—"simply to reaffirm their place in the hierarchy," whereas Bataille seeks equal opportunity access for all to create so that they may then destroy.[13] He would lose anyone who would lose loss.

Roland Barthes, in "The Pleasure of the Text," makes a similar move: "I need to distinguish euphoria, fulfillment . . . from shock, disturbance, even loss, which are proper to ecstasy, to bliss."[14] Jouissance is a disturbing pleasure, a dark glamour of rapture and disruption. It shines and cuts and leaves its bearer not knowing what to make of herself—or her pleasure. She is left beside herself, severed from herself. Bliss is a word for painful over-pleasure, *felt* and *grasped* as such. Something tremendous coursing through the body, bending the mind. Then, on a dime: rapid, luminous deteriorations. If per chance it didn't exist, queers would invent it. Along with irony, bliss is a quintessential queer accoutrement: it's hedonistic and wedded to pain; it's clearly buoyant, yet it is dark; it's provocatively sexy, intimate, scandalous, and bodily, while it's evasive of capture and speech. With its shadows and ties to loss, societies deny this extreme pleasure in favor of tamer, paler "fulfillment."

But I pet loss. I love fertile loss. Much of my recent work explores queer, unexamined forms of growth, even fertility, that spring from negativity. In a piece on queer Shakespeare, *The Winter's Tale*, specifically, I argued that children do not issue solely from parental intercourse or parental love.[15] Children bodily, shockingly, profoundly, just as forcefully are the result of parents' lost and cast-away attractions: all of the people one has *not* had sex with, or has slept with but not bred with, or has stopped pursuing. (My ex-girlfriend wouldn't have had her specific children without our relationship breaking up.) Thus, I propose, your child is the fertility of your negativity (if you end up having children). Your specific child, whoever she will be, will be caused by *lost* attachments, all of your prior failed attractions, and your other unpursued pursuits. At least in part.

Do we as a culture allow children access to the kind of loss from which they are made? Do we allow them dizzy pursuit of Lantz's tightrope, which he tethers to destruction tied to gaming? In one realm we certainly do. Call it the allowable economy of candy.

Gaming Works Like Candy?

Clearly, a chocolate bar is not a game. But is it like a game in effect not in fact? What are its effects? According to *Charlie and the Chocolate Factory,* the Tim Burton film from 2005, the effects of candy are libidinal, captivating, repetitive, time wasting, grandly lateralizing of adults and children, and linked to the pleasures of self-destruction.[16] Indeed, we should note that, at this point in gaming's history, digital games are becoming more like candy: quickly consumed, "eaten" in snatches, snacked on in the cracks of our time, especially as they migrate increasingly to smartphones, which are a pantry in our pockets. Games are candy without the calories and as accessible to kids as adults.

Thus, one could marvel over the prescience of Burton's making candy seem so interactive. In this film, for the children in the movie, candy, like a game, is a world you enter, but they go through the screen. Call it Toca Candy Tour meets Toca Candy Romp. You stomp on candy, wear it, and become it; you move it on a screen. You puzzle it out. Where does chocolate come from, the child appears to question, making candy more mysterious than babies and as libidinal as sex itself. Wonka says it "triggers the release of endorphins that give the feeling of being in love." Children, unsurprisingly, want to grasp this luxury that delivers pleasures, ones where they have agency, choice, access, and clear permission to overindulge. In fact, Willy Wonka (played by Johnny Depp), parodying "parents" (a word he can't say), playfully warns the little child hedonists, "Don't lose your heads; don't get overexcited"—by which of course he means *do* get excited to the extreme. Wonka himself has a Wildean look—top hat, velvety long purple coat, a subtle shade of lipstick, and pageboy haircut—and when the children meet him, it's on the heels of his Disney-style display of dolls bursting into flames, leaving the figurines with melting plastic flesh and hanging eyes. "Wasn't that just magnificent?" Wonka asks the group.

This is the film's introduction to destruction, an interest that Willy and the children share. And here is where the film breaks out on two rails, as if it's of two minds about the game of candy, as if it's also asking: "What is it doing to children's brains?" "Might our family lose our child to chocolate?" Indeed, quite strikingly, the film pits Willy against family values, as it were. He doesn't like families and can't pronounce "parents." Yet the film also, without apparent irony, even though with comedy, presents the cheerful sweetness and downright coziness of Charlie's family unit (his parents and grandparents). Then there's the notable, full-on contrast between the other children's dramatic interactions with Willy's candy and Charlie's different, wide-eyed wonder, as if he were simply watching a game of SimsCandy played by Willy Wonka. Are we meant to take these dualities ironically? Are they a wonderfully sly inoculation against the film's perversions?

I really don't know. Perhaps there is a clue in Wonka's childhood. It is shown in flashbacks, where young Willy appears as a ghost, dressed as a goblin on the night of Halloween. Underneath this sheet, he wears a set of braces that looks like a muzzle more than anything else. And his dentist father throws the "evil candy" into the fireplace where he burns it; so candy, of course, is the sign of the boy's forbidden pleasures, whatever they encompass, whatever else is ghosted in Willy's young life, making young Wonka a stranger in his family, before he runs away. (He never "grows up" to have a wife and children.)

Lateralization—or, as I prefer, sideways growth—nonetheless is on display on the Wonka factory tour. It appears as a fanciful wedding of destruction to a connection that runs between Willy and young Charlie, logically joining "the child" to "the queer" via jouissance. Building on the sense that "candy is a waste of time," as Willy's father once had told him, one child asks at Willy Wonka's factory, "Why is everything here completely pointless?" Charlie answers, "Candy doesn't have to have a point—that's why it's candy." More important still is Wonka's special elevator: "[It's] not an ordinary up and down elevator," he tells the kids. "It can go sideways, slantsways, [and] any way you can think of." Sideways movements conduct the children into each new room, where they see fanciful modes of manufacturing. For example, they see a cow being whipped—hence, the making of whipped cream—in a light masochistic joke for children. Then, pink cotton-candy sheep come into view: "I'd rather not talk about this one," Willy slyly offers. He is also working on other new motions—how to send a chocolate bar by TV.

But it is the film's last two moves that hold queer Willy and innocent Charlie in a relation that speaks volumes. At the end, only Charlie and his grandpa (Charlie's chaperone) remain on Willy's tour. Wonka takes them to an unsought climax. Shot to the heights of his "Up and Out" room, in the elevator with mysterious powers, Willy and his guests (the boy and his grandfather) look like they are on a ride to self-destruction. They shoot through the smokestack of Willy Wonka's factory, in a novel version of Icarean flight, and free-fall to earth, where they land unharmed. Now Willy Wonka propositions Charlie: if he leaves his family to come to live with Willy, Charlie can own the world of chocolate—take it from Willy and run it himself. Willy wants an heir, which he pronounces "hair." As we can predict, Charlie says no to this queer choice. Instead, he takes Willy, even given Johnny Depp's performance as a flamer, to the family dinner table. (Guess who's coming to dinner, it appears?)

Here, as if they are nodding to the child inside Willy Wonka—this queer man who is a queer child, who will make an unrelated child his legal "hair"—the family invokes Willy Wonka as a "boy" by Charlie's side. Charlie, the innocent, now has something in his future to expect: a productive factory for making wasteful pleasures, with sideways spread and vertical motions that play with destruction, bequeathed to a child by a Wildean queer.

Surely these relations beg to be a game.

Coda and Climax: My Queer Games

In conclusion, with an eye to lateralization, jouissance, and the dark fertility, for oneself and others, of one's sliding self-differentiations, let me end by saying: if queer children were a video game, here are games I'd like to see.

Game #1: Inspired by the film *The Hanging Garden* (from 1996). *Premise of the game*: Your avatar is a gay man at his sister's wedding, ten years after he's left his family's home. A fat teen ghost, the ghost of the gay man, is haunting everyone, since this family has kept him alive as a suicidal image hanging from a tree. *Objective of the game*: Cut your teenage self from the tree, against the efforts of the family's father to keep you hanging there, strung up in sorrow; then, reach the goal of escaping from the house with your little sister who's actually your daughter (raised by your mother—all without your knowledge). *Game-design challenge*: Though this is essentially a free-the-prisoner game—a kind of *Super Mario Bros.* with a queer twist—it's a prisoner game that spreads to the *side* and *backward* in time. The gay man's traversing levels of *himself,* comprising different times he must first collect then carry from the home. The player's avatar thus must gather a fat teenager and a little boy (himself as a child), along with the sister who will prove to be his daughter, while he steers a course through a cynical bride, bisexual groom, drunken father, and miserable mother. Somehow the game's face should register these synchronies as layerings of time and growth through breadth. And the design should include flower icons that show growing taking place in suspension.

Game #2: Inspired by the film *Heavenly Creatures,* the Peter Jackson movie from 1994 about a real-life New Zealand murder. *Premise of the game*: Two young girls are in love with each other but face major obstacles to being together. Their own parents stand against their wish to run with abandon and feel with each other to the point of exhaustion and scary pleasure. *Objective of the game*: Making use of *two* girl avatars that you must *separately* move in tandem, remove the right obstacle to the girls' love. Is it one girl's working-class mother or comical dad? Is it the other girl's beautiful mother or nerd professor father? (Hint: it's the professor.) *Game-design challenge*: There should be hand-eye-coordination feats the players must perform as they move the girls physically, mentally, and emotively. (Two different players may play as a pair.) Try to bring the girls' creations in clay—a royal family of characters they animate—into how they move or how they fight their obstacles. Additionally, the game should somehow convey the girls' emotion building, such that it pressures their desire to murder. If they kill a parent besides the professor, the game will end with their being separated (as it did in life). If they kill the scholar, they get to die of pleasure.

Game #3: Inspired by the film *Six Degrees of Separation* (from 1993), based on the drama of the same name. *Premise of the game*: A young black hustler leads a white mother to love him and mourn him and redirect her life. *Objective of the game*: Get a wealthy woman, a rich white woman, to break from her husband and have a social conscience, all through encounters with a black gay con, who is our protagonist and wants to be her son. *Game-design challenge*: Quite a bit like *Braid*, this specific game is rich in allusions—not to *Prince of Persia* but to *Guess Who's Coming to Dinner*—and works through levels that piece together narratives that discomfort players and question liberal platitudes. Moves that separate husband and wife slowly should reveal—think of *Braid* here—that our protagonist is not who he seems: not the son of Sidney Poitier but a more aggressive (I would say more satisfying) child queered by color. In its design, the game should craft a room that has red walls, soft light, good art, and plentiful horizontal windows that capture views of Manhattan—which, at night, reflect the room back onto itself, mixing the outside views with all the interior ones, making the occupants look as if they're walking in the sky above the street, as if they are safely ensconced in the views they think they are above. The game should also reference Kandinsky and Cézanne and deploy ironically repeated lines like "I love museums," "I love art." The avatar on-screen should be Will Smith and carry some mark of that actor's homophobic resistance to his part, a prejudice perhaps he, by now, having grown fatter and broader in his thinking, has dramatically, happily differentiated *from*.

Notes

1. I am of course deploying the standard linguistic definition of "queer" that exists at this time: "*adj.* 1) deviating from the expected or normal; strange; 2) odd or unconventional in behavior; eccentric; 3) arousing suspicion; 4) *Slang.* Homosexual"; "*n.* A homosexual" (*American Heritage Dictionary,* New College Edition). The phrase "no promo homo" is a coinage by my colleague, Clifford Rosky, professor of law at the University of Utah.

2. The assertion that all children are queer, via their various forms of strangeness, is the thesis of my book, *The Queer Child, or Growing Sideways in the Twentieth Century* (Durham, N.C.: Duke University Press, 2009).

3. For my article-length essay on *jouissance,* see "*Jouissance,* the Gash of Bliss," in *Clinical Encounters in Sexuality: Psychoanalytic Practice and Queer Theory,* ed. Noreen Giffney and Eve Watson (New York: Punctum Books, in press).

4. Quoted in Kenneth Lewes, *The Psychoanalytic Theory of Male Homosexuality* (New York: Simon & Schuster, 1988), 149. Freud is the one who says perversions are characteristic of people who either extend themselves beyond the normal "path" of "copulation" or linger at midpoints. See Sigmund Freud, *Three Essays on the Theory of Sexuality,* in *The Freud Reader,* ed. Peter Gay (New York: Norton, 1989), 247.

5. Oscar Wilde's *The Picture of Dorian Gray* would be an obvious touchstone on this point, as would Wilde himself (in the public's sense of him).

6. Sam Anderson, "Just One More Game . . . How Time-Wasting Video Games Escaped the Arcade, Jumped into Our Pockets and Took Over Our Lives," *New York Times Magazine,* April 8, 2012, 29, 30, 55.

7. Hanna Rosin, "The Touch-Screen Generation: What's This Technology Doing to Toddlers' Brains?" *The Atlantic,* April 2013, 60.

8. Ibid., 57, 58.

9. Ibid., 60, 58, 64.

10. Georges Bataille, *Visions of Excess: Selected Writings, 1927–1939,* ed. and trans. Allan Stoekl (Minneapolis: University of Minnesota Press, 1985), 21. Some material in this section draws on my essay "*Jouissance,* the Gash of Bliss" and on the conclusion in *The Queer Child.*

11. Ibid., 8, 75, 116.

12. Ibid., 119–20.

13. Ibid., xvi.

14. Roland Barthes, *The Pleasure of the Text,* trans. Richard Miller (New York: Hill & Wang, 1975), 19.

15. See Kathryn Bond Stockton, "*Lost,* or 'Exit, Pursued by a Bear': Causing Queer Children on Shakespeare's TV," in *Shakesqueer: A Queer Companion to the Complete Works of Shakespeare,* ed. Madhavi Menon (Durham, N.C.: Duke University Press, 2011), 421–28.

16. The material that follows draws on my conclusion in *The Queer Child*.

Chapter **23**

Queer Growth in Video Games

CHRISTOPHER GOETZ

Video games need to grow up. For games studies, at least, this seems to be the consensus. Perhaps to protect what we study, or to legitimize it, we ask that games be more artful or at least more like other arts (e.g., cinema).[1] We wonder why more games don't contain "adult" content, ranging from the overtly sexual to the thematically serious (e.g., *Heavy Rain*).[2] We even ask that games "change the world" or at least make play productive and educational.[3] As scholars, we are especially drawn to games that address us as *mature* adults, and that do something other than just show us a good time.

The emerging field of queer games studies has formed behind a similar call for games to "grow up," insofar as growing up means doing more to welcome the presence of *others* in a culture that is putatively male (and definitely heteronormative, immature, homophobic, misogynistic, and reactionary). Queer games studies questions commercial gaming's pleasure economy by linking the pleasure of masculine empowerment in games to the violent overreaction in game communities whenever anybody challenges this pleasure. Writer and video game critic Leigh Alexander, in her unfavorable review of

Grand Theft Auto V, ties masculine empowerment in games to the immaturity at the heart of the reflex to lash out at critics: "What, you want to leave me death threats? Go for it! Games are about feeling powerful, and about you getting your way!"[4] Here, empowerment means *entitlement* for a particular kind of insecurity mended by the egocentric, male empowerment fantasy.[5] And "growing up" means outgrowing the expectation of this masculine entitlement.

But there is also a vein in queer games studies that asks games to *never grow up*—at least when the "up" in "growing up" relates to what Kathryn Bond Stockton identifies as "marriage, work, reproduction, and the loss of childishness."[6] Stockton describes queer growth as "sideways growth," a move intended to recuperate unacknowledged development, the "energy, pleasure, vitality, and emotion in the back-and-forth of connections and extensions that are not reproductive" and that grow "to the side of cultural ideals."[7] Samantha Allen connects games to this notion of queer growth with the term "reproductive futurism," meaning the pressure exerted by heteronormative culture in order to check actions that don't appear to contribute to legitimate forms of upward growth. In this vein of queer games studies, video games are "queer" precisely for their embrace of blissful *jouissance,* for their association with activities that are perceived as immature, and for the pure wastefulness of energy and time spent outside the narrow strictures of hetero-reproductivity. In what Marsha Kinder described as games' abrupt beginnings, "extended middles," and infinitely deferred endings, games are both a cause of and an emblem for the many delays that characterize childhood.[8]

In one sense, there is no tension here between these two attitudes toward growth in games: asking games to stop being homophobic and misogynistic does not necessarily mean calling for an end to fun. But there is a definite tension here around the term "empowerment." One vein of queer games studies seems down on the pleasures of game empowerment. The other seems to embrace it, or at least to preserve a space for guilty indulgence of such pleasures. This chapter's goal is to address this tension and frame empowerment in commercial games in terms of "sideways growth."

As with the eponymous youth of Stockton's book, *The Queer Child,* there is unacknowledged, sideways growth to be found within commercial gaming, too, and often games are empowering precisely because they allow for exploration of this growth. I draw on psychoanalysis for its models of growing up that perhaps unintentionally provide helpful wiggle room for thinking about nonnormative fantasy and empowerment. These models at least help demonstrate how often commercial video game empowerment is based on a kind of growth that will never look like "growing up" (because it is better thought of as growing sideways) and that is empowering specifically because it is a *masochistic* pleasure. As masochistic empowerment, it does not fit with the rubric of the immature, fractured male-ego "entitlement fantasy" under which it is often classed. Pausing to see it in its difference from masculine–sadistic empowerment can benefit queer games studies by preserving a space for thinking *positively* about the empowerment of queer communities through sideways growth.

Many video games occasion a return to anxieties and wishes predating the Oedipus complex's concerns about sexual and social difference, making these games appear to be about anything but growing up.[9] But, in fact, these games externalize and develop these "preoedipal" wishes and anxieties, opening up new possible structures in adult life for play and, perhaps, for fostering a better understanding of our relationship to the spaces and people around us. The specific "preoedipal" concern that the video games in this chapter allow us to explore is the tether fantasy.

Salman Akhtar coined the term "fantasy of a tether"[10] to describe a response to "unresolved separation–individuation," the name for the process of the infant's developing sense of separateness from the parent. Separation–individuation is like Freud's *fort/da* but broken down into subphases in which the infant's autonomy (unevenly) increases. In each phase, the child is variably "tethered" to the parent, who remains an anchor (or point of security) from which the child can feel confident exploring the world outside.

When the "fantasy of a tether" manifests—and this can happen at any time in life—it generally takes the form of imagining connectivity to some safe space, like imagining the route home after a long day of work. It can also take the form of imagined exposure to danger, and thinking about how you might flee some threat, and to where. Exposure can mean the excitement of getting caught out of doors during a thunderstorm, or the dread of having to take shelter from a terrorist attack. It can take the form of opening up—letting a breeze enter the home—or closing down, a pleasure taken in the click of a door lock. Even more simply, it can mean the emotional use of a smartphone as a kind of lifeline to loved ones.[11]

To think of the tether fantasy as a kind of growth, it is helpful to note its role in a variety of cultural productions, from backyard bomb shelters to design contests for zombie-apocalypse strongholds.[12] As a fantasy of home invasion, the tether fantasy intersects with class and race stratification through the structures of gated communities and home alarm systems. It is related to historically changing definitions of homes as private spaces for withdrawal, especially as entertainment media and communications technologies have entered the home and made it into a kind of entertainment "fortress" (mirrored in films like *Panic Room*).[13] Dwelling on a tether fantasy and giving it new form, multiplying the pleasures taken from it, constitutes a kind of sideways growth. This growth shares an affinity with the oft-noted experience of queer gamers who, while young, see games as a kind of refuge from the harsh and judgmental social world.

Tether fantasies are an important part of both independent and blockbuster, or "AAA,"[14] commercial game development. Games like *Minecraft, Terraria, Rust, Starbound, Dark Souls,* and many others across the broad genre of the role-playing game (RPG), from the familiar Japanese RPG to popular cooperative dungeon crawlers like *Diablo III,* operate on the premise of the tether fantasy. Video games are often described as a spatial medium,[15] which makes them well suited for thinking about the tether fantasy's interest in experiences of boundedness and openness. In other words, space is not just a metaphor for identity in games (the way being "in the closet" and "coming out" are spatial metaphors for expressing queer identities to hetero-culture). Rather, space in games becomes the site of a literal wish fulfillment about spatializing (externalizing) deep-seated concerns about threat and safety, similar to the way Otto Rank makes sense of a "womb fantasy" as the desire, literally, to return to the nirvanic womb and resolve the "trauma of birth."[16]

Both *Minecraft* and *Terraria* begin by asking players to build and seek refuge within shelter before the game's first nightfall—venturing out when things seem safe, and returning again as the sun sets. Players are "tethered" to these safe spaces throughout play; in turn, patterns of stretching out into danger and returning shape the boundaries of home base. In *Super Metroid,* play involves imagining the exploration of space from the safety of energy-restoring save points scattered across the map. Players find the next safe place when their tethers are stretched to the limit, and the game plots scenarios to specifically emphasize the urgency of making it to one of these save points. Every save point is a kind of provisional substitute for the ultimate, womb-like safety of game protagonist Samus's own spaceship, which awaits Samus's last-minute escape. A much more recent commercial game, *Dark Souls,* employs a lifeline tether like *Metroid*'s, wherein players stretch out only so far (as current upgrades permit) from the safety of a bonfire, until they are finally able to connect to the next bonfire. I have argued elsewhere that the "tether fantasy" is crucial for understanding the highly porous boundaries of the genre of the RPG, in which heroes leave the protective enclosure of the walled city for the adventure beyond, returning to safety to rest and recover in order to venture farther the next day.[17] Some games emphasize the act of stretching out *(Dark Souls, Super Metroid),* and some the return to a state of fortification *(Minecraft, Terraria).*

These games all, to some degree, involve self-determined exposure to threat and anxiety. In short, they are about dwelling on vulnerability. The tether fantasy is a masochistic empowerment fantasy. It is a thrill in exposure, a pleasure taken in a momentary loss of stability and certainty—a brush with danger or death. Freud emphasized the return to warmth (or comfort) in his anecdote about the "cheap enjoyment . . . obtained by putting a bare leg from under the bedclothes on a cold winter night and drawing it in again."[18] But a game like *Dark Souls,* I think, dwells on the coldness of exposure, reveling in what Francis Spufford called a "tingling disruption of the domestic" in his study of Victorian culture's fascination with narratives of polar exploration. Spufford recounts a broad cultural pleasure in narratives in which nature overtakes humanity, a fantasized "sublime of defeat," or "a dreamed-of conquest *by* raging elements."[19] *Dark Souls* is notoriously difficult—but there is something celebratory of loss and pain in the way in which the unavoidably high number of player character deaths is touted by game publisher Bandai Namco's own promotional efforts (additional content was released in 2012, rebranded as the "Prepare to Die" edition).

This fact could be linked easily to Jesper Juul's *The Art of Failure* as more evidence of our complicated relationship with winning and losing in video games. But I want to suggest that the structure of the game itself figures loss as a failed extension into danger, a tether stretched too far. Stretching the tether into danger is a core pleasure of the game, one the game requires be regularly recalibrated. Since death can mean losing all carried currency and experience, the threat of loss and the thrill of exposure are intertwined. The game dwells in its own excessive darkness by organizing play as a *perpetual departure* from the warmth of the bonfires (the fire, the hearth, is a cultural image for the "womb"). And, for those who are no longer intimidated by the game's various monsters, the looming threat always remains of being "invaded" by other players who are tasked by the game with hunting you down.

It is possible to view the "masochism" here as a drive for mastery. Freud flirted with the idea that the compulsion to repeat painful experiences was masochistic in nature (i.e., a pleasure in its own right), but he concluded that repetition compulsion had the goal of "binding" traumatic experiences, meeting a need for stability and control that was more important than the psyche's general aversion to pain. In a similar sense, the sublime of defeat in *Dark Souls,* rather than a masochistic thrill, might be part of the pleasure of overcoming or mastering pain.

But masochism is especially appropriate for thinking about a tether fantasy when viewed as relational psychologists do, as an empowering evocation of absent parents: "If parental figures have become identified with the pain they cause, then aggravating such pain can magically evoke their presence and overcome separation anxiety."[20] Similarly, pain can be thought of as a kind of autonomy from parents, an ability to endure.[21] This is, at least, how Akhtar makes sense of the tether fantasy, as a "gradual deflation and relinquishment of the sense of omnipotence experienced in the symbiotic dual unity with the mother."[22]

The idea that a key commercial play fantasy is masochistic conflicts with the assumed male-sadistic organization of AAA gaming, which Anna Anthropy sums up well: "Mostly, videogames are about men shooting men in the face."[23] As games scholars, we are right to condemn a culture of violence and entitlement. But since the tether fantasy is prominent in commercial gaming,[24] it is important to argue that there are aspects of mainstream empowerment worth preserving as a topic of study, aspects of empowerment that cannot be reduced to male entitlement, and that might likely be shared by a wider group of people seeking expression (through fantasy) for what psychoanalysts call the "symbiotic orbit," or a stable balance of exposure and withdrawal. The question of the relation between queerness and fantasies of empowerment remains important, and one that we should not simply dismiss.

Thinking about tether fantasies in video games poses the question of what it means to dwell on a preoedipal fantasy about separating from and merging with spaces of comfort. How is this oscillation a kind of sideways growth that is relevant for the study of queerness? This, I think, raises the related question of what kind of progress we make when we play games and how this progress is recognized by the culture of our parents. Is the time really just *wasted*? Or is it, rather, seen as a waste because it is not "productive" from the point of view of "reproductive futurism"? I'm not suggesting that LGBTQ gamers necessarily experience tether fantasies differently than others do— quite the opposite. I'm suggesting that this kind of empowerment is a vibrant and important part of the pleasure taken in video games both inside and outside queer communities. Games that attack fun, that force us to question the privilege in video game pleasure, are crucial for queer games discourse. But the spirit of growing sideways can help recuperate at least parts of the mainstream games we grew up loving, as well as the guilty time spent playing ever since. Queer games studies entails accepting the co-presence and mutual reflexivity of the childish and the adult in games, and this applies to avant-garde games as well. This flexibility is part of what is so broadly compelling about the notion of queer growth in video games.

Notes

1. For a thorough primer on art and video games see Felan Parker, "An Art World for Artgames," *Loading . . . The Journal of the Canadian Game Studies Association* 7, no. 11 (2012): 41–60; Patrick Jagoda, "Between: An Interview with Jason Rohrer," *Critical Inquiry,* May 2011, http://criticalinquiry .uchicago.edu/the_jason_rohrer_interview/.

2. For a discussion of art and adult sexuality see Rob Gallagher, "No Sex Please, We Are Finite State Machines: On the Melancholy Sexlessness of the Video Game," *Games and Culture* 7, no. 6 (2012): 399–418; Brenda Brathwaite, *Sex in Video Games* (Boston: Charles River Media, 2006).

3. Jane McGonigal, *Reality Is Broken: Why Games Make Us Better and How They Can Change the World* (New York: Penguin, 2011); James Paul Gee, *What Video Games Have to Teach Us about Learning and Literacy* (New York: Palgrave Macmillan, 2007).

4. Leigh Alexander, "Review of GTA V*," September 16, 2013, http:// leighalexander.net/review-of-gta-v/.

5. Queer games scholar and historian Zoya Street, who quotes Alexander in his book, *Delay: Paying Attention to Energy Mechanics* (Rotherham, U.K.: Rupazero, 2014), persuasively links the idea of "empowerment" in commercial games to "entitlement," noting that white, heterosexual, male players mistake empowerment for entitlement in games built around experiencing spatial freedom (an experience not shared equally across all gender and racial divides).

6. Kathryn Bond Stockton, *The Queer Child, or Growing Sideways in the Twentieth Century* (Durham, N.C.: Duke University Press, 2009), 4.

7. Ibid., 13.

8. Marsha Kinder, *Playing with Power in Movies, Television, and Video Games: From Muppet Babies to Teenage Mutant Ninja Turtles* (Berkeley: University of California Press, 1991).

9. "Oedipal" here refers of course to Freud's well-known investigations of the Oedipus complex, a cornerstone of his theories of psychoanalysis (the heterosexual boy's repressed wish to kill the father and marry the mother). But in the context of developmental psychology, specifically, "oedipal" issues simply have to do with permutations of gender and sexual identity, as well as where one "fits" into the institutions of family, community, and industry.

10. For a discussion of the clinical dynamics of a tether fantasy, see Akhtar's *The Damaged Core: Origins, Dynamics, Manifestations, and Treatment* (North Vale, N.J.: Jason Aronson, 2009).

11. Sherry Turkle, in *Alone Together: Why We Expect More from Technol-*

ogy and Less from Each Other (New York: Basic Books, 2012), calls this kind of connection a "tethered self," describing the present-day phone user continuously connected to loved ones through digital mobile devices. Turkle's worries about adolescents who never experience adulthood's rite of passage: feeling "truly alone."

12. "Zombie-Proof Architecture: When the Dead Start to Walk You'd Better Start Building," *Economist Blog,* August 17, 2012, http://www.economist .com/blogs/prospero/2012/08/zombie-proof-architecture.

13. Barbara Klinger's term for domestic transformations in America following 9/11. See *Beyond the Multiplex: Cinema, New Technologies, and the Home* (Berkeley: University of California Press, 2006).

14. "AAA" here refers to games with especially high production value, made with large development teams over the course of several years, and with budgets in the tens of millions of dollars.

15. Henry Jenkins, "Game Design as Narrative Architecture," in *First Person: New Media as Story, Performance, and Game,* ed. Noah Wardrip-Fruin and Pat Harrigan (Cambridge, Mass.: MIT Press, 2004), 118–30; Mark Wolf, *The Medium of the Video Game* (Austin: University of Texas Press, 2001).

16. Otto Rank, *The Trauma of Birth* (Dover, U.K.: Courier, 1929).

17. In "Tether and Accretions: Fantasy as Form in Videogames" (*Games and Culture* 7, no. 6 [2012]: 419–40) I argue that the genre of the RPG is made up of the intersection of a tether fantasy and a "fantasy of accretions." I make sense of the latter as a pleasure taken in accruing objects, currency, treasure, and power from the game's worlds in a way that augments one's ability to stretch out into and explore that world. I link the fantasy to a kind of death drive, a compulsion to, bit by bit, become impervious to the threats of the outside world. The fantasy, by design, has no "end," because if it did, then it would realize what Freud said of the aim of "conservative instincts" to return to a prior state of being, to become "inorganic" once again; in other words, the best way to forestall death is to be dead.

18. Sigmund Freud, *Civilization and Its Discontents,* trans. James Strachey (New York: Norton, 1930), 40.

19. Francis Spufford, *I May Be Some Time: Ice and the English Imagination* (New York: Palgrave Macmillan, 1996), 26.

20. John Kucich, "Olive Schreiner, Masochism, and Omnipotence: Strategies of a Preoedipal Politics," *Novel: A Forum on Fiction* 36, no. 1 (2002): 83.

21. Derek Burrill's study on masculinity in video games, *Die Tryin': Videogames, Masculinity, Culture* (New York: Peter Lang, 2008), asserts that masochistic trials of enduring pain are indeed a staple of masculine gaming culture. However, it is likely that Kucich would not necessarily recognize

the masochism described in this chapter, which might more accurately be described via Kucich's emphasis on "preoedipal masochism," which "sustain[s] omnipotence in the absence of a powerful or punitive other," meaning that "sensations of self-sufficiency may come simply from the ritualization of suffering," a kind of autonomy through perseverance (Kucich, "Olive Schreiner, Masochism, and Omnipotence," 83). This form of masochism is preoedipal and could exist "alongside subsequent distortions of the Oedipus complex" without necessarily disrupting that symbolic order (or "mental health").

22. Salman Akhtar, *Inner Torment: Living between Conflict and Fragmentation* (North Vale, N.J.: Jason Aronson, 1999), 8.

23. Anna Anthropy, *Rise of the Videogame Zinesters: How Freaks, Normals, Amateurs, Artists, Dreamers, Drop-Outs, Queers, Housewives, and People Like You Are Taking Back an Art Form* (New York: Seven Stories Press, 2012), 3.

24. Seven games structured at their core around a tether fantasy have appeared in the last three annual lists of top-ten-grossing software titles *(Pokemon X&Y, Assassin's Creed IV: Black Flag, The Last of Us, Tomb Raider, Monster Hunter 4, Minecraft, Fallout 4)*. And *Minecraft* has been on this list for the last two years. Many other titles from these lists, while not exemplary of tether play, do contain RPG elements *(Grand Theft Auto V, Call of Duty: Ghosts, FIFA 14, BioShock Infinite, Call of Duty: Advanced Warfare, Destiny, Madden NFL 15, WATCH_DOGS, NBA 2K15, Call of Duty: Black Ops 3, Madden NFL 16, Star Wars: Battlefront, NBA 2K16, FIFA 16)* (lists available online at http://venturebeat.com/ and http://www.thefiscaltimes.com/).

Chapter **24**

Finding the Queerness in Games

COLLEEN MACKLIN

We must dream and enact new and better pleasures, other ways of being in the world, and ultimately new worlds.

—José Esteban Muñoz, *Cruising Utopia*

Where Is the Queerness in Games?

When we say a game is queer, what do we mean? How does one go about locating the queerness in games? Do we find queerness through the characters we play, or the worlds we inhabit? Do we find it when a game lets us enact queerness through what we do in the game? Do we find it when we play as queer-identified players and/ or form player communities? Or is a game queer when the designer crafts the game with queer intentions? Where is the queerness in games? I've been interested in this question as a game designer, player, and queer practitioner for a while, so here are some of my thoughts on the matter and some games and the people who make them to consider along the way.

Is the Queerness Found in a Game's Characters and Story-Worlds?

Often, when we think about contemporary video games, we think of the stories they tell: space marines shooting aliens, marines shooting other marines, or, for something completely different, Italian plumbers attempting to rescue a princess in distress. These are the tropes in popular video games and their narratives could be considered, with few exceptions, hyper-hetero. Video games are a backwater for progressive sexual politics, more so than other forms of narrative media where LGBTQI characters and lives are increasingly depicted. However, if we look more closely at some of the games out there, we might uncover some forms of queerness.

Mass Effect and *Dragon Age,* both games by the company BioWare, let you play gay. If you choose the right branches on the dialogue tree, you can enjoy a same-sex hookup with a fellow elf, alien or a space marine. The *Fable* series, by famed Lionhead Studios designer Peter Molyneux, allows for same-sex marriage and polygamy. I think it's great to have different romantic options in these highly popular games, and it's certainly promising to see major "AAA" games include gay options.

But when I play through the options in these games it becomes clear that the nature of these same-sex relationships are, for the most part, the same as the opposite-sex ones. The story, more or less, remains the same. The only differences are encoded in the game's interchangeable variables (male or female), leading to slight variations in character skins and animations—and if we're lucky, dialogue. It's interesting to me how the implementation of gay and lesbian romance in these games mirrors the political arguments underlying same-sex marriage—that everyone should be given the same rights following the same dominant social structures. Perhaps these games have not found their queerness yet, at least queerness defined by a polymorphous politics that often questions the norm. What if, instead of a simple variable switch in the code, there were options not just for the gender of the person or alien we might woo, but the way we woo them? It's laudable that these same-sex romance options exist, but do they represent a game gaywash, promising LGBTQI options but with little flexibility in our actual play? What can game characters and narratives let us explore beyond what might be considered homo/heteronormative politics? Polyamory? Asexuality? Kink?

Games are more about world building than about linear story-telling. If it's worlds that we are exploring with games, then isn't it possible for these algorithmic worlds to evolve to allow for more flexibility and diversity in player desire? Could our game worlds include queer utopias? Mainstream game companies may argue that it's not financially viable to build in queer possibilities for what they believe is a predominately conservative, straight player demographic. At the same time, indie designers and alt-game creators are already making it happen, building games and building player communities that exist outside the mainstream. There's certainly more to explore in queer world building, and games seem ripe with potential to allow players special access to José Esteban Muñoz's ideas of a queer utopia, which allows us to "dream and enact new and better pleasures, other ways of being in the world, and ultimately new worlds."[1]

Is a Game's Queerness Found in What It Lets Us Do?

merritt kopas, game designer and theorist, has pointed out that many media scholars consider video games "texts" in the same way one might look at a novel, film, or television series.[2] Through this lens, a game is a container, where meaning is found in character, story, and events. The previous paragraphs also examined video games in this way—finding the queerness in game worlds, stories, and characters. But this perspective overlooks one of the most unique features about games: that they also create meaning through our choices as players. In fact, many games have no story at all in the conventional sense (think basketball, *Tetris,* or checkers). In these games, the story is created on the fly by the player, their actions, and the game's feedback to those actions. In other words, what I get to do in the game and what the game does back to me. So, what does a queer game *do*?

Anna Anthropy's *dys4ia* is an interesting example of what I think a queer game does. It uses the structure of the popular Nintendo *WarioWare* series (perhaps we should call Anthropy's game a form of "queerioware"), a game comprising mini-games where one simple action is required to get to the next game in the set. It demands quick reactions to short vignettes, each requiring the player to perform different tasks in response to the situation. When considered together, the mini-games in *dys4ia* tell an autobiographical story about Anna's experiences with hormone replacement therapy. On the game's surface the content involves queer themes, and the game's designer (and, by extension, the protagonist) self-identifies as queer.

But what makes *dys4ia* do what a queer game does is it subverts our expectations of control and agency as players, which is the seamless interactive foundation of most games. *dys4ia* is full of what at times seem like interactive glitches, propelling the player through its mini-games by forcing failure, ending mini-games prematurely, and leaving us wondering if we have any chance to win at all. As we play, we realize that the power is not ours. Instead of playing the game we are played by the game. In the main menu, we can even choose to start at any level, jettisoning the standard progression through levels that we are used to in video games. However, we can't choose where the story goes. It's not ours to choose, anyway. Our character is Anna, and we're like an empathetic witness, standing in her shoes, retracing her steps. Because of this, I believe it moves us more than if we had full control. The game takes control and says, "Here, join me." We fail along with Anna and we experience her transformation through our shared failure. In most games failure is a tool for feedback on the journey toward the goal. In *dys4ia,* failure is the game.

In his book *The Queer Art of Failure* Jack Halberstam says, "The queer art of failure turns on the impossible, the improbable, the unlikely, and the unremarkable. It quietly loses, and in losing it imagines other goals for life, for love, for art, and for being."[3] In *dys4ia,* we play at failing and through it we see new possibilities for living—through the designer's lived experience.

Is the Queerness in Games Found in Who Makes Them and How They Were Made?

Most games are designed in a play-centric mode—one that puts the player experience at the top of a designer's list of things to consider. It's almost doctrine that designers use an iterative method with plenty of play-testing as a baseline for design refinements. But there's a burgeoning queer resistance to this mode of working. *dys4ia* is one interesting example of subverting traditional notions of what makes a "good" game (interesting choices, player agency, challenge). In fact, public criticism of the game centered on whether one could consider it a game at all. We've heard these kinds of questions aimed at works of art, too.

In her essay "Death of the Player," a turn on the classic Roland Barthes essay "Death of the Author," designer and critic Mattie Brice opens with this simple statement: "Players are overrated."[4] In it, Brice suggests that authorship in games needs to be reconsidered with more weight. She suggests an author-centric approach over the dominant player-centric game design mode, which emphasizes play-testing with players and iterating the game's design to make it more fun. Brice goes on to explore some of the reasons she didn't play-test her autobiographical game *Mainichi,* which explores a day in her life as a trans woman. Mattie describes her motivation for making the game as a way for her friend to experience the world through her eyes. She says that play-testing the game would defeat the purpose of it: "I couldn't playtest the game with [my friend] and then 'release' it after. It would be like asking your crush to read and edit the love note you want to pass to them one day."[5]

merritt kopas's *Hugpunx* questions whether games need players at all. It's a short and sweet game about hugging people and cats on the street, set to a bouncy tune. We could call this a "hug 'em up" instead of a "shoot 'em up." There's really no skill involved in the hugging, no "leveling-up," per se, and no win state (although the game does progress to an ending, which coincides with the end of the song). It simply involves moving toward cats and people and pressing a button to hug them. In fact, if you choose to not move or hug anyone, you still get the postgame reward message "yr totally rad! Go hug yrself!" You can't fail, unless you think you did based on whatever goal you set for yourself (in my case, hugging only cats). It's a game that plays itself, questioning the norms of most video games based on progress and player interaction: a lean-back experience over a lean-forward one. Both of these examples seem to say that the game is here, and it's queer, whether we play it or not.

Is a Game's Queerness Found in Players and Communities of Play?

When we play a game, we often take on a new persona like Lara Croft, Gordon Freeman, or Sonic the Hedgehog. At times, we have choices about the types of characters we play. Female or male? Night Elf? Paladin? Khajiit? Whether by choice or by default, many players have engaged in "gender play"—playing as a character of another gender. This is one way games give us opportunities and choices that are ripe for exploring different identities and experiences. Gender play is a form of meaning made somewhere in the air between the game and us, through a playful conversation between the possibility space of the game and our own subjectivity. Gender play is something many of us fondly recall as a form of self-expression in our early days as queers.

What about what happens between players, in a queer play community? There's an emerging queer critical community in games (as exemplified by this collection and many great conferences and conversations) and I'm excited about it. While the personal may be political, it's when these personal experiences come together to form a public that I think we have the power to cultivate new, queered forms of games and influence the growth of games as a creative field. At IndieCade 2012, the cofounder of the 1970s countercultural New Games movement Bernie De Koven said, "All play in public is political."[6] What happens when that public is a queer gaming public?

"Everyone games" is the motto for GaymerX (now known as simply GX), an annual fan conference dedicated to the public celebration of queerness in games.[7] It comprises conference sessions about games and game making, an expo floor with queer game-related merchandise and game demos, dance parties, cosplay, and events and sessions about topics as wide-ranging as wrestling and the furry community. I have had the pleasure to attend and the thing that struck me was how diverse it was—not only in terms of bodies and backgrounds, although this is significant, especially for a very homogenous industry. GaymerX was also diverse in the sense that fan interests were diverse. Almost any game title out there had a queer fan and their stories and cosplay depictions of these popular games imbued the games with a new queer life. Whether it was a couple sporting authentic leather-daddy mustaches dressed as Mario and his brother Luigi or an androgynous Zelda, the queering of these game characters was a celebration of the games they star in as well as a sly realization of the way these characters and games can signify queerness when viewed in the right light.

Another interesting note about the diversity of the attendees at GaymerX is that many of the people I encountered played multiple roles. They were designers and critics and fans. These individuals are forming a new games criticism by writing and making games from their own personal play experiences and also taking on issues of representation and social justice in the industry. They include Anna Anthropy, Mattie Brice, merritt kopas, Liz Ryerson, Zoya Street, Robert Yang, and others. This is a community that not only plays games, it creates and circulates ideas about them, fueling a growing queer indie game scene with broad representation at other industry conferences and festivals. These burgeoning communities of queer players, makers, and critics are putting pressure on a game industry where women, people of color, and the LGBTQI community are noticeably underrepresented. Just as playing in public is political, we're seeing the beginnings of the formation of a politically powerful counterpublic in the game community. A counterpublic, to use Michael Warner's term, "formed by their conflict with the norms and contexts of their cultural environment."[8] There is a movement afoot, one that is speaking out through words and making games and playing them, alone and together.

Where Is the Queerness . . . in Games?

We can find traces of queerness—or at least its potential—in the characters and worlds of games. We can find it in the actions of the game, in the people who make them, how they are made, in how we play, in who plays, and how we talk about games. We can find the queerness in many aspects of games, not just these ones we have just explored. We might find it in the tools of game making, for instance—tools like Twine, which have enabled an explosion of new, queer games and interactive narratives. We might find it in the way we share games, in how they are distributed, and in queer games made for the queer community. In looking at the parts, however, I think we may have lost sight of the whole. Ultimately, I believe games are predisposed toward queer explorations. Instead of the question "Where is the queerness in games?" we can ask, "Where is the queerness?" and answer "In games!"

Games are queer, indeed. How? They encourage and let us revel in (the queer art of) failure. In fact, failure, often painful in life, is often one of the more pleasurable elements in games, as Jesper Juul has pointed out in his aptly named book *The Art of Failure*.[9] Failure encourages us to try out new, unexpected strategies—ones that a game's designer may have never anticipated. Games release us from ourselves and let us try on new identities. They give us the space to explore unfamiliar pleasures and desires. They permit—in fact they encourage—transgression, a quality inherent to play. To a modern world obsessed with productivity and achievement, games are a "waste of time," "totally unproductive," for "kids," To quote radical play designer Bernie De Koven once more, when we play games together, we create "an embellishment, a useless, spontaneous, joyous human decoration on the shape of necessity."[10] If we think of society clothing itself in the things it designs, then games are society's costume jewelry, strap-on, and studded collar. An embellishment, yes, but one that is absolutely necessary for our own pleasure.

I opened this essay with a quote from José Muñoz describing a queer utopia, a new world of possibility that is not here yet, but one for which we can strive. I'll close with the thoughts of Bernard Suits, who wrote about games and utopia thirty years earlier. In the book *The Grasshopper: Games, Life and Utopia,* the grasshopper has a dialogue with his disciples, including Skepticus, the hardworking ant. The Grasshopper describes the role of games in Utopia, a place where work and all instrumental activities are no longer relevant: "I believe that Utopia is intelligible, and I believe that game playing is what makes Utopia intelligible."[11] His disciple Skepticus replies, "What you are saying is that in Utopia the only thing left to do would be to play games, so that game playing turns out to be the whole of the ideal of existence." The Grasshopper responds, "So it would appear, at least at this stage of our investigation."[12]

At this stage in our investigation, I would propose that games are queer because they provide us with a notably different way of looking at and living in the world. The queer utopia may already be here, in our games. In his playful exploration, Suits coined the phrase "lusory attitude" to describe a willingness to play: to adopt the rules of the game not in order to achieve something "useful" in the world, but to enjoy the inherent pleasures of play itself—to revel in playing games as "the voluntary attempt to overcome unnecessary obstacles."[13] This essay revels in its attempt to overcome the unnecessary obstacle of trying to find the queerness in a medium that, by its nature, is queer already. So let's play.

Notes

1. José Esteban Muñoz, *Cruising Utopia: The Then and There of Queer Futurity* (New York: New York University Press, 2009), 1.

2. I first heard merritt kopas's ideas on this at a workshop she ran called "Interrupting Play: Queer Games and Futurity" at New York University on February 18, 2014.

3. Jack (Judith) Halberstam, *The Queer Art of Failure* (Durham, N.C.: Duke University Press, 2011), 88.

4. Mattie Brice, "Death of the Player," *Alternate Ending*, October 29, 2013, http://www.mattiebrice.com/death-of-the-player/.

5. Ibid.

6. This statement by Bernie De Koven comes from a session at IndieCade in October 2012 called "A Conversation with Eric Zimmerman and Bernie DeKoven." A video recording of this session is available at https://www.youtube.com/watch?v=Wr6b3_sFMCs.

7. See http://gaymerx.com/.

8. Michael Warner, *Publics and Counterpublics* (New York: Zone Books, 2002), 63.

9. Jesper Juul, *The Art of Failure: An Essay on the Pain of Playing Video Games* (Cambridge, Mass.: MIT Press, 2013).

10. Bernie De Koven, *The Well-Played Game: A Player's Philosophy* (Cambridge, Mass.: MIT Press, 2013), 136.

11. Bernard Suits, *The Grasshopper: Games, Life and Utopia* (Peterborough, Ont.: Broadview Press, 2005), 154.

12. Ibid., 154.

13. Ibid., 55.

Chapter **25**

Organizing New Approaches to Games
An Interview with Chelsea Howe, Toni Rocca, and Sarah Schoemann

MODERATED BY BONNIE RUBERG

The past few years have seen an unprecedented surge in video game events that directly speak to issues of queerness and games. Some are oriented toward the gaming industry. Others are oriented toward academics. Still others offer queer-identified gamers a chance to meet and form community. What unites these events is their drive to bring discussions about LGBT issues and gaming out into the open, and to provide a place for those who feel passionate about these important intersections to share and create ideas.

Chelsea Howe's, Toni Rocca's, and Sarah Schoemann's stories each speak to issues far beyond the events they co-run. For activists and community organizers like these, thinking differently about games and making games differently also requires organizing differently. The experiences of the three leaders interviewed here illuminate new paths for video games more broadly. Their insights can help guide others to approach game events, and video games in general, in unexpected ways. This interview, conducted through shared text document, took place in the spring of 2014, at a pivotal moment for the emergence of queer games communities.

RUBERG: How would you describe the games event that you organize? What would you say are your individual roles and goals?

HOWE: The Queerness and Games Conference (QGCon) is about bridging the gap between two groups that have an infinite amount to teach each other but sometimes rub each other the wrong way. It's about two very different paths of inquiry into the lives of queer-identified folks and the systems that affect and influence queerness—one of art and self-expression and creation, and another of research and analysis and synthesis. My goal in helping organize QGCon was twofold: selfishly, I wanted to be around the fascinating people in games and academia thinking about queer topics, and more broadly, I wanted those people to have a chance to meet one another in a safe, uplifting, forward-looking environment.

ROCCA: GaymerX takes the topic of the interwoven relationship between queerness and gaming to the casual weekend convention setting. Despite its relatively large academic and industry attendance, the convention actually focuses on its majority audience, which consists primarily of geek fans and gamers along the LGBTQ spectrum. This is where we can take a lot of these very important topics of discussion to a more casual audience who might never be exposed to them. Meanwhile, the convention boasts plenty of games, parties, cosplay, and celebrities, to keep the event setting one of fun and entertainment, all under the assurance of safety and comfort, which many people cannot find in other fan-facing conventions. My job is to oversee the entire project and to manage the staff running it to ensure that we are creating something in the image of what attendees will truly love. I keep a close ear to our communities and keep tabs on every criticism . . . and try to make sure I'm constantly keeping myself in tune with what our audience wants.

SCHOEMANN: Like the Queerness and Games Conference, one of our goals for Different Games is bringing together academics and designers in the same space, as well as folks from other overlapping areas, like artists, journalists, critics, and fans.

In New York City, all of these roles are pretty closely intertwined in the games scene, so it was really about designing
an event that would facilitate the kinds of conversations we
wanted to see happen while including the broadest range of
stakeholders . . . Early on in thinking about Different Games,
the issue I personally was most connected to was the need for
more feminism and gender diversity in games-related spaces,
but I decided that I would focus on that in smaller projects.
For Different Games, we ultimately decided we wanted to take
on the issue of inclusivity more broadly, to try to facilitate
an event that was about highlighting the work being done by
folks of all different identities that wasn't being represented
at most conferences and events. We saw the event as a way to
model a space with alternative values . . . I started scheming
about doing a conference in 2011. #1reasonwhy hadn't even
happened yet. It felt really urgently needed.

RUBERG: What inspired you to start or join the event? Was there
something specific about games or the industry that you
wanted to celebrate, or maybe change?

HOWE: I am not the sort of activist who yells from rooftops or
posts Twitter diatribes. I don't have the stomach, the skin,
or the courage. Organizing QGCon, however, felt like a way
that I could make a difference. It is a softer kind of activism,
less focused on overturning what's outside and more focused
on nurturing, encouraging, and growing what's inside. That,
and my own belief in the potency of games to create change,
sparked a desire to explore their overlap with queer themes.

ROCCA: I was actually scouted by the founder of GaymerX, Matt
Conn. In the first year, I intended to take on a smaller role in
the company, but as things started happening I slowly began
to take over the entire project. As a person who is very deeply
affected by empathy, I saw the demand for something like
this very quickly. Countless retellings of friends harassed and
shamed at larger conventions, stories of queer gamers losing
interest in play simply because they felt it wasn't made for
queer people, these things fueled my need to make GaymerX.

I wanted a safe place for people to have fun and be geeky and queer and not feel bad about it, a place where creeps and pickup artists and homophobic misogynistic gamer-bros were not only scarce, but would be dragged off the premises for offending. More than anything, I wanted to create a fun space where the default was treating others with respect.

SCHOEMANN: I come from a background in education and studio art where my focus had always been social justice concerns, and when I got into games I started to feel like it was divorcing me from the community of artists and activists that I had been part of. Suddenly I was in grad school around lots of engineers and in the games scene, around a lot of dudes making indie games, and I found that I was constantly confronting all of these unchecked assumptions that I had been insulated from by being among people who cared about doing things for the same reasons I did. So for me, a lot of the energy behind creating Different Games was about trying to manifest a games community that I would want to be part of.

RUBERG: How would you describe the process of putting together the event? Did you meet resistance or receive support from any group in particular?

HOWE: Putting QGCon together was a matter of thinking about it, saying you were going to do it, telling everyone you were going to do it, and then just doing it. The "just do it" had so many factors: website/social presence buildup, formal academic CFP (call for papers), the agonizing process of fund-raising, securing space, handling scheduling, creating signage, schedules, and other paraphernalia, and then actually facilitating the forty-eight hours of the event itself. We were incredibly lucky to have four organizers, each with different specialties.

ROCCA: In the beginning it was kind of rough. We had some people come along who made a lot of promises but in the end weren't really willing to put in any work. Scouting people who were really excited for the cause and good at what they did took a ton of work. Also, despite having done a Kickstarter, we also literally had no money to run the event other than the amount that would go toward things like the hotel, supplies, travel, et cetera. Our founder, Matt Conn, actually had to foot the bill for a lot of GaymerX's expenditures. This actually continues to be the case, as we have a very hard time getting sponsors, due to us being involved in two things that seem to clash in the public's eyes. At the end of the day, the people who came to GaymerX were our true supporters and sponsors.

SCHOEMANN: I also can't overstate how supportive and generous the department of Technology, Culture, and Society at NYU Polytechnic School of Engineering has been. A lot of people seem to mistake this for an NYU Game Center event, but it's very much a project of the Integrated Digital Media Program. Game Center has certainly helped us, but really, their identity as an institution is quite distinct from what we are trying to do. This conference was about creating an identity for games outside of a design-focused, formalist approach that many academics in New York City favor. I think that's partly what has really helped define it and it's one of the reasons that the community in New York has responded so positively to the project.

RUBERG: What was your experience like of the event itself? Did things go according to plan? Did you accomplish what you wanted to? Did anything surprise you?

HOWE: I never expected the emotional outcome of QGCon to be quite what it was. The immense amount of talent, being surrounded by others who not only were aware of what you were going through but understood it in a visceral, personal way: it all added up into this surreal, wonderful feeling of home and belonging. Those were my people. Things were chaotic, as always. Nothing went quite as planned but nothing went horribly awry. We were all improvising, and the overall result was wonderful.

ROCCA: I couldn't believe it was happening when it finally did. After spending an entire year working on it, actually being at the convention was very surreal. I spent most of my time running around trying to make sure little loose ends were tied

up and things ran smoothly. Of course, we ran into some unexpected turns but we managed to fix all of them quickly and
the event actually ran smoothly. It was wonderful being there,
too, because it was great to see how important this was to a
lot of our attendees. One man came to tell me he was visiting
from Saudi Arabia and that he was a gay gamer and he never
imagined something like this existed. It just all went better
than we could have dreamed.

SCHOEMANN: In some ways the 2013 event was a strange mash-
up. It felt a little divided, with half the audience clearly gravi-
tating toward the design-focused programming and different
attendees at the panels that were more academic. But I think
identifying those schisms was an important step toward
making the next year's conference feel more integrated. The
2014 conference felt really good in that respect. If part of the
point of the event was to model a different kind of community for games, we all definitely succeeded in coming together
and doing that, which was humbling and amazing. Even if
they're only temporarily able to exist in person, the connec-
tive networks that are activated through that kind of space
outlive themselves and are such an important and sustaining
resource.

RUBERG: What has the afterlife of the event been like? Are you
planning to run the event again, and if so how will it be different? Do you think the event has made a wider impact?

HOWE: We're going to run the event again, but I'm terrified about
next year! QGCon was so perfect in my mind. It's going to be
hard to do it again. It's going to be hard to do it better. This
year we will try to have more developers, to broaden the arcade, to be able to fly more people out and keep the costs as
minimal as we can. We'll try to add more opportunities for
people to just relax and be together. We'll try to make sure
there's a fundamental, ground-level understanding of game
design and queer theory for everyone to grow from. But I
think that just the fact that QGCon existed, just the fact that
it will continue to exist, will mean something to many, many

people out there in the world. That is our quiet good. We're here, we're queer . . .

ROCCA: There was a lot of pressure for a second year, so we really had to do it! As it is, money is so very tight and ticket sales do little to fix that. Last year about 50 percent of our total revenue came from last-month ticket sales. Meaning the money is there . . . eventually. We are currently running a Kickstarter to try to make people spend some money sooner rather than later, so that we can have some cash on hand to pay for some of the expenses/deposits. Feedback is also really strange. Most of the feedback I've gotten is really touching and great; some of it is kind of ridiculous and entitled. But I've learned to separate the people who want a fun, safe space from the people that say things like "I wish there weren't any men there" or "I'm straight and I was uncomfortable 'cause everything was about gay stuff" or other just odd selfish stuff. Other than that, it's just still strange realizing that GaymerX already happened. But I can't really think of that, since I've got next year to focus on!

SCHOEMANN: There has been so much positive momentum around the conference in our second year that I'm feeling hopeful that we'll find a way to do it again. It's hard to make something that runs primarily on people's passion sustainable, because scaling is always going to be an issue. One of the things we did this year that I was really proud of was that we offered travel grants to everyone that was coming from out of state for the event, and we'd like to keep that practice going for the future. It's so, so important to financially support people if we want to create a sustainable community for folks who have been pushed to the margins. We've also all accumulated so much knowledge and experience from the last two years that it would be a shame not to keep building on all we've learned.

Chapter **26**

Forty-Eight-Hour Utopia
On Hope and the Future of Queerness in Games

BONNIE RUBERG

Two weeks before the inaugural Queerness and Games Conference (QGCon), I found myself on the phone with a reporter from the *San Francisco Bay Guardian*. He had chosen our event (conference mission: "to explore the intersection of LGBT issues and video games") as the subject of an upcoming cover story. It seemed like an honor. The reporter and I talked about the exciting mix of academics and game developers who were coming to present. We talked about the indie designers who were exhibiting queer work in our arcade. But then the big questions started, questions I couldn't always answer. What about, for example, discrimination in games, one of the many topics the conference claimed to address? What exactly, the reporter wanted to know, did we intend to do about it? How were we going to make things better?

It's not an unreasonable question, and I realize in retrospect that all the reporter wanted was an upbeat, uplifting sound bite. From his perspective, I should have responded with confidence, command, and a surefire plan. "Homophobia runs rampant in games," the perfectly quotable me would have said. "My conference is here to make sure that changes, and fast." Or maybe I would have promised a utopian light at the end of the tunnel. "Crusaders like me are on the path to fixing systemic problems in the video game industry," I could have self-righteously assured him. "The present is bleak, but the future is coming. It is equality. It is happiness." There were even rainbows on the Queerness and Games Conference logo.

I couldn't bring myself to say any of those boldly idealistic things though. For years before I became an academic, I worked as a video games journalist. I knew well that anything I said to a reporter might appear on the pages of Wednesday's alt weekly irrevocably decontextualized, sure to insult or misrepresent . . . someone. Co-organizing the conference, which was set to take place at UC Berkeley in October 2013, had already proven an extremely delicate operation. Though we organizers came from diverse backgrounds, many potential speakers expressed concern that the conference would feel like an unsafe space. Scholars feared they would find themselves lost among the jargon of game developers. Developers feared that scholars would look down their noses and dissect their games with three-dollar words. After many carefully crafted e-mails and (thankfully only one) public Twitter spat, I knew to think before making bold statements on behalf of our community.

Understandably, this didn't please the reporter from the *Bay Guardian*. "You sound like a PR rep," he told me. "You're always on message. Come on, you obviously think there's something wrong with how queer characters are being represented in games. If you could wave a magic wand, what would you *want* games to be like?"

Imagine a perfect world. As Ursula Le Guin reminds us in "The Ones Who Walk Away from Omelas," her meditation on utopia, that's easier said than done.

I made excuses. "It's really not that simple . . ." The truth was that I had no idea how to answer. I had spent months planning the conference, creating a platform for others to speak, and I knew that I wanted to open new dialogues, to inspire new ways of seeing games queerly. But what did I personally want for the future of video games? Not me as a representative of the Queerness and Games Conference, but me as a player, as someone passionate about the medium? Even lingering over the question felt selfish. By day, I study expressions of

sexuality and gender in digital media. In theory, the scholar eluci-
dates culture; she doesn't prescribe. Yet it goes without saying that I
think that video games would be a better place if more mainstream
games represented LGBT characters as whole people instead of side-
line stereotypes, if we put an end to homophobia in video games and
the games industry, and if we made space for queer gamers like myself to call video games our own.

Optimism, however, does not come easy to me. It makes me feel
unrealistic. Staying cynical means that my hopes don't have too far
to fall each time someone on the Internet calls me a "stupid dyke" for
talking about homoerotics in *Portal,* or threatens to hunt me down
with a handgun for questioning racial representations in *Resident
Evil 5* (to name only a few of the incidents from my years writing
about games). As long as the Queerness and Games Conference went
smoothly and sparked fresh ideas, I would consider it a success. After
all, what's the point of dreaming impossibly big, of dreaming utopia,
the "no place" that science fiction long ago taught us only exists as
the dystopia in disguise?

I left the reporter with the least committal of parting remarks:
"The future will bring something different."

What I didn't know until the Queerness and Games Conference began,
or perhaps until after it ended, was that my co-organizers and I had
created our own forty-eight-hour paradise—not perfect, because nothing is perfect—but impossibly beautiful and also impossibly brief.

In many ways, the conference resembled any number of other
university conferences and/or small-scale "alternative" game events.
Held in UC Berkeley's impressively collegiate South Hall, home of the
School of Information, it began with a speaker dinner on a Friday
night, continued for a full day of talks on Saturday, included a Saturday night pizza party and "play session," and ran on through Sunday
evening with more panels and workshops. We had keynotes. We had
badges. Business cards exchanged hands. References to Foucault
were made. Volunteers on break in the hallways played games on the
Nintendo DS. As organizers, we ran around shaking hands, plugging
in AV equipment, directing attendees to our gender-neutral bathroom, putting out fires: the usual.

However, somewhere along the way, something happened that made the Queerness and Games Conference different from any other event I've attended. Something—and the cynic in me can't quite believe I'm saying this—downright magical.

Maybe it was the collaboration. We opened the conference with a session called "What Is Queerness and Games?" Each of the organizers spoke about their hopes for the weekend (mine: to stop being seen as that "one weird grad student" who works on queer game studies). Each of the audience members wrote their own goals down on index cards, shared them with their neighbors, and then posted them by the entrance to the building. Later in the day, keynote speaker Colleen Macklin challenged listeners to imagine different ways of conceptualizing queer games. Co-organizer Chelsea Howe ran a paper prototyping workshop that ended in the creation of a new tabletop RPG based on dragons in drag. Sunday's micro-talk session, which opened the floor to any attendee to speak on any subject, buzzed with excitement. Our final panel, "The Future of Queerness and Games," roused enthusiastic feedback and created dialogue across disciplines and industries.

Maybe the magic came from a kind of intellectual alchemy. We didn't know what would happen when we put academics and game designers in a room (well, a building) together for the weekend. The resulting organic, emergent, and generative chemistry far exceeded my most secret and optimistic expectations. Keynote speaker Jack Halberstam, well-known for his writing on queer failure, joined in for a public conversation with Jesper Juul, well-known for his writing on game failure—a combination I may have described, when I introduced the two, as an "academic slash fiction." Keynote speaker Kathryn Bond Stockton used the term *jouissance* in her talk on gaming and queer children. "Oh no," I thought as I eyed the audience from the back of the room, "game folks can smell fancy French terminology a mile away. I hope no one is complaining about this on Twitter." Not only did no one complain, Stockton's talk had a huge impact. In one of the Sunday afternoon sessions, a designer who had previously vocalized his distrust of academics took the stage earnestly and ecstatically chanting, "Jouissance! Jouissance!"

Or maybe the magic came from visibility and acceptance. Showing up at gaming events and showing up queer is so often an emotionally (and potentially physically) dangerous combination. We organizers tried our best to address this explicitly, and while there is always room for improvement, it largely seems to have worked. Our program featured an "inclusivity statement," inspired by a similar statement written for New York University's Different Games, which stressed the importance of respecting every individual's chosen identity. Again and again, over the course of the weekend, the sight of so many gender nonnormative gamers and scholars meeting under one roof moved me. In my own life, I encounter many moments when I feel pressured to either tone down my queerness (Bonnie, don't mention that you're kinky in front of other academics) or to perform it (Bonnie, do mention your ex-girlfriend so that others won't mistake you for straight). For the first time in academia, the first time in games, and possibly the first time ever, I felt like I had found a community where I could be the version of myself that I am on the inside.

However you explain the magic of the Queerness and Games Conference, I wasn't the only one who felt it. Attendees and speakers came to us many times over the course of the weekend to thank us, to hug us, to share their stories. By Saturday night a large circle of folks had formed in the hallway to discuss their own complicated gender identities. By Sunday night the audience was collectively daydreaming about all the queer games events we could organize to keep our wonderful but temporary community together. In the days after the conference, I received an amazing and humbling landslide of e-mails from scholars and developers who shared my warm, glowing sentiments about the conference.

When my colleagues back in the Berkeley Department of Comparative Literature asked me how the weekend had gone (they'd seen me stress about it for weeks prior), I couldn't help but put aside my academic persona and beam. "It was short," I murmured wistfully, "but it was wonderful." Many of them looked back at me with polite but puzzled smiles. It was time to stop hugging, I realized. It was time to stop grinning. The utopia had come and gone.

The words of my co-organizer Mattie Brice, who'd addressed the crowd caringly in conference's final moments, came to mind: "Take care of yourself. This has been a wonderful weekend. But it's a very different world out there."

In the months that passed after the first Queerness and Games Conference, once my bliss had mellowed into general good feeling, once we decided to take the plunge and organize the conference again in 2014, I found myself again wondering about the value of hope and the notion of a queer games utopia. Even as I reflected on the magic of the event, I couldn't help but hear the questioning voice of the *Bay Guardian* reporter. What did you accomplish? What about LGBT issues and video games did you actually change? Why struggle to replicate your forty-eight-hour haven if you're not certain it did any good? Even the notion of "striving to do good" was potentially problematic. Did "making video games a better place" mean instrumentalizing the members of our newly forming queer games community?

In part he's right, that straw man. Many things looked much the same in that next year as they had the year before. There was still homophobia in video games, still homophobia in the video games industry. There were still quarrels over queer representation, still queer players who felt abandoned by the art form they love. Still glowing from the inclusivity and warmth of the Queerness and Games Conference, I discovered that I had more trouble than ever stomaching events like the Game Developers Conference (GDC). In a short time, I had grown so accustomed to speaking with other people who are passionate about LGBT issues that I'd forgotten the snickering dismissiveness of mainstream games cultures. At a GDC cocktail party, a friend of a friend scrunched up his face and glared at me when I told him I co-organize the Queerness and Games Conference. "Queerness? And games?" he asked with a twinge of sarcasm and disgust. "Okay, I just wanted to make sure I heard you right." Long after he'd sauntered off to another part of the bar, my mind replayed his comment. Why did it make me so angry? I used to face the firing squad of online commenters every time I published an article. I used to have a thick skin. My temporary no-place had opened my mind and my heart, but it had also made me soft, vulnerable. It had made me happy, but it also made me lose track of what was, in some sense, real.

However, to that reporter, I could have also said, "Yes, some things have changed." I would have been exaggerating if I claimed they had changed specifically because of the Queerness and Games Conference. The diversity track at GDC in 2014 featured a number of talks about queerness and games, bringing the topic to a much wider industry audience. I was also working with coeditor Adrienne Shaw to put together this collection, which emerged in part from QGCon 2013.

Now, in 2016, the Queerness and Games Conference is entering its fourth year. Back at that first conference, I had felt like the "weird grad student" who studied queer issues in games. Today I am an incoming professor of digital games and queer game studies has become a burgeoning area of research. The intersection of queerness and video games is being recognized as a crucial topic for discussion and activism by more and more game designers, players, and academics every day. For me, it all began with that one weekend, one building, and the two hundred people inside its walls. It began with cautious optimism, with anxious hope, and it has become something bigger than me or any individual, bigger than QGCon, far more complicated than utopia but also far more rich and full of potential.

As always, the fearful cynic in me is still wary of hoping too much, but I now see the value of even the most fleeting of welcoming spaces. A temporary community is still a community, and the powerful feeling of belonging lasts long beyond any given place or time. I have also come to see the value of optimism, of idealism, and of happiness, even if these, too, are fleeting. When we share these feelings, if only for an instant, we believe that anything is possible. Real change is hard, but this initial inspiration is still crucial. It shapes us, drives us, and fuels us to work toward a feasibly different tomorrow. It allows us to push forward because we feel we are pushing together, challenging and supporting one another, making new worlds.

If I could wave a magic wand, what future would I wish for queerness and games? My perspective has changed considerably since I first stumbled through an answer to that question. My idea of utopia has also changed. I still wish for video games that represent queer folks fairly and fully, for a video games industry marked by acceptance and diversity, for an academy engaged in heated discussions around queer games. In the meantime, though, I've come to find great meaning in the temporary moments that reconnect me to the people with whom I share my passion for the power of video games and those who play them.

The evening after that GDC cocktail party that had left me spinning, I sat outside an industry-oriented dance party watching the crowd and wondering if video games would ever be *okay,* and what that even meant. Suddenly a friendly face appeared in the crowd, a Queerness and Games attendee I hadn't seen since our closing panel in October. "Bonnie!" he shouted, running to pull me up into a hug. When I told him about our yet-unannounced decision to organize the conference again in 2014, he literally jumped with joy. "QGCon is back! QGCon is back!" In his voice I heard reflected my own excitement, my own happiness, and my own feeling that the "no place" of utopia had become some place after all.

Looking back from 2016, the questions of optimism and utopia that we Queerness and Games Conference organizers wrestled with in those first moments seem far away—not because we have found the answers, and not because equality has finally come to games, but because now we know beyond a doubt that the issue of difference and video games matters. It matters to the hundreds of people who have attended QGCon and its associated programs. It matters to the many thousands more who are rallying for social justice in so many corners of the games world. The Queerness and Games Conference no longer feels like magic. Now it feels real: a real community, a real set of labors, a real accomplishment. We may never find our utopia, and that is how it should be. There is no perfection, only change—in games, in our communities, and in ourselves. That is what I hope for.

Contributors

LEIGH ALEXANDER is the editor in chief of *Offworld*. Her writing has been published in *The Guardian, The Atlantic, Slate,* and *Time.*

GREGORY L. BAGNALL is a doctoral candidate in English at the University of Rhode Island.

HANNA BRADY writes stories for video games.

MATTIE BRICE is a play and games critic, designer, and activist. She has written for such publications as *Kotaku, Paste Magazine,* and *PopMatters.*

DEREK A. BURRILL is associate professor of media and cultural studies at the University of California, Riverside. He is the author of *Die Tryin': Videogames, Masculinity, and Culture* and *The Other Guy: Media Masculinities within the Margins.*

EDMOND Y. CHANG is visiting assistant professor in women's and gender studies at the University of Oregon. His areas of interest include technoculture, gender and sexuality, cultural studies, digital games, popular culture, and contemporary American literature. He has written on queergaming and is contributor to the forthcoming *Digital Pedagogy in the Humanities: Concepts, Models, and Experiments.*

NAOMI CLARK is an independent game designer in New York City and teaches game design at the NYU Game Center.

KATHERINE CROSS is a doctoral student in sociology at the City University of New York.

KIM D'AMAZING is a doctoral candidate at the School of Media and Communication at the Royal Melbourne Institute of Technology.

AUBREY GABEL is a doctoral candidate in French at the University of California, Berkeley.

CHRISTOPHER GOETZ is assistant professor of film studies and new media in the Department of Cinematic Arts and the Public Humanities in a Digital World cluster at the University of Iowa.

JACK HALBERSTAM is professor of American studies and ethnicity at the University of Southern California. He is the author of five books, including *Female Masculinity* and *The Queer Art of Failure.*

TODD HARPER is assistant professor in the Simulation and Digital Entertainment program at the University of Baltimore.

LARISSA HJORTH is in the School of Media and Communication at the Royal Melbourne Institute of Technology. She is the author of *Mobile Gaming in the Asia-Pacific* and *Games and Gaming.*

CHELSEA HOWE is a creative director at Electronic Arts, an educator, and a member of the Game Developers Conference advisory board.

JESPER JUUL is associate professor of design at the Royal Danish Academy of Fine Arts. He is the author of *Half-Real, The Casual Revolution,* and *The Art of Failure.*

MERRITT KOPAS is the author of more than two dozen digital games. She is the editor of *Videogames for Humans.*

COLLEEN MACKLIN is associate professor of art, media, and technology at Parsons School of Design.

AMANDA PHILLIPS is assistant professor of English at Georgetown University.

GABRIELA T. RICHARD is assistant professor of learning, design, and technology at the Pennsylvania State University. Her research focuses on the intersections of culture, media, learning, and socialization, particularly in video games, computing education, and makerspaces. She is coeditor of *Diversifying Barbie and Mortal Kombat: Intersectional Perspectives and Inclusive Designs in Gaming* and has written extensively on games, learning, and online gaming communities, especially on experiences across gender, race, ethnicity, and sexuality.

TONI ROCCA is the president of GaymerX.

BONNIE RUBERG is a postdoctoral scholar in the Interactive Media and Games division at the University of Southern California.

SARAH SCHOEMANN is a doctoral student in digital media at Georgia Institute of Technology.

ADRIENNE SHAW is assistant professor of media studies and production at Temple University. She is author of *Gaming at the Edge: Sexuality and Gender at the Margins of Gamer Culture* (Minnesota, 2014).

KATHRYN BOND STOCKTON is distinguished professor of English, associate vice president for equity and diversity, and dean of the School for Cultural and Social Transformation at the University of Utah. She is the author of three books, including *Beautiful Bottom, Beautiful Shame: Where "Black" Meets "Queer"* and *The Queer Child, or Growing Sideways in the Twentieth Century*.

ZOYA STREET is a doctoral student in sociology at the University of Lancaster. His writing looks at play, labor, and games within material and symbolic systems of every scale: from the tiny emotional loops of caring for a virtual pet to the massive macronetwork of meaning making in late capitalism.

PETER WONICA is an educational game developer.

ROBERT YANG is an artist and game developer. He teaches game design at NYU Game Center and at Parsons School of Design.

JORDAN YOUNGBLOOD is assistant professor of English and new media studies at Eastern Connecticut State University. His research focuses on the intersections of gender, sexuality, and game play, particularly in terms of spatial and narrative design. He has published in *ADA: A Journal of Gender, New Media, and Technology* and the collection *Rated M for Mature: Sex and Sexuality in Gaming.*

Index

Page numbers in italics refer to illustrations.